Roster of
CIVIL WAR
SOLDIERS

from
Washington County,
Maryland

Revised Edition

———

Roger Keller

CLEARFIELD

First Edition, 1993

Revised Edition printed for
Clearfield Company, Inc. by
Genealogical Publishing Co., Inc.
Baltimore, Maryland
1998

International Standard Book Number: 0-8063-4821-6

Made in the United States of America

THE ROSTER OF HEROES

This <u>Roster of Civil War Soldiers from Washington County, Maryland</u> began as a short appendix to another work by the author. <u>Events of the Civil War in Washington County, Maryland</u> was to have included "several pages" of names only because a list of names was not available in any known form at the time it was being written.

Only after making several visits to the Maryland State Archives and researching the state adjutant general's reports of that period, along with the special 1890 census and other sources, were these names uncovered by the author and published separately. A first for Washington County!

This second publication has about fifty new names provided by relatives of the men who did not appear in the first listing. This is why the recruiting stations in Hagerstown, Williamsport, Clear Spring, and elsewhere about the county recruited from "all over." Williamsport, for instance, attracted volunteers not only from Washington County but from the three panhandle counties of Virginia (now West Virginia): Berkeley, Morgan, and Jefferson. Men and boys also came from Frederick and Allegheny counties in Maryland as well as from Franklin and Fulton counties in Pennsylvania. Only those men whose place of residence was identified as a Washington County site were included in the first roster. There were many soldiers whose home towns were not given, and these names are now included, thanks to their descendants.

There are more names, I am sure.

Roger Keller
December, 1997

List of Major Sources and Keys

ANDERSONVILLE LISTINGS: Names of Union soldiers who died at the Andersonville, Ga., prison and their grave numbers. The list appears in The Soldier's Story by Warren Lee Gross, published in 1875.

CAPTAIN MAXWELL'S ROSTER: Roster of soldiers who served in Co. C, 3rd Regiment Potomac Home Brigade Infantry, under Captain Robert Maxwell, of Hagerstown. The complete roster in the possession of Dr. David Foltz, of Hagerstown. It was originally Co. A, 4th Regiment P.H.B. Infantry until merged into the 3rd Regiment as Co. B, then later as Co. F. The company was known as the "Blue Hen's Chickens of Hagerstown."

C.V.M.: Confederate Veteran Magazine. Bound volumes are available at the Western Maryland Room of the Washington County Free Library, at Hagerstown, Md.

DORRANCE DIARY: The wartime diary of Private James Dorrance of Clear Spring. Md., a private in Co. A, 7th Maryland Infantry. (US). Loaned by Mrs. Hilda Cushwa, of Clear Spring, Md.

1860-C: The regular National Census of Washington County, Md., for 1860. Available from the Washington County Free Library, at Hagerstown, Md.

1890-C: The special census of 1890 listing the surviving soldiers, sailors, marines and widows of the Civil War. Micro film available from the Washington County Free Library, at Hagerstown, Md.

HARTZLER: <u>Marylanders in the Confederacy,</u> authored by Daniel D. Hartzler, listing several thousand Marylanders who served the South.

H.R.M.V.: <u>History and Roster of Maryland Volunteers in the War of 1861-1865.</u> Two volumes plus index.

HUNTZBERRY: <u>Marylanders in the Civil War: The South.</u> Book 1. By Thomas V. and JoAnne M. Huntzberry. A listing of Marylanders serving the Southern cause.

I.J.F.C.: The Independent Junior Fire Company, of Hagerstown. Members names are shown on pages without numbers. Available at the Western Maryland Room of the Washington County Free Library, at Hagerstown, Md.

KEALHOFER DIARY: The personal diary of Miss Mary Louise "Lutie" Kealhofer, of Hagerstown, Md., for 1863. Published in the <u>Maryland Historical Society Magazine, December, 1945.</u>

MCCLANNAHAN PAPERS: Wartime diary of Matthew McClannahan, Co. I, 1st Maryland Federal Cavalry, 1861-1864. Washington County Historical Society, 973.78 M.

M.F.D.: <u>The Merchants and Farmers Directory for Hagerstown and Washington Co., Md., for 1871.</u>

M.S.A., A.G.R.: Maryland State Archives, the Adjutant General's Rosters of servicemen. Two volumes. Vol. 1, infantry, Vol. 2, cavalry. MSA-S 936-17. Also the official muster-in and muster-out rolls are noted. The Maryland Hall of Records, Annapolis, Md.

S.H.S.P.: <u>Southern Historical Society Papers,</u> in the Western Maryland Room of the Washington County Free Library, at Hagerstown, Md.

U.S.C.T: United States Colored Troops.

W.C.C.R.: <u>Washington County Cemetery Records.</u>
Seven volumes.

W.C.H.S.: Washington County Historical Society,
at Hagerstown, Md. References are noted from
vertical files (VF) etc.

V.R.C. The Veteran Reserve Corps. Wounded men who
served in non-combat rolls, releasing able-
bodied men for service.

THE ROSTER OF SOLDIERS AND SAILORS

(THIS IS AN ALPHABETICAL ROSTER OF MEN FROM OR WHO LIVED IN WASHINGTON COUNTY AND SERVED IN THE CIVIL WAR. WHILE IT IS IMPOSSIBLE TO SAY THAT IT IS COMPLETE, OR THAT EACH RESIDENCE IS CORRECT, IT CAN BE CONSIDERED GENERALLY RELIABLE. IN SOME INSTANCES SOLDIERS FROM WASHINGTON COUNTY ARE BURIED ELSEWHERE AND RECORDED IN STATE RECORDS AS RESIDENTS OF THE SECOND TOWN. THOSE RECORDED IN THE 1860 CENSUS AS RESIDENTS OF A PARTICULAR TOWN OFTEN RELOCATED TO ANOTHER BETWEEN THE WAR'S END AND THE TIME THE 1890 SPECIAL CENSUS WAS TAKEN, TWENTY-FIVE YEARS LATER. THIS ROSTER HAS ATTEMPTED TO CORRECT THE RECORD WHERE THE INFORMATION WAS AVAILABLE.)

(Unless otherwise noted, ages given are at time of enlistment)

~ ~

-- A --

ADAMS, Charles W. (Pvt.) "Alexander's" Baltimore Battery, Light Artillery. (US) Smithsburg. Served from 12 August, 1862 to 15 August, 1865. Buried in Mountain View Cemetery, Sharpsburg. Enlisted in 1862. Severely wounded in the Battle of Winchester, Va., in 1863, as the Confederates advanced to Maryland and Pennsylvania. Taken prisoner at Winchester and paroled to a Baltimore hospital. After the war Adams served as a publisher of the Hagerstown Herald and Torchlight newspaper, and in 1889 he was elected doorkeeper of the 51st Congress. (Williams, Vol. 2, 858) (H.R.M.V., Vol. 1, 820) (WCCR 1, 31) (1890-C)

ADAMS, George. (Pvt.) Co. A, 7th Regiment Maryland Infantry. (US) Age 36. Conococheague. Served from 9 August, 1862 to 31 May, 1865. Discharged at Arlington Heights, Va.

1

(H.R.M.V., Vol. 1, 278) (Scharf, Vol. 1, 226)
(MSA-AGR, Vol. 1, page 6 and MSA-S-936-17)

ADAMS, Jacob H. T. (Pvt) Co. H, 6th Regiment
Maryland Infantry. (US) Age 18. Enlisted at
Hagerstown, 21 August, 1862. Taken prisoner at
Loudoun Valley, Va., July, 1863. Died of
starvation and "civil mistreatment" at
Andersonville, Ga., Prison, 14 May, 1864.
(Grave No. 1928-Andersonville listings, page
293) (H.R.M.V., Vol. 1, page 241) (MSA-AGR,
936-2; AGR-1, 10)

ADAMS, John. (Pvt.) Co. H, 6th Maryland Infantry.
(US) Age 23. Williamsport. Enlisted at
Hagerstown, 21 August, 1862. Wounded in action
27 November, 1863 at Mine Run, Va. Discharged
with disability 24 April, 1865. Became a
confectioner at Williamsport. (MSA-AGR-1, page
10, and (MSA-AGR, 936-2) (H.R.M.V., Vol. 1,
page 241) (M.F.D., 749)

ADKINS, Alexander. (Pvt.) Co. I, 1st Regiment
"Russell's" Maryland Cavalry. (US) Enlisted at
Williamsport, 17 December, 1862. Deserted 26
May, 1864. (H.R.M.V., Vol. 1, page 732) (MSA-
AGR-S-936-38)

ALBERT, William H. (Sgt.) Co. I, 7th Regiment
Maryland Volunteer Infantry. (US) Age 39.
Hagerstown. Entered at Hagerstown 28 August,
1862. Died 2 November, 1863, from disease
contracted in service. Buried in Zion Reformed
Church Cemetery, Hagerstown. (WCCR, Vol. 6,
112) (H.R.M.V., Vol. 1, 297) (1890-C)(MSA-AGR-
1, 12)

ALLEN, Thomas. (Pvt.)6th Pennsylvania Cavalry.
(US) Hagerstown. (1890-C)

ALLISON, Joseph S. (Pvt.) Co. A, 2nd Maryland
Cavalry. (CSA) Hagerstown. Enlisted in 1862 at
age 16. Brother of Perry J. Allison.
(Hartzler, 76) (Portrait and Biographical
Record of the Sixth Congressional District of
Maryland, page 166)

ALLISON, Dr. Marcus W. (Pvt.) (CSA) Hagerstown.
Served in Co. F, 10th Virginia Infantry, in the
famous "Stonewall" Brigade, later commanded by
Gen. Richard Ewell. Veteran of the battles of
First Bull Run, Pea Ridge, Cross Keys, Seven
Days, Cedar Mountain, Second Bull Run,
Fredericksburg, Chancellorsville and at
Gettysburg, where he was captured. Sent to Fort
Delaware where he escaped on a boat in 1864. At
Cedar Mountain a shell fell among his company,
killing four men. The concussion knocked Dr.
Allison to the ground, unconscious. Believing
their comrade to be dead, he was left on the
field as his company relocated. A medical staff
officer noticed signs of life in him later and
took him to a field hospital. He was fully
revived and participated in the latter stages
of the fight. He was never seriously wounded in
the war, but later nearly died from the typhoid
fever after the Battle of First Bull Run. Prior
to the Battle of Chancellorsville, in 1862 Dr.
Allison had a most unusual experience that he
carried with him for the remainder of his very
productive life. Because of sickness, sore feet
and hunger, Allison fell out of the line of
advance on one occasion and reported to his
captain that he could not continue. He sat down
with his bayoneted gun on his lap and watched
the passing troops. At the end of the long line
came General "Stonewall Jackson." Studying the
doctor for a moment, he dismounted his horse
and with saber in hand walked toward the jaded
doctor. Jackson, well aware that the doctor was
in disobedience to his order that his men must
keep up, asked why he was sitting. Allison
explained. Jackson thought a moment then made
an offer. Allison could ride his horse, and he,
the general would walk, explaining that he
would need every man in the coming battle.
Allison accepted and was helped into the saddle
by Jackson. The bearded general then took a
small Bible from his pocket and began to read
aloud. The other soldiers mused at the scene,
well aware of the great general's unusual
behavior. After a while a courier arrived with

a dispatch for Jackson. Reading it, he announced to Allison that he had urgent need of his horse, and that the doctor must be sufficiently rested to continue the march. He dismounted and rejoined the other soldiers as Jackson rode away. In only a few hours, work came that Jackson had been mortally wounded by his own men as he scouted the lines in a heavily wooded area nearby. Dr. Allison returned safely to Hagerstown when the war ended, serving his many patients from his office at 322 West Washington Street. H.R.M.V., Part 1, 114. Boonsboro Odd Fellow, 11/25/65.

ALLISON, Perry J. (Pvt.) Served in the Army of Northern Virginia. (US) Hagerstown. Captured at Spotsylvania Court House by the forces of Gen. U. S. Grant. Held until the end of the war at Fort Delaware. He was the eldest son of William L. and Ann (Hisey) Allison, of Hagerstown. (Portrait and Biographical Record of the Sixth Congressional District of Maryland, 1898, page 166) (Hartzler, 76)

ALLISON, William H. (Pvt.) Co. B, 3rd Regiment Potomac Home Brigade Infantry. (US) Age 43. Wagoner. Clear Spring. Enlisted at Hagerstown, 11 December, 1861. Discharged 11 December, 1864. (H.R.M.V., Vol. 1, page 575) (Captain Maxwell's roster) (MSA-S-936-24)

ALSIP, John. (Pvt.) Co. E, 13th Regiment Maryland Infantry. (US) Smithsburg. Served from 17 December, 1861 to 17 December, 1864. (H.R.M.V., Vol. 1, 444) (1890-C)

ALSIP, Silas D. (Pvt.) Co. E, 13th Regiment Maryland Infantry. (US) Sharpsburg. Served from 7 February, 1865 to 29 May, 1865. (H.R.M.V., Vol. 1, 444) (1890-C)

ANDERSON, David. (Pvt.) Co. I, 1st Regiment "Russell's" Maryland Cavalry. (US) Williamsport. Served from 17 December, 1862 to 8 August, 1865. (H.R.M.V., Vol. 1, 732)

ANDERSON, Ephraim F. (Lt. Col.) Co. I, 7th
Regiment Maryland Infantry, (US) Clear Spring.
Wounded in action. Brevet-Major, 13 March, 1865
for gallantry in the Battle of the Wilderness,
VA; Brevet Lt. Col. 13 March, 1864 for
conspicuous gallantry at the battle of
Spottsylvania Court House, VA. (Scharf, 327)
(H.R.M.V., Vol. 1, 297) (Camper and Kirkley,
123)

ANDERSON, James. (Pvt.) Co. A, 3rd Maryland
Infantry. (US) Williamsport. Age 24. Enlisted
at Williamsport, 15 July, 1861. Mustered out 15
July, 1864. (MSA-AGR, 1, page 6) (H.R.M.V.,
Vol. 1, 116)

ANDERSON, James P. (Pvt.) Co. F. 1st Maryland
Potomac Home Brigade. (US) Washington Co.
Served from 4 September, 1861 to 5 October,
1864. Buried in St. Paul's Reformed Cemetery,
at Clear Spring. (H.R.M.V., Vol. 1, 510) (WCCR,
Vol. 5, 271)

ANDERSON, John H. (Pvt.) Co. I, 1st Regiment
"Russell's" Maryland Cavalry. (US)
Williamsport. Served from 3 September, 1861 to
3 September, 1864. Buried in Rose Hill
Cemetery, Hagerstown. (H.R.M.V., Vol. 1, 732)
(1890-C) (WCCR, Vol. 7, 227)

ANDERSON, Robert. (Pvt.) Co. I, 1st Regiment
"Russell's" Maryland Cavalry. (US) Enlisted at
Williamsport, 17 December, 1862. Deserted 22
December, 1862. (H.R.M.V., Vol. 1, page 732)
(MSA-AGR-S-936-38)

ANDERSON, William. (Pvt.) Co. B, 1st Regiment
Potomac Home Brigade "Cole's" Cavalry. (US)
Leitersburg. Served from 24 August, 1861 to 15
September, 1864. Right foot wounded in action
and later amputated. (H.R.M.V., Vol. 1, 671)
(1890-C)

ANDRESS, Adam. (Pvt.) Co. B, 3rd Regiment Potomac

Home Brigade Infantry. (US) Hagerstown.
Enlisted at Hagerstown, 23 Oct., 1861.
Discharged 23 Oct., 1863. (H.R.M.V., Vol. 1,
445)

ANDREW, William. (Pvt.) Co. E, 1st Regiment
Potomac Home Brigade Infantry. (US) Age 22.
Laborer. Huyett's. Served from 14 September,
1861 to 29 May, 1865. Reenlisted 23 February,
1864, at Sandy Hook, Md. Transferred to Co. E,
13th Maryland Infantry. (H.R.M.V., Vol. 1, 506)
(1890-C) (MSA-S-936-23)

ANDREWS, Peter. (Pvt.) Co. I, 7th Regiment
Maryland Infantry. (US) Enlisted at Hagerstown,
26 Aug., 1862. Age 21. Served until 31 May,
1865. (MSA-AGR, Vol. 1, 12) (H.R.M.V., Vol. 1,
297)

ARMBRISTER, J. H. (Pvt.) Co. A, 7th Maryland
Infantry. (US) Hagerstown. Enlisted at age 22,
on 14 November, 1862, at Hagerstown. Detached
on 15 April, 1864 to 2nd Division, 5th Army
Corps ambulance train, special order 102. Also
transferred to Co. C, 1st Maryland Infantry.
Discharged 31 May, 1865. (H.R.M.V., Vol. 1,
278) ((MSA-AGR-1, page 12)

ARMSTRONG, Jacob H. (Pvt.) Co. A, 7th Regiment
Maryland Infantry. (US) Washington County. Age
25. Served 18 August, 1862 to 31 May, 1865.
Deserted 25 February, 1863. Returned to unit 5
November, 1863 and made up time. Later
transferred to Co. C, 1st Maryland Infantry.
(H.R.M.V., Vol. 1, 278) (Scharf, Vol. 1, 226)
(MSA-AGR, Vol. 1, page 10 and MSA-S-936-17)

ANTHONY, James. (Pvt.) Co. I, 1st Regiment
"Russell's" Maryland Cavalry. (US)
Williamsport. Began service 2 December, 1861.
Killed in action at Brandy Station, Va., 9
June, 1863. (H.R.M.V., Vol. 1, 732)
(McClannahan papers, 4)

ANTHONY, Joseph P. (Pvt.) "Alexander's" Baltimore
Battery, Light Artillery. (US) Hancock. Served

from 14 August, 1862 to 17 June, 1865.
(H.R.M.V., Vol. 1, 820) (1890-C)

ARMBRISTER, J. H. (Pvt.) Co. A, 7th Maryland
Infantry. (US) Age 22. Enlisted at Hagerstown,
14 November, 1862. Detailed to 2nd Division,
5th Army Corps ambulance train 28 August, 1862.
(MSA-AGR-1, page 12)

ARTZ, Thomas. (Pvt.) Co. H, 1st Regiment Potomac
Home Brigade "Cole's" Cavalry. (US)
Downsville. Served from 25 March, 1864 to 28
June, 1865. (H.R.M.V., Vol. 1, 689) (1890-C)

ATWOOD, William. (Pvt.) Co. A, 3rd Regiment
Maryland Infantry. (US) Age 28. Enlisted at
Williamsport, 1 February, 1862. Taken prisoner
11 May, 1864. Paroled, August 1864. Died of
wounds and complications at City Point
Hospital, Virginia, 15 April, 1865. (MSA-AGR-1,
page 9) (H.R.M.V., Vol. 1, 116)

AUSHERMAN, Hamilton. (Pvt.) Co. F, 5th Regiment
Maryland Infantry. (US) Williamsport. Served
from 11 December, 1861 to 11 December, 1864.
(H.R.M.V., Vol. 1, 202) (1890-C)

AUSTIN, Brown Lancaster. (Pvt.) Co. H, 1st
Regiment Maryland Cavalry. (US) Williamsport.
Age 21. Enlisted at Williamsport December 3,
1861. Discharged December 3, 1864. Died 1898.
(H.R.M.V., Vol. 1, 728)

AUSTIN, John T. (Pvt) Co. D, 2nd Virginia
Infantry Regiment. (CSA) Williamsport. Enlisted
at Martinsburg, Virginia (now West Virginia),
4/18/61, as a private. Last official entry
shows him present for duty Nov/Dec 1861.
(Roster, *2nd Virginia Regiment*, Frye)

-- B --

BACHTELL, Lewis L. (Pvt.) Co. H, 6th Regiment
Maryland Infantry. (US) Age 21. Smithsburg.
Enlisted at Hagerstown, 21 August, 1862.
Wounded in right side at Locust Grove, Va., 27

7

November, 1863. Transferred to V.R.C.
Discharged 20 June, 1865 at Washington, D.C.
Reported to census taker, in 1890, that the
ball was still in his body. (1890-C) (H.R.M.V.,
Vol. 1, 241) (MSA-AGR, Vol. 1, page 40, and
(MSA-AGR, 936-2)

BAILEY, Samuel E. (Cpl.) Co. G, 130th
Pennsylvania Infantry Regiment. (US)
Hagerstown. Served from 6 August, 1862 to May,
1863. Disabled with wound of right leg.(1890-C)

BAIN, John. (Pvt.) Co. H, 6th Regiment Maryland
Infantry. (US) Age 21. Enlisted at Hagerstown,
7 April, 1865. Transferred to 1st Regiment
Maryland Infantry 20 June, 1865. (MSA-AGR,
Vol. 1, page 40) (H.R.M.V., Vol. 1, page 50)

BAIRD, Andrew. (Pvt.) Co. I, 1st Regiment
Maryland Cavalry. (US) Age 18. Farmer.
Williamsport. Enlisted at Williamsport, 26
March, 1864. Deserted 25 May, 1865. (H.R.M.V.,
Vol. 1, page 741) (MSA-AGR-S-936-36)

BAKER, David. (Pvt.) Co. G, 3rd Regiment Maryland
Infantry. (US) Leitersburg. Served 27 February,
1864 to 22 July, 1864. (1890-C)

BAKER, David H. (Pvt.) Co. G, 99th Pennsylvania
Infantry Regiment. (US) Leitersburg. Served
from 27 February 1865 to 22 July, 1865. (1890-C)

BAKER, Emmanuel. (Pvt.) Co. G, 1st Regiment
Potomac Home Brigade "Cole's" Cavalry. (US)
Clear Spring. Served 25 February, 1864 to 28
June, 1865. Buried at St. Peter's Lutheran
Cemetery, Clear Spring. (H.R.M.V., Vol. 1, 687)
(WCCR, Vol. 2, 70)

BAKER, Joshua. (Pvt.) Co. I, 39th Regiment
Infantry. (U.S.C.T.) Maryland Volunteers. (US)
Hancock. Served from 31 March, 1864 to 4
December, 1865. Suffered gunshot wound.
(H.R.M.V., part 2, 281) (1890-C)

BAKER, Levi. (Pvt.) Co. E, 1st Regiment Maryland

Cavalry. (US) Age 37. Boonsboro. Enlisted at
Boonsboro, 7 March, 1864. Discharged 8 August,
1865. Sustained a flesh wound of the leg.
Buried in Benevola United Brethren Church
Cemetery, Benevola, Md.. (H.R.M.V., Vol. 1,
720)(1890-C) (WCCR, Vol. 2, 292) (MSA-S 936-36)

BAKER, Newton D. (M. D.) (Pvt.) Co. F, 1st
Virginia Cavalry, (CSA) Washington County.
(Hartzler, 80)

BAKER, William H. (Pvt.) Co. B, 1st Regiment
Potomac Home Brigade "Cole's" Cavalry. (US)
Sharpsburg. Age 24. Master painter. Entered
service at Hagerstown, serving from 22 October,
1864 to 28 June, 1865. (H.R.M.V., Vol. 1, 671)
(1890-C) (Scharf, Vol. 1, 226) (1860-C, page
41) (MSA-AGR, Vol. 1, page 41)

BALL, (Reverend) Benjamin F. (Cpl.) Co. C, 43rd
Virginia Cavalry. (Mosby's) (CSA) Washington
County. (Hartzler, 81)

BALL, Charles E. (Pvt.) Co. D, 1st Regiment
Potomac Home Brigade "Cole's" Cavalry. (US)
Boonsboro. Served from 8 September, 1861 to 8
September, 1864. Taken prisoner and confined to
Libby Prison, Richmond, for three months.
(H.R.M.V., Vol. 1, 678) (1890-C)

BALL, Wallace M. B. (2nd Lt.) Co. I, 2nd
Regiment Maryland Infantry. (US) Washington
County. Entered service at Hagerstown, 2
August, 1861 as sergeant. Promoted second
lieutenant 3 January, 1863. Resigned 30
September, 1864. (H.R.M.V., Vol. 1, 102) (MSA-
AGR-S-324)

BALTZ, John. (Pvt.) Co. A, 7th Regiment Maryland
Infantry. (US) Washington County. Age 21.
Served from 16 August, 1862 to 31 May, 1865.
(H.R.M.V., Vol. 1, 278) (Scharf, Vol. 1, 226)
(MSA-AGR, Vol. 1, page 41 and MSA-S-936-17)

BALTZ, Thomas. (Pvt.) Co. A, 7th Regiment
Maryland Cavalry. (US) Hagerstown. Age 18.

Served 11 August, 1862 to 31 May, 1865.
(H.R.M.V., Vol. 1, 278) (Scharf, Vol. 1, 226)
(MSA-S-936-17)

BAMFORD, Robert C. (Capt.) Co. H, 1st Regiment
Potomac Home Brigade Infantry. (US) Age 33.
Sharpsburg. Entered the service 10 September,
1861 as first lieutenant, promoted captain 25
April, 1862. Born 27 March, 1831, near
Sharpsburg, on what would later be a part of
the Antietam Battlefield, and became a
carpenter's apprentice for two years under
Aaron Frye. Later, he worked for the Baltimore
and Ohio Railroad constructing bridges, and
after much study became a master bridge
builder. In 1859 he went to Cuba, working for a
Baltimore firm to erect bridges for a railroad
company, and supervised the building of six
structures in an eight month period. He
returned to Sharpsburg as the war broke out in
1861, resigned his position with the Baltimore
firm and organized a company for service that
did not enter the army. Later, he helped
organize Co. H, 1st Maryland Infantry and was
named captain. His term of service covered
three years and three months. In January, 1861,
Bamford and one hundred picked men erected a
telegraph line from Hagerstown to Hancock at a
time when "Stonewall" Jackson's men were making
raids in that area. His men were diverted to
Winchester, Va., where they participated in the
fighting and earned commendations for their
actions. Bamford's men also took part in
fighting during the Confederate siege of
Harper's Ferry in September, 1862. Bamford was
taken prisoner when Gen. Miles surrendered to
the Rebels, led by Gen. Jackson. He was sent to
Annapolis and paroled for six months. After
duty on the lower Potomac, he went with the
army to Gettysburg, participating in the second
and third day's fighting. In that great battle
he received several minor flesh wounds, and his
clothing was pierced by shot five different
times without injury. Bamford was mustered out
of service, as he was disabled with serious
abdominal problem. He received $20 a month

pension. returned to Sharpsburg and went into business dealing in horses and hay. In 1868 he moved to Hagerstown where he became storekeeper for Spickler's distillery, for the government. He became sheriff of Washington County in 1871 and later served two years on the Hagerstown Town Council and was also elected to the state legislature. His family associated with St. Paul's Methodist Episcopal Church, in Hagerstown. (Portrait and Biographical Record of the Sixth Congressional District of Maryland, 1898, pages 559-61) (Scharf, 327) (H.R.M.V., Vol. 1, 523) (1890-C) (MSA-S-936-23) (Pension Records, page 157)

BANTZ, William H. (Sgt.) Co. B, 7th Regiment Maryland Infantry. (US) Hagerstown. Age 20. Enlisted 18 August, 1864. Discharged 31 May, 1865. (H.R.M.V., Vol. 1, 281) (MSA-AGR, Vol. 1, 41)

BANZHOF, Frederick W. (Pvt.) Co. B, 1st Regiment Maryland Cavalry. (US) Williamsport. Served from 22 February, 1864 to 8 August, 1865. (H.R.M.V., Vol. 1, 709) (1890-C)

BARBER, George W. (Pvt.) Co. B, 3rd Regiment Potomac Home Brigade. (US) Washington Co. Served from 11 October, 1861 to 11 October, 1864. Buried in Rose Hill Cemetery, Hagerstown. (H.R.M.V., Vol. 1, 575) (WCCR, Vol. 7, 238) (MSA-S-936-23)

BARBER, John H. (Pvt.) Co. B, 3rd Regiment Potomac Home Brigade Infantry. (US) Age 34. Hagerstown. Enlisted at Hagerstown, 30 October, 1861. Discharged 30 October, 1864. (H.R.M.V., Vol. 1, page 576) (Captain Maxwell's roster) (MSA-S-936-23)

BARBER, John Richard. (Pvt.) (CSA) Washington County. Rode with the cavalry of John Hunt Morgan. After the war he owned extensive holdings in real estate in Maryland and West Virginia. (Confederate Veteran Magazine, Vol. XVIII, page 148)

11

BARGER, Leander. (Pvt.)Co. F, 1st Regiment
Potomac Home Brigade Infantry. (US) Age 22.
Laborer. Washington County. Enlisted 4 Sept.,
1861. Reenlisted 28 February, 1864, at
Frederick, Md. Transferred Co. F, 13th Regiment
Maryland Infantry. Discharged 29 May, 1865.
(H.R.M.V., Vol. 1, page 510) (MSA-S-936-23)

BARGER, Nelson. (Pvt.) Co. I, 1st Regiment
"Russell's" Maryland Cavalry. (US) Enlisted at
Williamsport, 17 December, 1862. Discharged 8
August, 1865. (H.R.M.V., Vol. 1, page 732)
(MSA-AGR-S-936-38)

BARKDOLL, George H. (Pvt.) Co. E, 1st Regiment
Potomac Home Brigade Infantry. (US) Age 18.
Laborer. Washington County. Enlisted at Sandy
Hook, Md., 12 December, 1864. Transferred to
Co. E, 13th Regiment Maryland Infantry.
Discharged 29 May, 1865. (H.R.M.V., Vol. 1,
page 506) (MSA-S-936-23)

BARKDOLL, John. (Sgt.) Co. H, 6th Maryland
Regiment. (US) Smithsburg. Age 22. Enlisted 21
August, 1862. Wounded in Loudoun Valley, Va.,
imprisoned in Andersonville, Ga., Prison, where
he died 15, June, 1864. Military records allude
to reports that he died of "starvation and
mistreatment." (H.R.M.V., Vol. 1, 241)
(Williams, Vol. 2, 715) (MSA-AGR-S-936-2)

BARKER, Lewis. (Pvt.) Co. A, 3rd Regiment
Maryland Infantry. (US) Age 40. Enlisted at
Williamsport, 15 July, 1861. Served until 15
July, 1864. (H.R.M.V., Vol. 1, page 117) (MSA-
AGR, Vol. 1, page 29)

BARKER, Mathias. (Pvt.) Co. A. 3rd Regiment
Maryland Infantry. (US) Age 39. Enlisted 15
July, 1861 at Williamsport. Served until 15
June, 1864. (H.R.M.V., Vol. 1, page 117) (MSA-
AGR, Vol. 1, page 29)

BARNES, George W. (Pvt.) Co. D, 126th Regiment
Pennsylvania Infantry. (US) Hagerstown. Served

from 6 August, 1862 to 30 May, 1865. (1890-C)

BARNES, John T. M. (Major) 3rd Louisiana Light
Artillery, Washington Co. (CSA) (Hartzler, 81)

BARNES, Richard M. (Sgt.) Co. B, 21st Virginia
Infantry. (CSA) Washington Co. (Hartzler, 81)

BARNES, Ruben T. (Pvt.) Co. D, 13th Regiment
Maryland Infantry. (US) Sharpsburg. Served
from 12 August, 1862 to 29 May, 1865. (1890-C)

BARNETT, James. (1st Lt.) Co. A, 3rd Regiment
Maryland Infantry, (US) Washington County.
Entered the service 15 June, 1861 as sergeant
in the 1st Virginia Union Infantry. Promoted to
second lieutenant 30 October, 1862. First
lieutenant 1 Feb., 1863. Mustered out 8 Feb.,
1864. (Scharf, 327) (H.R.M.V., Vol. 1, 116)

BARNETT, George W. (Lt.) Co. H, 3rd Regiment
Maryland Cavalry. (US) Hancock. Served from 16
October, 1863 to 5 October, 1864. (H.R.M.V.,
Vol. 1, 116, 136) (1890-C)

BARNETT, George W. (2nd Lt.) Co. H, 3rd Regiment
Maryland Cavalry. (US) Hancock. (Scharf, 327)
(H.R.M.V., Vol. 1, 774)

BARNEY, Lawrence. (Pvt.) Co. H, 6th Regiment
Maryland Infantry. (US) Age 21. Entered
service 28 August, 1862 at Hagerstown.
Deserted 2 September, 1862. (MSA-AGR, Vol. 1,
page 40) (H.R.M.V., Vol. 1, page 243)

BARNHART, William H. H. (Pvt.) Co. A, 7th
Regiment Maryland Infantry. (US) Chewsville.
Age 21. Served from 18 August, 1862 to 31 May,
1865. (H.R.M.V., Vol. 1, 278,) (Scharf, Vol.
1, 226) (1890-C) (MSA-AGR, Vol. 1, page 41 and
MSA-S-936-17)

BASFORD, John H. (Pvt.) Co. B, 7th Regiment
Maryland Infantry. (US) Hagerstown. Served from
14 August, 1862 to 31 May, 1865. Wounded.
(H.R.M.V., Vol. 1, 281) (1890-C)

13

BAXTER, Andrew J. (Pvt.) Co. F, 2nd Regiment
Potomac Home Brigade Infantry. (US) Hancock.
Served 13 October, 1861 to 1 February, 1863.
Buried in Mt. Olivet Cemetery, west of Hancock.
(H.R.M.V., Vol. 1, 558) (WCCR 1, 139)

BAYNE, John. (Pvt.) Co. F, 1st Regiment Potomac
Home Brigade Infantry. (US) Age 21. Laborer.
Hancock. Served from 4 September, 1861 to 4
September, 1862. (H.R.M.V., Vol. 1, 510) (1890-
C) (MSA-AGR, Vol. 1, page 40 and S-936-23)

BAZEL, Moses. (Pvt.) Co. I, 1st Virginia Cavalry.
(CSA) Keedysville. Service dates not available.
(1890-C)

BEACHLEY, Jones E. (Cpl.) Co. E, 131st Regiment
Ohio Infantry. (US) Funkstown. Served from 2
May, 1864 to 25 August, 1864. Also, Co. H,
179th Regiment Ohio Infantry, from 9 September,
1864 to 30 June, 1865. (1890-C)

BEAN, Charles F. (Major) Co. G, 5th Texas
Infantry Regiment. (CSA) Washington County.
Bean was born near Hagerstown in 1839, and
later moved with his family to Milam County,
Texas. There he joined a ranger company,
participating in frontier service before the
war. His unit was disbanded when the war began,
allowing its members to enter the Confederate
military. Bean became a member of Gen. John B.
Hood's famous "Texas Brigade." He saw action at
Seven Days, Second Manassas, Boonsboro, or
South Mountain, and Sharpsburg. At Gettysburg
he lost his right arm in the brutal fighting
south of town. He was captured and held
prisoner in a government hospital until he was
moved to Point Lookout Prison, Md., for ten
months. On his release he went to Richmond and
was authorized to raise a battalion of five
companies. His men were recruited and had just
finished training when the war ended. Bean
attained the rank of major at this time. After
the war he returned to Texas and served in
public office as assessor and county

commissioner. (Williams, Vol. 2, 1138)

BEARD, David L. (Cpl.) Co. F, 2nd Regiment
Maryland Infantry. (US) Hancock. Served from 17
September, 1861 to 30 September, 1864. (1890-C)

BEARD, John. (Lt.) Co. F., 1st Regiment Maryland
Potomac Home Brigade Infantry. (US) Washington
Co. Entered service 21 August, 1861, as second
lieutenant in Co. F. Promoted to first
lieutenant 13 February, 1863. Mustered out 4
September, 1864. Buried in cemetery on the Etta
Daniels farm on Elbow Ridge, near Millstone.
(H.R.M.V., Vol. 1, 1, 510) (WCCR, Vol. 4, 88)

BEARD, John. (Pvt.) Co. I, 7th Regiment Maryland
Infantry. (US) Age 22. Hagerstown. Enlisted at
Hagerstown, 28 August, 1862. Transferred to
V.R.C. 16 August, 1864. Discharged 13 July,
1865. (MSA-AGR, Vol. 1, 41) (H.R.M.V., Vol. 1,
page 297)

BEARD, John. (1st Lt.) Co. F, 1st Regiment
Potomac Home Brigade Infantry, (US) Boonsboro.
Entered the service as second lieutenant, Co.
F, 21 August, 1861. Promoted to first
lieutenant 13 February, 1863. (Scharf, 327)
(H.R.M.V., Vol. 1, 510)

BEARD, Samuel M. (1st Lt.) Co. F, 1st Regiment,
Potomac Home Brigade Infantry, (US) Age 19.
Farmer. Clear Spring. Entered the service as
corporal 21 August, 1861, later promoted to
sergeant and then to first lieutenant 24
February, 1865. A veteran volunteer, he
transferred to Co. F, 13th Maryland Infantry.
(Scharf, 327) (H.R.M.V., Vol. 1, 446, 510)
(MSA-S-936-23)

BECKETT, John M. (Pvt.) Co. A, 1st Regiment
Maryland Cavalry, (CSA) Washington County.
(Hartzler, 85) (Huntsberry, 83)

BEDECKER, John R. (Pvt.) Co. H, 6th Regiment
Maryland Infantry. (US) Age 21. Enlisted at
Hagerstown, 7 August, 1862. Transferred June,

1865 to V.R.C. Discharged at Baltimore, 16
October, 1865. (MSA-AGR, Vol. 1, page 40)

BELL, Alcemus. (Pvt.) Co. A, 3rd Regiment
Maryland Infantry. (US) Age 20. Entered service
15 June, 1861. Served to 15 June, 1864.
(H.R.M.V., Vol. 1, page 117) (MSA-AGR, Vol. 1,
page 30)

BELL, George D., Jr. (Brevet Brig. Gen.) Born in
Hagerstown, he was the second son of William
Duffield and Susan Harry Bell. (Mrs. Bell's
family, originally spelled "Harrie," was among
the early settlers of Washington County. The
development directly east of Hagerstown, along
Jefferson Blvd., was once known as "Harry's
Town," after her relatives.) (see 1859 Taggert
Map of Washington County) Mr. Bell was a co-
founder of "Torch Light and Public Advertiser"
newspaper. George Bell Jr. received an
appointment to the United States Military
Academy, at West Point, by a member of Congress
from his district, J. Dixon Roman, of
Hagerstown. Bell graduated in 1853 and served
at Fort Hamilton, New York. He sharpened his
military skills on the frontier at Fort
McIntosh, Texas and later as a scout against
the Seminole Indians, in Florida. Bell
returned to the frontier for service at Fort
Brown, Texas and on commissary duty in charge
of the ordinance department at San Antonio,
Texas. He also served at Ft. McHenry,
Maryland, Fort Worth, Texas and performed Coast
Survey duty. During the Civil War he was active
as a bearer of dispatches between the General-
in-Chief and the commanding officer, Indianola,
Texas. Returning to the east, he was assigned
to a light artillery battery in defense of the
Nation's Capital, then to commissary and
quartermaster duty at Annapolis Junction, duty
in the Manassas campaign and at many other
stations. The following brevets, for war
service, were received by Bell:
Brev. Major -- U. S. A., 13 March, 1865.
Brev. Lt. Col.--U. S. A., 13 March, 1865.
Brev. Col. U. S. A., 13 March, 1865.

Brev. Brig. Gen. U. S. A., 9 April, 1865.
All were for "faithful and meritorious services
during the rebellion."
   General Bell's younger brother, Harry, served
in the 1st Maryland Confederate Cavalry.
(Williams Vol. 1, 238) (O.R. Series 1, Vol.
2, 337; Vol. 5, 28; Vol. 11, 167, 168, 169, and
176) (Kealhofer Diary, 256fn)

BELL, Henry C. (Pvt.) Co. A, 1st Regiment
   Maryland Cavalry, (CSA) Hagerstown. Son of
   William D. Bell, founder of the Hagerstown
   Torch-Light newspaper. His brother George Bell
   graduated from the United States Military
   Academy and was breveted brigadier general in
   the Union Army. Buried Rose Hill Cemetery,
   Hagerstown. (Hartzler, 85) (WCCR, Vol. 6, 167)
   (Huntsberry, 83)

BELL, William T. (Pvt.) Battery H, 11th Heavy
   Artillery. (U.S.C.T.) (US) Hagerstown. Served
   from 6 November, 1863 to 2 October, 1865.
   (1890-C)

BELLMAN, Oscar. (Pvt.) Co. I, 1st Regiment
   "Russell's" Maryland Cavalry. (US) Hagerstown.
   Served from 3 September, 1861 to 22 September
   1861. (H.R.M.V., Vol. 1, 732) (1890-C)

BELTZHOOVER, Daniel. (Col.) 1st Regular Louisiana
   Artillery Regiment. (CSA) Hagerstown. Son of
   the Beltzhoover family, operators of the
   popular Globe Tavern, on West Washington
   Street. Graduated from West Point in 1847,
   along with A. P. Hill and Henry Heth, two men
   who would play active rolls in the war for the
   South. He served with distinction in the
   Mexican War, but resigned his commission in
   1856, and was appointed professor of geometry
   and higher math at Mount Saint Mary's College,
   in Emmitsburg, Md. At the outbreak of the war
   he offered his services to the South, and was
   appointed to the staff of Gen. David E. Twigg,
   at New Orleans. In 1862, Beltzhoover became
   chief of artillery, Western Department, and in
   1864 commanded a brigade in J. H. Forney's

Division of the Trans-Mississippi Department.
As captain of the famous "Watson's" Artillery
Battery he was breveted major for gallant
conduct under Gen. Albert Sidney Johnson.
Promoted lieutenant-colonel, in 1864, he was
placed in charge of all artillery at Vicksburg,
and while there was commissioned colonel of
artillery. Beltzhoover received praise for his
gallant and heroic work during the siege of
Fort Powell, in Mobile Bay, during August,
1864. After the war he devoted himself to the
instruction of youth. He was proficient in
music and a composer of many pieces of
instrumental merit. He died at Mobile, in
November, 1870. (Scharf, Vol. 2, 1046) (Crute,
CSA Units, 138) (S.H.S.P., Vol. XXX, page 56)

BENSHOF, Lewis. (Cpl.) 165th Pennsylvania
Volunteer Infantry. (US) Downsville. Service
dates not reported to census. (1890-C)

BENCHOFF, Columbus. (2nd Lt.) Co. D. 1st Regiment
Potomac Home Brigade "Cole's" Cavalry. (US)
Washington County. Entered service 25 February,
1865, as a private. Promoted second lieutenant
10 April, 1865. Discharged 28 June, 1865.
(H.R.M.V., Vol. 1, 678)

BENDER, Augustas, (Pvt.) Co. A., 1st Regiment
Potomac Home Brigade Infantry. (US) Sharpsburg.
Served from 19 September, 1861 to 27 August,
1864. Buried at Mountain View Cemetery,
Sharpsburg. (H.R.M.V., Vol. 1, 486) (WCCR 1,
49)

BENDER, Benjamin. (Pvt.) Co. D, 1st Regiment
Potomac Home Brigade Infantry. (US) Age 25.
Boatman. Sharpsburg. Served from 19
September, 1861 to 27 August, 1864.
Transferred to Co. D 13th Regiment Potomac Home
Brigade Infantry. Buried at Mountain View
Cemetery, Sharpsburg. (H.R.M.V., Vol. 1, 486,
503)) (WCCR 1, 37) (1890-C) (Scharf, Vol. 1,
226) (MSA-AGR-S-936-22)

BENDER, Jacob. (Pvt.) Co. D., 1st Regiment

Potomac Home Brigade Infantry. (US)   Age 21.
Boatman.   Enlisted at Sharpsburg, 15 August,
1861.   Veteran. Transferred to Co. D, 13th
Regiment Infantry.   (H.R.M.V., Vol. 1, page
502)   (MSA-AGR-S-936-22)

BENDER, Michael. (Pvt.) Co. D, 13th Regiment
Maryland Infantry.   (US)   Boonsboro. Served
from 2 February, 1865 to 29 May, 1865.
(H.R.M.V., Vol. 1, 441) (1890-C)

BENNER, Bently Aaron. (Pvt.) Co. H, 1st Regiment
Potomac Home Brigade Infantry.   (US)
Sharpsburg.   Served from 25 October, 1861 to 25
October, 1864. (H.R.M.V., Vol.   1, 524) (1890-
C) (Scharf, 226)

BENNIX, William C. (Pvt.) Co. I, 7th Maryland
Infantry.   (US) Washington Co. Age 20.   Served
from 31 August, 1862 to 31 May, 1865.   Buried
in Rose Hill Cemetery, Hagerstown.   (H.R.M.V.,
Vol.   1,297) (WCCR, Vol. 6, 259) (MSA-AGR, Vol.
1, page 44)

BERNARD, Michael. (Pvt.) Co. H, 6th Regiment
Maryland Infantry.   (US)   Age 29.   Enlisted at
Hagerstown, 1 September, 1862.   Deserted at
Williamsport, Md., 20 November, 1862. (MSA-AGR,
Vol. 1, page 40)

BERRY, Nimrod.   (Pvt.) Co. H, 6th Regiment
Maryland Infantry. (US)   Age 21.   Enlisted at
Hagerstown, 4 August, 1864.   Deserted at
Williamsport, Md., 11 December, 1862. (MSA-AGR,
Vol. 1, page 40)

BERRY, Silas. (Pvt.) Co. A, 3rd Regiment Maryland
Infantry. (US)   Enlisted at Williamsport, 15
June, 1861.   Age 29.   Served until 15 June,
1864.   (H.R.M.V., Vol. 1, page 116) (MSA-AGR,
Vol.   1, page 29)

BEYARD, Samuel M. (1st Lt.) Co. F, 13th Regiment
Maryland Infantry. (US) Clear Spring. Enlisted
21 August, 1862 with rank of corporal.
Initially served with Capt. John T. Whitter's

Company attached to Lockwood's Independent
Brigade of the Federal 8th Corps. Taken
prisoner at Harper's Ferry, 15 September, 1862
and paroled to Annapolis. Later served guard
duty on lower Potomac. In 1863 prior to the
Battle of Gettysburg, Beyard was sent to
Baltimore to help build entrenchments. He
arrived at Gettysburg in time to take part in
the second and third day's fighting. Discharged
February, 1864. Reenlisted with Co. F, 13th
Maryland Infantry as a first lieutenant. Taken
prisoner at Duffield Station, Va., sent to the
notorious Andersonville, Ga., prison where he
was confined seven months. After the war he
returned to Washington County and turned to
farming. In 1892 he was killed in a train wreck
on the Baltimore and Ohio line, near Cherry
Run, W. Va. (H.R.M.V., Vol. 1, 446, 510)
(Williams, Vol. 2, 804)

BICKLE, Christian F. (spelled Bickley in HRMV)
(Sgt.) Co. E, 1st Regiment Potomac Home Brigade
Infantry. (US) Hagerstown. Served from 1
October, 1861 to 1 October, 1864. (H.R.M.V.,
Vol. 1, 506) (1890-C)

BICKLE, Ferdinand H. (Cpl.) Co. H, 6th Regiment
Maryland Infantry. (US) Smithsburg. Age 20.
Enlisted at Hagerstown 21 August, 1862. Served
to 31 May, 1865. Taken prisoner on 15 June,
1863, at Winchester, Va. Mustered out while at
McClellan U.S.A. Hospital, Philadelphia, Pa.,
31 May, 1865. (H.R.M.V., Vol. 1, 241) (1890-C)
(MSA-AGR, Vol. 1, 40 and S-936-2)

BINGAMAN, John B. (Pvt.) Co. A, 7th Regiment
Maryland Infantry. (US) Washington County.
Age 18. Served from 14 August, 1862 to 31 May,
1865. Discharged at Arlington Heights, Va.
(H.R.M.V., Vol. 1, 278) (Scharf, Vol. 1, 226)
(MSA-AGR, Vol. 1, page 41 and MSA-S-936-17)

BINGAMAN, Levi F. (Cpl.) Co. B, 3rd Regiment
Potomac Home Brigade Infantry. (US) Hagerstown.
Entered service at Hagerstown 9 November, 1861.
Discharged 9 November, 1864. (H.R.M.V., Vol.

1, 575) (Captain Maxwell's roster) (MSA-S-936-23)

BINGHAM, David. (Pvt.) Co. D, 2nd Regiment Maryland Cavalry. (US) Weverton. Served from 6 July, 1863 to 6 February, 1864. (H.R.M.V., Vol. 1, 754) (1890-C)

BINGHAM, George H. (Pvt.) Co. D, 2nd Maryland Cavalry. (US) Weverton. Bingham and his family, living near Harper's Ferry at the time, witnessed the John Brown raid in 1859. He served throughout the conflict and was later appointed postmaster at Weverton, by President Harrison. (Williams, Vol. 2, 1289)

BISHOP, John. (Pvt.) Co. H, 3rd Regiment Maryland Cavalry. (US) Hancock. Served 28 September, 1863 to 7 September, 1865. Buried in Mt. Olivet Cemetery, west of Hancock. (H.R.M.V., Vol. 1, 774) (WCCR, Vol. 2, 139.)

BISON, Henry. (Pvt.) Co. B, 3rd Regiment Potomac Home Brigade Infantry. (US) Age 20. Washington County. Enlisted 9 December, 1861. Veteran. Discharged 29 May, 1865. (H.R.M.V., Vol. 1, page 576) (MSA-S-936-23)

BLAIR, Andrew J. (Pvt.) Co. G, 1st Regiment Potomac Home Brigade "Cole's" Cavalry. (US) Bugler. Williamsport. Served from 26 February, 1864 to 28 June, 1865. (H.R.M.V., Vol. 1, 687) (1890-C)

BLAIR, Phillip D. (Pvt.) Co. L, 22nd Pennsylvania Volunteer Cavalry. Buried in Rose Hill Cemetery, Hagerstown. (WCCR, Vol. 7, 233)

BLANK, Jacob P. (Pvt.) Co. K, 1st Regiment Maryland Infantry. (US) Eakle's Mill. Served from 28 May, 1861 to 2 July, 1865. Suffered with inflammatory rheumatism. (H.R.M.V., Vol. 1, 66) (1890-C)

BLESSING, John H. (Pvt.) Co. F, 13th Regiment Maryland Infantry. (US) Age 31. Stonemason.

Enlisted at Sandy Hook, Md., 26 January, 1865.
Discharged 29 May, 1865. (H.R.M.V., Vol. 1,
page 446) (MSA-AGR-S-936-22)

BLOOM, George D. (Pvt.) Co. H, 1st Regiment
Maryland Cavalry. (US) Hagerstown. Served
from 3 December, 1861 to 8 August, 1865.
(H.R.M.V., Vol. 1, 729) (1890-C)

BOGARD, Samuel M. (Lt.) Co. F, 13th Regiment
Maryland Infantry. (US) Age 19. Clear Spring.
Served from 21 May, 1860 to 25 May, 1864.
Transferred to 1st Regiment Maryland Home
Brigade. (1890-C)

BOLINGER, John C. (Pvt.) Regimental Band, 1st
Maryland Infantry. (US) Hagerstown. Served
from 29 September, 1861 to 25 August, 1862.
(H.R.M.V., Vol. 1, 18) (1890-C)

BOLMER, David T. (Pvt.) Co. A, 7th Regiment
Maryland Infantry. (US) Washington County.
Age 36. Entered service 16 August, 1862.
Deserted 30 January, 1863, at Maryland Heights.
(H.R.M.V., Vol. 1, 278) (Scharf, Vol. 1, 226)
(MSA-AGR, Vol. 1, page 41 and MSA-S-936-17)

BONEBRAKE, Andrew S. (Pvt.) Co. H, 6th Regiment
Maryland Infantry. (US) Age 21. Enlisted 21
August, 1861, at Hagerstown. Taken prisoner.
Exchanged. Discharged at Washington, D.C., 20
June, 1865. Government paid him $10 for
rations owed while a prisoner of war.
(H.R.M.V., Vol. 1, page 241) (MSA-AGR, Vol. 1,
page 40, and (MSA-AGR-S-936-2)

BONER, John H. (Cpl.) Co. D, 1st Regiment
Potomac Home Brigade "Cole's Cavalry." (US)
Leitersburg. Enlisted 24 August, 1861. Taken
prisoner. Exchanged. Discharged 15 September,
1864. (H.R.M.V., Vol. 1, 671) (Bell, 67)

BOOTH, John. (Pvt.) Co. I, 1st Regiment
"Russell's" Maryland Cavalry. (US) Washington
County. Enlisted 3 September, 1861. Killed in
action at High Bridge, Va., 5 April, 1865.

(H.R.M.V., Vol. 1, 732) (McClannahan papers, 4)

BORNUM, Charles. (Sgt.) Co. H, 10th U.S. Cavalry.
(US) Washington Co. Buried in Beautiful View
Cemetery, near State Line. (WCCR, Vol. 6, 61)

BOSWELL, George M. (Pvt.) Co. G, 1st Regiment
Potomac Home Brigade "Cole's" Cavalry. (US)
Sharpsburg. Served from 4 August, 1864 to 25
May, 1865. H.R.M.V., Vol. 1, 687) (1890-C)
(Scharf, 226) (MSA-AGR-S-936-22)

BOVEY, William H. (Pvt.) Co. A, 7th Regiment
Maryland Infantry. (US) Washington County.
Age 22. Entered service 14 August, 1862,
discharged 31 May, 1865, at Arlington Heights,
Va. (H.R.M.V., Vol. 1, 278) (Scharf, Vol. 1,
226) (MSA-AGR, Vol. 1, page 41 and MSA-S-936-
17)

BOWARD, Denton. (Pvt.) Co. B, 7th Regiment
Maryland Infantry. (US) Hagerstown. Musician.
Age 18. Served from 18 August, 1862 to 31 May,
1865. Member Independent Junior Fire Company,
of Hagerstown. Buried in Rose Hill Cemetery,
Hagerstown. (H.R.M.V., Vol. 1, 281) (WCCR,
Vol. 7, 254) (1890-C) (MSA-AGR, Vol. 1, page
41) (I.J.F.C. roster)

BOWARD, Joseph. (Pvt.) Co. I, 7th Regiment
Maryland Infantry. (US) Hagerstown. Age 39.
Served from 26 August, 1862 to 31 May, 1865.
(H.R.M.V., Vol. 1, 297) (1890-C) (MSA-AGR, Vol.
1, page 44)

BOWARD, William W. (Pvt.) Co. I, 7th Regiment
Maryland Infantry. (US) Hagerstown. Served
from 19 August, 1862 to 29 March, 1865. Buried
in Rose Hill Cemetery, Hagerstown. (1890-C)
(WCCR, Vol. 7, 254)

BOWDEN, Charles W. (Pvt.) Co. A, 3rd Regiment
Maryland Infantry. (US) Age 44. Enlisted at
Williamsport, 15 July, 1861. Served until 15
July, 1864. (H.R.M.V., Vol. 1, page 117) (MSA-
AGR, Vol. 1, page 29)

23

BOWER, Andrew. (Pvt.) Co. A, 7th Regiment
Maryland Infantry. (US) Washington County.
Age 21. Served from 8 August, 1862 to 31 May,
1865. Discharged at Arlington Heights, Va.
(H.R.M.V., Vol. 1, 278) (Scharf, Vol. 1, 226)
(MSA-AGR, Vol. 1, page 41 and MSA-S-936-17)

BOWERS, George W. (Pvt.) Co. B, 3rd Regiment
Potomac Home Brigade Infantry. (US) Age 23.
Washington County. Enlisted at Hagerstown, 3
December, 1861. Discharged 1, November, 1865.
(H.R.M.V., Vol. 1, page 576) (MSA-S-936-23)

BOWERS, James. (Pvt.) Co. A, 1st Regiment
Maryland Cavalry. (US) Indian Springs.
Teamster. Enlisted 28 September, 1861.
Discharged 16 April, 1863. (1890-C) (H.R.M.V.,
Vol. 1, page 706) (MSA-S-936-23)

BOWERS, John C. (Sgt.) Co. H, 3rd Maryland
Cavalry Regiment. (US) Hagerstown. Served from
28 September, 1863 to 7 September, 1865.
Transferred to non-commissioned officers staff.
(H.R.M.V., Vol. 1, 774) (1890-C)

BOWERS, William. (Pvt.) Co. B, 3rd Regiment
Potomac Home Brigade Infantry. (US) Age 22.
Chewsville. Enlisted at Hagerstown, 20
January, 1862. Transferred to Co. F.
Discharged 30 January, 1865. (H.R.M.V., Vol.
1, page 576) (Captain Maxwell's roster) (MSA-S-
936-23)

BOWIE, Washington. (Pvt.) (CSA) Unit unknown.
Buried in Rose Hill Cemetery, Hagerstown.
(WCCR, Vol. 7, 454)

BOWLES, John C. (Cpl.) Co. A, 3rd Regiment
Maryland Infantry. (US) Enlisted at
Williamsport 15 June, 1861. Age 22. Mustered
out 15 June, 1865. (MSA-AGR, Vol. 1, 29)
(H.R.M.V., Vol. 1, 117)

BOWMAN, David. (Pvt.) Co. D, 3rd Regiment
Maryland Infantry. (US) Smoketown. Served

from May, 1864 to August, 1865. Discharged due
to loss of fingers on right hand. (1890-C)

BOWMAN, David A. (Pvt.) Co. F, 13th Regiment
Maryland Infantry. (US) Smithsburg. Served
from 15 February, 1865 to 29 May, 1865.
(H.R.M.V., Vol. 1, 446) (1890-C)

BOWMAN, John. (Pvt.) Co. C, 5th Regiment Maryland
Infantry. (US) Age 26. Farm laborer.
Smoketown. Served from 29 October, 1864 to 1
September, 1865. Discharged at Frederick, Md.
(H.R.M.V., Vol. 1, 191) (1890-C) (Discharge
papers in possession of Mr. Bill Fuss, of
Williamsport)

BOWMAN, John C. (Pvt.) Co. A, 7th Regiment
Maryland Infantry. (US) Smoketown. Age 20.
Entered service 18 August, 1862. Wounded in
action 27 June, 1864, at Petersburg, Va. Taken
prisoner 31 March, 1865 at White Oak Road, Va.
(H.R.M.V., Vol. 1, 278) (Scharf, Vol. 1, 226)
(MSA-S-936-17)

BOWMAN, Joseph. (Pvt.) Co. D, 12th Regiment
Maryland Infantry. (US) Smithsburg. Served
from 27 July, 1864 to 6 November, 1864.
(H.R.M.V., Vol. 1, 427) (1890-C)

BOWSER, Charles W. (Pvt.) Co. B, 3rd Regiment
Potomac Home Brigade Infantry. (US) Age 18.
Shoemaker. Beaver Creek. Enlisted at
Hagerstown, 1 December, 1861. Veteran.
Transferred to Co. F. Discharged 29 May, 1865.
(H.R.M.V., Vol. 1, page 592) (Captain
Maxwell's roster) (MSA-S-936-23)

BOYD, Andrew G. (Pvt.) Co. A, 1st Maryland
Cavalry. (CSA) Washington County. (Hartzler,
93) (Huntsberry, 83) (Goldsborough, 229)

BOYER, Andrew. (Pvt.) Co. E, 1st Regiment Potomac
Home Brigade Infantry. (US) Age 20. Laborer.
Enlisted at Hagerstown, 1 October, 1861.
Reenlisted 23 February, 1864 at Sandy Hook, Md.
Discharged 29 May, 1865. (H.R.M.V., Vol. 1,

page 506) (MSA-S-936-23)

BOYERS, Jacob F. (Pvt.) Co. E, 3rd Regiment
Potomac Home Brigade Infantry. (US)
Brownsville. Served from 31 March, 1864 to 29
May, 1865. (H.R.M.V., Vol. 1, 588) (1890-C)

BRADY, Joshua, J. (Pvt.) Co. F, 2nd Regiment
Potomac Home Brigade Infantry. (US) Age 20.
Farmer. Washington County. Enlisted 31 August,
1861. Transferred to Co. C. Discharged 29 May,
1865. (H.R.M.V., Vol. 1, 558) (MSA-S-936-24)

BRANDENBERG, Amos. (Sgt.) Co. H, 6th Regiment
Maryland Infantry. (US) Age 21. Enlisted at
Hagerstown 14 August, 1862. Accidentally
wounded April, 1864. Wounded in action 2 April,
1865, near Petersburg, Va. Lost one leg.
Promoted to sergeant on same date. (MSA-AGR,
Vol. 1, 40) (H.R.M.V., Vol. 1, 241 and (MSA-
AGR-S 936-2)

BRANE, Granison G. (Pvt.) Co. G, 1st Regiment
Potomac Home Brigade Infantry. (US)
Brownsville. Served 2 September, 1862 29 May,
to 1865. Transferred to Co. G, 13th Maryland
Infantry. (H.R.M.V., Vol. 1, 517) (1890-C)

BREATHED, James. (Lt. Col.) Stuart Horse
Artillery. Born in Morgan County, Va., 15
December, 1838. When very young he moved with
his family to Washington County and was
educated at St. James College. Later he
graduated from the University of Maryland
Medical School. His apprenticeship was served
in Hagerstown under Dr. James Macgill, of
Hagerstown. Dr. Breathed moved to Missouri to
begin his practice, but returned to Washington
County when the war began. His companion on the
trip home was J. E. B. Stuart, soon to become
famous for his exploits as Gen. Robert E.
Lee's resourceful cavalry commander.
Breathed expressed great dissatisfaction with
the Maryland General Assembly's vacillation
over the war and determined he would act in
favor of the south. He enlisted at Martinsburg,

26

Virginia (now West Virginia) on 31 August,
1861, as a private in Company B of the 1st
Virginia Cavalry, commanded at that time by
Stuart. Later, Stuart recognized Breathed and
gave him special service work as a scout. On 23
March, 1862, Breathed was selected first
lieutenant under Capt. John Pelham in a
battalion of horse artillery organized by
Stuart. The young doctor was promoted to
captain on 9 August, 1862, after he recruited
more than one hundred Marylanders into the
horse artillery. He advanced to the rank of
major on 22 February, 1864. During his
brilliant, but short military career, he became
one of the finest artillery officers in the
southern army. When a battle was over he
applied his medical skills to the wounded of
both sides. Breathed's battery fought in the
thick of almost all actions of the Army of
Northern Virginia including the Peninsula
campaign, Fair Oaks, Seven Days near Richmond,
Antietam and Gettysburg. Breathed saw action
throughout Washington County as Lee's army
retreated from Gettysburg, in 1863. He was
seriously wounded at the Battle of Yellow
Tavern, Virginia, near Richmond, on 11 May,
1864, where his friend Stuart was killed.
During the furious action there he was cut from
the saddle and fell among the hoofs of charging
horses. When his men returned for him they
discovered he had pulled a Federal officer from
his horse, climbed on it, and galloped away to
safety. On another occasion he used his great
skills in hand-to-hand combat to defeat two
enemy officers who charged him. Fitz Lee, a
Confederate brigade commander and nephew of
Gen. Robert E. Lee, often referred to
Breathed's "Proverbial intrepidity and
recklessness," upon every battlefield. He was
wounded again in the fighting around Richmond
at the close of the war. After Yellow Tavern he
received a personal letter from Gen. Robert E.
Lee, which read in part, "Major,- I heard with
great regret that you were wounded and
incapacitated for regular duty. I beg to
tender you my sympathy, and to express the hope

that the army will not long be without your
valuable services." Earlier, on 21 March, 1864,
a highly complimentary letter was received from
Stuart, "I am sensible of the distinguished
gallantry which you have always displayed when
brought in contact with the enemy, and can also
assure you of its appreciation by the
commanding general. I feel confident you will
soon be promoted." Breathed was paroled at
Winchester on 24 April, 1865. Returning to
Washington County he established his medical
practice at Hancock. While some citizens
initially objected to treatment from a "Rebel"
doctor, he was finally accepted and practiced
on both sides of the Mason-Dixon line. His
gentle demeanor and dedication to his
profession resulted in many families naming
their babies after him. Breathed died from the
lingering effects of war wounds on 14 February,
1870, at the age of thirty-two. He is buried in
St. Thomas' Graveyard, in Hancock. (1)

BREATHED, John W. Jr. (Pvt.) Co. B, 35th
Virginia Cavalry, (CSA) Washington County.
Brother of Col. James Breathed of Stuart's
Horse Artillery. (Hartzler, 95)

BRECKLEMAN, Augustas. (Pvt.) Co. L, 1st Potomac
Home Brigade "Cole's" Cavalry. (US) Washington
Co. Bugler. Served from 31 March, 1864 to 28
June, 1865. Buried in Rose Hill Cemetery,
Hagerstown. (H.R.M.V., Vol. 1, 696) (WCCR, Vol.
7, 388)

BRENEMAN, Martin. (Pvt.) Co. F, 3rd Regiment
Potomac Home Brigade Infantry.(US) Beaver
Creek. Enlisted at Hagerstown, 1 December,
1862. Taken Prisoner 9 July, 1864, at battle of
Monocacy, Md. Discharged 29 May, 1865.
(H.R.M.V., Vol. 1, page 592) (Captain Maxwell's
roster.)

BREWER, James H. C. (1st Lt.) Also Regimental
Quartermaster, 6th Maryland Infantry. (US)
Clear Spring. Entered the service as second
lieutenant, Co. H. Promoted to first lieutenant

11 February, 1863 and to first lieutenant and regimental quartermaster 17 November, 1864. (Scharf, 327) (H.R.M.V., Vol. 1, 224, 240)

BREWER, Valentine G. (1st Lt.) Co. A, 7th Regiment Maryland Infantry. (US) Clear Spring. Age 22. Entered at Hagerstown as private, 8 August, 1863 and moved rapidly through the ranks to first Lieutenant, 10 November, 1864. (Scharf, 327) (H.R.M.V., Vol. 1, 278) (MSA-AGR, Vol. 1, page 40 and MSA-S-936-17)

BRIAN, James H. (Pvt.) Co. H, 4th Regiment Maryland Infantry. (US) Clear Spring. (1890-C)

BRIDENDORF, Harrison. (Pvt.) Co. H, 6th Regiment Maryland Infantry. (US) Age 32. Enlisted at Hagerstown for three years on 14 August, 1862. Deserted, caught and returned. Ordered to forfeit all bounty and pay due, or that may be due, and to be confined in Fort McHenry prison for two years and six months. Drummed out of service. (MSA-AGR, Vol. 1, 17 and (MSA-AGR-S-936-2) (H.R.M.V., Vol. 1, pages 20, 241)

BRIDENDOLPH, John D. (Pvt.) Co. F, 1st Regiment Potomac Home Brigade Infantry. (US) Age 25. Farmer. Washington County. Enlisted 27 Feb., 1864. Transferred to Co. F, 13th Regiment Maryland Infantry. Discharged 29 May, 1865. (H.R.M.V., Vol. 1, page 511) (MSA-S-936-23)

BRIDENDOLPH, William H. (Pvt.) Co. F, 1st Regiment Potomac Home Brigade Infantry. (US) Age 18. Farmer. Washington County. Enlisted 27 February, 1864. Transferred to Co. F, 13th Regiment Maryland Infantry. (H.R.M.V., Vol. 1, page 511) (MSA-S-936-23)

BRIETNESSER, Samuel Leonard. (Pvt.) Co. H, 6th Regiment Maryland Infantry. (US) Age 22. Enlisted at Hagerstown, 21 August, 1862. Wounded in action at the Wilderness, 6 May, 1864. Discharged 26 June, 1865. (H.R.M.V., Vol. 1, page 241) (MSA-AGR, Vol. 1, page 40, and (MSA-AGR-S-936-2)

BRILL, George. (Pvt.) Co. D, 13th Regiment
Maryland Infantry. (US) Hagerstown. Musician.
Served from 4 September, 1861 to 29 May, 1865.
Veteran. (H.R.M.V., Vol. 1, 442) (1890-C)

BRILL, John. (Pvt.) Co. B, 13th Regiment Maryland
Infantry. (US) Hagerstown. Musician. Served
from 1 March, 1865 to 29 May, 1865. (H.R.M.V.,
Vol. 1, 435) (1890-C)

BRINE, Samuel G. (Pvt.) Co. A, 1st Maryland
Infantry, (CSA) Hagerstown. (Hartzler, 96)
(Huntsberry, 83)

BROGUNIER, Aaron H. (Pvt.) Co. A, 7th Regiment
Maryland Infantry. (US) Hagerstown. Age 27.
Member Independent Junior Fire Company of
Hagerstown. Enlisted Hagerstown, 13 August,
1862. Shot through ankle in action, 27 June,
1864, at Petersburg, Va. Hospitalized at
Frederick, Md. Discharged there 26 May, 1865.
(H.R.M.V., Vol. 1, 278) (Scharf, Vol. 1, 226)
(1890-C) (MSA-AGR, Vol. 1, page 41 and MSA-S-
936-17) (I.J.F.C. roster) (Pension List, 157)

BROGUNIER, James D. (Pvt.) Co. A, 1st Regiment
Potomac Home Brigade "Cole's" Cavalry. (US)
Hagerstown. Entered service 10 August, 1861.
Transferred to Co. I, 1st Regiment Potomac Home
Brigade Infantry, 1 November, 1861. Mr.
Brogunier operated the State Toll Gate along
the National Pike, west of Hagerstown, for over
forty years. It was located about where the
industrial park, housing the Washington County
Detention Center, is today. When the toll gate
was closed he went into dairy farming. Mr.
Brogunier died at his home, 728 West Washington
Street, on 23 June, 1925 at age 82. Buried in
Rose Hill Cemetery, Hagerstown. (H.R.M.V., Vol.
1, 666) (Mrs. Annie Brew, his great-grand
daughter, of Hagerstown)

BROGUNIER, Joshua. (Pvt.) Co. I, 7th Regiment
Maryland Infantry. (US) Age 22. Enlisted at
Hagerstown, 28 August, 1862. Died of disease

contracted in service 15 July, 1863. (MSA-AGR, Vol. 1, page 44) (H.R.M.V., Vol. 1, page 297)

BROOKS, Benjamin. (Sgt.) Co. G, 7th Regiment Maryland Infantry. U.S.C.T. (US) Hagerstown. Also reported as 38th Regiment. Served from February, 1864 to February 1865. (1890-C)

BROOKS, Lloyd. (Sgt.) Co. B, 4th Regiment Maryland Infantry, U.S.C.T. (US) Williamsport. Served from 26 August, 1863 to 4 May, 1866. (H.R.M.V., Vol. 2, 134)

BROOKS, Nathanial. (Pvt) Co. B, 4th Regiment, USCT Maryland Volunteers. (US) Clear Spring. Entered service 26 Sugust, 1863. Lost left arm in action. Discharged 24 June, 1865. Received monthly pension of $18.00. (Pensions List, 157)

BROOKS, Samuel T. H. (Pvt.) Co. I, 1st Regiment "Russell's" Maryland Cavalry. (US) Hagerstown. Enlisted at Williamsport, 17 December, 1862. Discharged 8 August, 1865. (H.R.M.V., Vol. 1, 732) (1890-C) (MSA-AGR-S-936-38)

BROOKS, William H. (Pvt.) Co. B, 3rd Regiment Potomac Home Brigade Infantry. (US) Age 22. Hagerstown. Enlisted at Hagerstown, 23 December, 1861. Transferred to Co. F. Discharged 1 No. 1865. (H.R.M.V., Vol. 1, page 576) (Captain Maxwell's roster) (MSA-S-(936-23)

BROOM, Sanuel. (Pvt.) Co. F, 19th Regiment Maryland Infantry. (U.S.C.T.) (US) Hagerstown. Served from 21 May, 1863 to 15 January, 1867. (1890-C)

BROOKS, V. B. (Pvt.) 1st Regiment Maryland Infantry. (1890-C)

BROSIEUS, Benjamin. (Pvt.) Co. H, 3rd Regiment Maryland Cavalry. (US) Hagerstown. Served from 28 September, 1863 to 7 September, 1865. (H.R.M.V., Vol. 1, 775) (1890-C)

BROWN, Austin, (Sgt.) Co. H., 1st Maryland

Cavalry. (US) Sharpsburg. Age 26. Horse
dealer. Enlisted in Capt. Zeller's Company,
1st Regiment Virginia Volunteers, 25 September,
1861, at Williamsport, for three years. Later,
transferred to Co. H, 1st Maryland Cavalry.
Promoted corporal 1 May, 1862. Transferred to
Co. K, 1st Maryland Cavalry, 12 December, 1863.
Served as orderly at regimental headquarters in
July, 1863. Promoted sergeant in 1863 while on
detached service at Brandy Station, Va.
Transferred to Co. C, 1st Maryland Cavalry, 16
May, 1864 at Baltimore, Md. Served extra, or
daily duty temporarily at headquarters of 10
Corps in August, 1864. Discharged on expiration
of term of enlistment 3 December, 1864, at
Varina, Va. Died at Williamsport, Md., January,
1898. (National Archives service record and
family history prepared by Linda Austin West,
of Lancaster, Pa.)

BROWN, George W. (Pvt.) Co. A, 3rd Regiment
Maryland Infantry. (US) Age 30. Entered
service 15 June, 1861. Served until 15 June,
1864. (H.R.M.V., Vol. 1, page 117) (MSA-AGR,
Vol. 1, page 29)

BROWN, Henry A. (Pvt.) Battery B, "Snow's" First
Light Artillery. (US) Smithsburg. Served From
5 December, 1862 to 7 September, 1863.
(H.R.M.V., Vol. 1, 804) (1890-C)

BROWN, James F. (Pvt.) 1st Virginia Cavalry and
Stuart's Horse Artillery, Breathed's Battery.
(CSA) Hagerstown. Born at Pikesville, Md.,
moved at an early age with family to
Hagerstown. Educated at St. James College. In
1861 when Gen. Patterson made his move into
Virginia, Brown joined the Virginia cavalry.
Served initially as a courier for J. E. B.
Stuart until the horse artillery was formed.
Captured at Hagerstown 13 July, 1863 during the
Confederate retreat from Gettysburg. Exchanged
March, 1865. (CVM, Vol. 14, 65) (Hartzler, 98)

BROWN, James S. (Pvt.) Co. F, 1st Regiment
Potomac Home Brigade Infantry. (US) Age 23.

Carpenter. Weverton. Enlisted at Sandy Hook,
Md. Served from 19 January, 1865 to 29 May,
1865. Transferred to Co. F, 13th Regiment
Maryland Infantry. (H.R.M.V., Vol. 1, 446)
(1890-C) (MSA-S-936-23)

BROWN, John F. (Sgt.) Co. I, 38th Infantry
Regiment. (U.S.C.T.) (US) Hagerstown. Entered
15 February, 1865. Drowned 14 January, 1866.
(1890-C)

BROWN, John M. (Pvt.) Co. K, 126 Pennsylvania
Volunteer Infantry. (US) Williamsport. Served
from 15 August, 1862 to 1 March, 1863. (1890-C)

BROWN, John R. (Cpl.) Co. F. 2nd (U.S.C.T.) (US)
Buried at Red Hill Cemetery, near Keedysville.
(WCCR, Vol. 5, 180)

BROWN, Martin L. (Pvt.) Co. D, 4th Regiment
Maryland Infantry. (U.S.C.T.) (US)
Williamsport. Served from 28 August, 1863 to 4
May, 1866. (1890-C)

BROWN, R. E. (Pvt.) 1st Maryland Cavalry. (CSA)
Age 16. Hagerstown. Brother to James F.
Brown. (above) Killed at Winchester, Va., 19
September, 1864. (CVM, Vol. 14, 34)

BROWN, Talman J. (Pvt.) Co. H, 6th Regiment
Maryland Infantry. (US) Age 18. Enlisted at
Hagerstown, 21 August, 1861. Deserted at
Washington, D.C., 15 August, 1864. (H.R.M.V.,
Vol. 1, page 241) (MSA-AGR, Vol. 1, page 40)

BROWN, William. (1st Corp.) Co. K, 6th Regiment
Maryland Infantry. (US) Age 32. Enlisted 21
August, 1862 at Hagerstown. Wounded 2 April,
1865, in assault on enemy works near
Petersburg, Va. Sent to hospital in
Philadelphia. Discharged at Philadelphia 16
June, 1865. (MSA-AGR, Vol. 1, 40)

BRUFF, Joseph E. (Sgt.) Co. H, 6th Regiment
Maryland Infantry. (US) Age 21. Enlisted at
Hagerstown 12 August, 1862. Killed in action

at the Wilderness, Va., 5 May, 1864. (MSA-AGR, Vol. 1, 40) (H.R.M.V., Vol. 1, 243)

BRUTWEIZER (?), Peter. (Pvt.) Co. A, 7th Regiment Maryland Infantry. (US) Hagerstown. Served July, 1863 to 31 May, 1865. (1890-C)

BUCK, Jacob M. (Pvt.) Co. I, 1st Regiment Potomac Home Brigade Infantry. (US) Rohrersville. Served from 19 January, 1864 to 29 May, 1865. Transferred to Co. I, 13th Maryland Regiment. (H.R.M.V., Vol. 1, 530) (1890-C)

BUCK, Silas. (Pvt.) Co. I, 1st Regiment Maryland Infantry, Potomac Home Brigade. (US) Keedysville. Entered service in 1861. Served three years and two months. Was present when Harper's Ferry surrendered in 1862; fought at Gettysburg, discharged at Fredericksburg, Va., in 1865. Immediately joined Co. I, 13th Regiment Maryland Volunteers, and served until the war's end. After receiving his discharge at Baltimore he returned to Keedysville as a cabinet maker. (Williams, Vol. 2, 1167) (H.R.M.V., Vol. 1, 454)

BUCK, William. (Pvt.) Co. A, 7th Regiment Maryland Infantry. (US) Hagerstown. Age 20. The son of George Buck, a taylor, he entered at age 20. Served 8 August, 1862 to 3 June, 1865. Wounded in action 27 June, 1864, at Petersburg, VA. Taken prisoner 31 March, 1865. (H.R.M.V., Vol. 1, 278) (Dorrance Collection, letter 16 Feb., 1863) (Scharf, Vol. 1, 226) (1860-C, page 3) (MSA-S-936-17)

BUCKLAND, L. L. (Pvt.) (US) Unit unknown. Washington County. Buried in Rose Hill Cemetery, Hagerstown. (WCCR, Vol. 7, 248)

BULLEN, Jacob W. (Pvt.) Co. K, 6th Regiment Maryland Infantry. (US) Age 19. Entered service at Hagerstown 29 August, 1862. Discharged at Washington, D.C., 20 June, 1865. (MSA-AGR, Vol. 1, page 40) (H.R.M.V., Vol. 1, page 245)

BUNTZ, Charles S.W. (Pvt.) Co. H, 2nd Regiment
Potomac Home Brigade Infantry. (US) Age 18.
Farmer. Washington County. Enlisted at New
Creek, W. Va., 31 August, 1861. Transferred to
Co. A. Veteran. Discharged 29 May, 1865.
(H.R.M.V., Vol. 1, 562) (MSA-S-936-24)

BURGER, Conrad. (Pvt.) Co. F, 3rd Regiment
Potomac Home Brigade Infantry. (US) Age 25.
Hagerstown. Served from 28 February, 1864 to
29 May, 1865. (H.R.M.V., Vol. 1, 592) (1890-C)
(MSA-S-936-24)

BURGESS, John W. (Pvt.) Griffeth's Battery,
Stuart's Horse Artillery. (CSA) Hancock.
(1890-C)

BURGER, John G. (Pvt.) Co. F, 3rd Regiment
Potomac Home Brigade Infantry. (US) Age 27.
Hagerstown. Served from 28 February, 1864 to 29
May, 1865. (H.R.M.V., Vol. 1, 592) (1890-C)
(MSA-S-936-23)

BURGESS, John W. (Sgt.) Battery B, Baltimore
(2nd) Light Artillery. (CSA) Williamsport and
Hancock. His preparations for a professional
career were interrupted when the war began. He
enlisted in an artillery unit composed of many
Maryland volunteers, attached to the famous
"Stonewall" brigade. Burgess participated in
fighting at Port Republic, South Mountain and
Gettysburg. In 1862 he was near Gen. Jackson
when killed by his own men. He served to the
end of the war, then returned to Williamsport
and later moved to Hancock. He served as
Superintendent of the Chesapeake and Ohio
Canal. (Williams, Vol. 2, 976) (H.R.M.V., Vol.
1, 829) Hartzler, 102.

BURHAM, William H. (2nd Lt.) Co. K, 7th Regiment
Maryland Infantry. (US) Washington County.
Entered service at Hagerstown 4 April, 1864.
Discharged 31 May, 1865. (H.R.M.V., Vol. 1,
299) (MSA-AGR-S-453-5)

BUSSARD, Elias F. (Pvt.) Co. H, 3rd Regiment

Maryland Cavalry. (US) Hagerstown. Served from
28 September, 1863, to 7 September, 1865.
Injury to spinal column. (H.R.M.V., Vol. 1,
775) (1880-C)

BUTLER, Josiah. (Pvt.) Co. H, 1st Regiment West
Virginia Infantry. (US) Four Locks. Entered
service 19 June, 1863. No other dates
available. (1890-C)

BUXTON, John A. (Pvt.) Co. A, 7th Regiment
Maryland Cavalry. (US) Washington County. Age
40. Served 16 August, 1862 to 31 May, 1865.
Wounded in action 2 June, 1864, at Cold Harbor,
Va. Buried in Rose Hill Cemetery, Hagerstown.
(H.R.M.V., Vol. 1, 278) (Scharf, Vol. 1, 226)
(WCCR, Vol. 7, 384) (MSA-AGR, Vol. 1, page 41
and MSA-S-936-17)

BYER, William. (Pvt.) Co. B, 3rd Regiment Potomac
Home Brigade Infantry. (US) Hagerstown. Age
22. Enlisted 22 October, 1861. Discharged 22
October, 1864. Member Independent Junior Fire
Company of Hagerstown. (H.R.M.V., Vol. 1, 575)
(MSA-S-936-23) (I.J.F.C. roster)

BYREM, Elias. (Pvt.) Co. E, 13th Regiment
Maryland Infantry. (US) Smoketown. Served
from 1 February, 1865, to 9 May, 1865. (1890-C)

BYRNE, William E. (Pvt.) Co. G, 7th Virginia
Cavalry. (CSA) Maryland Heights. (Hartzler,
104)

BROWMLEY, John, (1st Lt.) Co. H, 3rd Regiment
Maryland Cavalry, (US) Washington County.
Served 28 September, 1863 to 5 January, 1865.
(H.R.M.V., Vol. 1, 774) (Scharf, 327)

BURK, Jerome B. (1st Lt.) Co. E, 1st Regiment
Potomac Home Brigade Infantry, (US) Washington
County. Served 23 August, 1861 to 1 Oct., 1864
(Scharf, 327) (H.R.M.V., Vol. 1, 505.)

BUSH, George W. (Cpl.) Co. B, 3rd Regiment
Potomac Home Brigade Infantry. (US) Hagerstown.

Served from 23 October, 1861 to 23 October, 1864. Bush also served in Co. C, 2nd Regiment Pennsylvania Infantry from 10 April, 1861 to 20 June. 1861. (H.R.M.V., Vol. 1, 575) (1890-C)

BUTLER, A.S. (Cpl.) Co. I, 22nd Regiment Pennsylvania Cavalry. (US) Hagerstown. Also Co. D, 110th Regiment Pennsylvania Infantry. Service dates not available. (1890-C)

BYERS, Charles E. (1st Sgt.) Co. A, 7th Regiment Maryland Infantry. (US) Hagerstown. Age 19. Enlisted at Hagerstown 18 November, 1862. Discharged at Arlington Heights, Va. 31 May, 1865. (H.R.M.V., Vol. 1, 278) (Scharf, 226) (MSA-AGR-936-17)

BYER, Samuel C. (Cpl.) Co. B, 3rd Regiment Potomac Home Brigade Infantry. (US) Age 23. Hagerstown. Enlisted at Hagerstown 11 October, 1861. Discharged 23 October, 1864. (H.R.M.V., Vol. 1, 575) (MSA-S-936-24)

--- C ---

CABLE, John W. (Pvt) Co. B, 51st Ohio Infantry. (US) Washington County. Born in Sandyville, Ohio, in 1844, Cable moved with his family to Washington County after the war. He enlisted Feb. 1864 and served in the Army of he Cumberland under Gen. George H. Thomas. Cable was severely wounded at the Battle of Kennesaw Mountain and later discharged. In Washington County he engaged in farming and distilling with his uncle, John Welty, in the Ringgold District. Cable served as a director of the Hagerstown Bank from 1873 to 1897. He was a stockholder in the Great Hagerstown Fair for over twenty years and also served as a special Deputy Naval officer at the Port of Baltimore. (Williams, Vol. 2, 783) (History of the Hagerstown Bank, 153-54)

CALLAHAN, Phillip.(Pvt.) Co. F, 1st Regiment
Potomac Home Brigade Infantry. (US) Age 25.
Farmer. Clear Spring. Enlisted 4 September,
1861. Reenlisted 28 February, 1864, at
Frederick, Md. Died 5 January, 1865.
(H.R.M.V., Vol. 1, page 511) (MSA-S-936-23)

CAMPBELL, William. (Pvt.) Co. F, 1st Regiment
Potomac Home Brigade Infantry. (US) Age 44.
Cooper. Washington County. Enlisted 4
September, 1861. Reenlisted 28 February, 1864,
at Frederick, Md. Taken prisoner 29 June, 1864
at Duffield Station, Va. No further record
available to the War Department. (H.R.M.V.,
Vol. 1, page 510) (MSA-S-936-23)

CARBAUGH, Daniel. (Pvt.) Co. H, 97th Regiment
Pennsylvania Infantry. (US) Hagerstown. Served
from 21 February, 1865 to 28 August, 1865.
(1890-C)

CARL, DANIEL A. (or David) (Pvt.) Co. A, 3rd
Maryland Infantry. (Sixteen months) Co. K, 6th
Regiment U.S. Cavalry. (US) Hancock. Served
from 15 July, 1861 to 15 July, 1864. Born in
Pennsylvania, Carl learned the harness-making
trade from John Culp, of Gettysburg, at a young
age. Moving to Warfordsburg in 1859 he
continued in the same business. When the war
started he enlisted in Co. A, 3rd Maryland
Infantry, serving sixteen months. In October,
1862 he enlisted on the 6th U. S. Cavalry as a
private and served with distinction for twenty
months. Carl participated in the battles of
Cedar Mountain, Va., Antietam and Gettysburg.
He was a member of the famous raiding party of
ten men under Capt. Ulric Dahlgren, that, on 1
July, 1863, at Greencastle, Pa., captured two
Rebel mail couriers, guarded by twenty-two
infantrymen. The mail contained important
troop information from Confederate President
Jefferson Davis to Gen. Robert E. Lee, at
Gettysburg. Dahlgren raced to Gen. Meade's
headquarters, and delivered the dispatches,
leading indirectly to the third day's results.
After the war, Carl brought his saddlery

business to Hancock. He purchased Bartlett and
Heller's store and established a reliable and
popular trade. He served honorably as
postmaster of Hancock during the administration
of President Harrison. One son, Charles E.
Carl, became principal of the Hagerstown Male
High School. (1890-C) (Portrait and
Biographical Record of the Sixth Congressional
District of Maryland, 1898, pages 624-26)
(H.R.M.V., Vol. 1, 117)

CARLIN, David J. (2nd Lt.) Co. B, 13th Regiment
Maryland Infantry. (US) Washington County.
Entered service 6 September, 1861 as private
in Co. B, 1st Potomac Home Brigade Infantry.
Promoted sergeant; second lieutenant 1 March,
1865. Veteran volunteer. (H.R.M.V., Part 1,
435) (MSA-AGR-936-24)

CARNEY, Richard. (Pvt.) 6th Regiment Pennsylvania
Volunteers. (US) Buried, 29 May, 1862 in Zion
Reformed Church Cemetery, Hagerstown. (Church
records) (WCCR, Vol. 6, 51)

CARR, Johnson. (Cpl.) Co. B, 3rd Regiment West
Virginia Infantry. (US) Hagerstown. Served from
June, 1861 to August, 1864. Lost hearing in
war. (1890-C)

CARSON, John C. (Pvt.) Co. F, 3rd Regiment
Potomac Home Brigade Infantry. (US) Hagerstown.
Served from 11 October, 1861 to 29 May, 1865.
Veteran. Member Independent Junior Fire
Company of Hagerstown. (H.R.M.V., Vol. 1, 592)
(1890-C) (I.J.F.C. roster)

CARSON, John T. (Sgt.) Co. B, 3rd Regiment
Potomac Home Brigade Infantry. (US) Age 28.
Chairmaker. Hagerstown. Enlisted at Hagerstown
11 October, 1861. Discharged 29 May, 1865.
(H.R.M.V., Vol. 1, 576) (Captain Maxwell's
roster) (MSA-S-936-24)

CARRIGAN, William. (Pvt.) Co. H, 1st Regiment
Maryland Infantry. (US) Age 34. Washington
County. Enlisted at Maryland Heights, 19

February, 1863. Transferred to Co. C, 7th Maryland Infantry. Discharged 2 July, 1865. (MSA-AGR, Vol. 1, page 66) (H.R.M.V., Vol. 1, 57, 283)

CARTY, Samuel. (Pvt.) Co. I, 7th Regiment Maryland Infantry. (US) Age 26. Entered service 1 September, 1863. Transferred to V.R.C. Discharged 29 June, 1865. (MSA-AGR, Vol. 1, page 66) (H.R.M.V., Vol. 1, 297)

CARTZ, Samuel. (Pvt.) Co. A, 7th Regiment Maryland Infantry. (US) Age 26. Enlisted at Hagerstown, 9 January, 1862. Later transferred to V.R.C. Discharged 17 June, 1863. (MSA-AGR, Muster-In Rolls, 936-17)

CARUTHERS, Isaac. (Pvt.) Battery B, 2nd Pennsylvania Artillery. (US) Hancock. Served from 21 December, 1863 to 29 January, 1866. (1890-C)

CARVER, John M. (Sgt.) Co. A, 7th Regiment Maryland Infantry. (US) Hagerstown. Age 27. Entered service 18 August, 1862. Discharged at Arlington Heights, Va., 31 May, 1865. (H.R.M.V., Vol. 1, 279) (Scharf, 226) (1890-C) (MSA-AGR, Vol. 1, 64 and (MSA-S-936-17)

CASSEL, John H. (Pvt.) Co. B, 3rd Regiment Potomac Home Brigade Infantry. (US) Age 27. Smithsburg. Enlisted at Hagerstown, 11 November, 1861. Transferred to Co. F. Discharged 11 November, 1864. (H.R.M.V., Vol. 1, page 576) (Captain Maxwell's roster) (MSA-S-936-23)

CASTLE, Daniel F. T. (Pvt.) Co. I, 1st Regiment "Russell's" Maryland Cavalry. (US) Washington County. Enlisted at Williamsport 17 December, 1862. Killed in action at Brandy Station, Va., 9 June, 1863. (H.R.M.V., Vol. 1, 732) (McClannahan papers, 4) (MSA-AGR-S-936-38)

CASTLE, William. (Pvt.) Co. D, 5th Regiment Maryland Infantry. (US) Boonsboro. Served from

27 October, 1864 to 1 September, 1865.
(H.R.M.V., Vol. 1, 194) (1890-C)

CASWELL, Andrew. (Pvt.) Co. H, 1st Potomac Home
Brigade Infantry. (US) Sharpsburg. Enlisted 14
September, 1861. Died 22 July, 1863. Buried in
Lutheran graveyard, Main Street, Sharpsburg.
(H.R.M.V., Vol. 1, 524) (WCCR, Vol. 1, 68)

CAW, John T. (Pvt.) Co. I, 1st Regiment
"Russell's" Maryland Cavalry. (US) Enlisted at
Williamsport, 17 December, 1862. Discharged 8
August, 1865. (H.R.M.V., Vol. 1, page 732)
(MSA-AGR-S-936-38)

CHANDLES, Oscar. (Pvt.) Co. B, 7th Regiment
Maryland Infantry. (US) Age 21. Enlisted at
Hagerstown, 14 August, 1862. Discharged 31
May, 1865. (MSA-AGR, Vol. 1, page 64)
(H.R.M.V., Vol. 1, page 281)

CHANEY, Charles W. (Pvt.) Co. C, 1st Regiment
Maryland Cavalry. (US) Age 17. Williamsport.
Locktender. Served from 22 February, 1864 to 8
August, 1865. Charles was the son of Lewis
Chaney, a lockkeeper on the C. & O. Canal.
(H.R.M.V., Vol. 1, 713) (1890-C) (1860-C, page
81) (MSA-S 936-36)

CHANEY, Christopher C. (Cpl.) Co. I, 7th Regiment
Maryland Infantry (US) Hagerstown. Age 24.
Enlisted at Hagerstown 5 September, 1862 for
three years and paid $25 bounty. Mustered out
5, September 1865. (MSA-AGR, -936-17)
(H.R.M.V., Vol. 1, 297)

CHANEY, Ezekiel. (Pvt.) Co. I, 1st Regiment
"Russell's" Maryland Cavalry. (US) Age 19.
Williamsport. Enlisted at Williamsport, 17
December, 1862. Wounded 16 August, 1864, at
Deep Bottom, VA. The older brother of Charles
Chaney. Discharged 8 August, 1865. (H.R.M.V.,
Vol. 1, 732. (McClannahan papers, 4) (1860-C,
page 81) (MSA-AGR-S-936-38)

CHAPTMAN, George R. (Pvt.) Co. G, 6th Virginia

Cavalry Regiment. (CSA) Hagerstown. (Service
dates not available) (1890-C)

CHASE, George W. (Pvt.) Co. A, 3rd Regiment
Maryland Infantry. (US) Clear Spring. Enlisted
15 June, 1861. Died May 3rd, 1864, of wounds
received in action near Richmond, Va.
(H.R.M.V., Vol. 1, 117)

CHASE, Samuel. (Pvt.) Co. F, 1st Regiment Potomac
Home Brigade Infantry. (US) Age 22. Laborer.
Washington County. Enlisted 4 September, 1861.
Reenlisted 28 February, 1864, at Frederick, Md.
Transferred to Co. F, 13th Regiment Maryland
Infantry. Discharged 29 May, 1865. (H.R.M.V.,
Vol. 1, page 510) (MSA-S-936-23)

CHESNER, William. (Pvt.) Co. I, 7th Regiment
Maryland Infantry. (US) Age 23. Enlisted at
Hagerstown, 21 August, 1864. Deserted at
Baltimore, 6 September, 1864. (MSA-AGR, Vol.
1, page 66) (H.R.M.V., Vol. 1, page 297)

CHIPPY, William. (Sgt.) Co. B, 3rd Regiment
Potomac Home Brigade Infantry. (US) Age 21.
Hagerstown. Enlisted at Hagerstown 19 October,
1861. Discharged 19 October, 1864. (H.R.M.V.,
Vol. 1, 576) (Captain Maxwell's roster) (MSA-S-
936-23)

CHRISINGER, Emmanuel. (Pvt.) Co. I, 7th Regiment
Maryland Infantry. (US) Hagerstown. Entered
at age 17. The son of bootmaker Emmanuel
Chrisinger, he served from 21 August, 1862 to 6
October, 1864. Transferred to V.R.C. 23 June,
1864. (H.R.M.V., Vol. 1, 297) (1890-C) (1860-
C, page 15)

CHRISSINGER, William. (Cpl.) Co. H, 6th Regiment
Maryland Infantry. (US) Age 19. Hagerstown.
Enlisted at Hagerstown 7 August, 1862. Wounded
in action, 4 April, 1865, near Richmond, Va.
Hospitalized at Fairfax, Va., General Hospital.
Discharged at Washington, D. C., 16 June, 1865.
(H.R.M.V., Vol. 1, 241) (MSA-AGR, Vol. 1, 63
and S-936-2)

CHRISTOPHER, Chaney. (Capt.) Co. I, 7th Regiment Maryland Infantry. (US) Age 34. Enlisted at Hagerstown, 31 August, 1863. (MSA-AGR, Vol. 1, page 66)

CHURCH, William H. (Pvt.) Co. D, 1st Regiment Potomac Home Brigade Infantry. (US) Hagerstown. Served from 18 September, 1861 to 29 May, 1865. Transferred to Co. D, 13th Maryland Regiment. (H.R.M.V., Vol. 1, 502) (1890-C)

CHURCHEY, Israel.(Pvt.) Co. D, 1st Maryland Potomac Home Brigade Infantry. (US) Age 30. Hagerstown. Fencemaker. Family emigrated to America from Ireland when he was 12, settling in Washington County. Entered service at Knoxville, 20 August, 1862. Transferred to Co. D, 13th Maryland Infantry. Discharged 29 May, 1865, at Baltimore, Md. Buried in Mt. Brier Church Graveyard, near Trego. (H.R.M.V., Vol. 1, 2, 502) (WCCR, Vol. 3, 139) (MSA-AGR, S-936-22) (Churchey Family History courtesy Rev. and Mrs. Carroll Churchey, Hagerstown) (letter to J. F. Churchey, Wilkinsburg, Pa., from Maj. Gen. Edward F. Witsel, USA, the Adjutant General's Office, Washington, D.C., dated 5 July, 1950)

CLAPP, Charles. (Pvt.) Co. F, 18th Louisiana Infantry, (CSA) Washington County. (Hartzler, 112)

CLARE, Lewis. (Pvt.) Co. A, 7th Regiment Maryland Infantry. (US) Hagerstown. Age 20. Entered 12 August, 1862. Deserted 25 August, 1865, at Baltimore. (H.R.M.V., Vol. 1, page 279) (MSA-AGR, Vol. 1, page 63 and MSA-S-936-17)

CLARK, John H. (Pvt.) Co. F, 1st Regiment Potomac Home Brigade Infantry. (US) Age 24. Coach maker. Washington County. Enlisted 4 September, 1861. Reenlisted 28 February, 1864, at Frederick, Md. Transferred to 13th Regiment Maryland Infantry. (H.R.M.V., Vol. 1, page 511) (MSA-S-936-23)

CLARK, John W. (Pvt.) Co. B, 7th Regiment
Maryland Infantry. (US) Age 21. Enlisted at
Hagerstown 11 May, 1862. Served until 31 May,
1865. (MSA-AGR, Vol. 1, page 64) (H.R.M.V.,
Vol. 1, page 281)

CLARK, W. D. (Pvt.) Musician Third Class, 1st
Brigade (Moxley's) Band. (U.S.C.T.) (U.S.)
Hagerstown. Enlisted at Hagerstown, mustered
in at Baltimore, 26 September, 1863. Served in
Maryland until mid-1864. Assisted army with
non-musical duties near Petersburg and
Richmond, Va. Mustered out 20 April, 1866, at
Brownsville, Texas. (Catherine T. McConnell
and Dr. Roland C. McConnell, Journal of Afro-
American Historical and Genealogical Society,
Vol. 12, No. 1 and 2, pages 11-15)

CLARY, James L. (2nd Lt.) Co. B., 3rd Regiment
Maryland Infantry. (US) Age 26. Smithsburg.
Entered service 23 July, 1861, as private in
Co. B. Promoted sergeant, second Lieutenant 1
February, 1863. Died 10 March, 1864. Buried
in St Paul's Church Cemetery, Smithsburg.
(H.R.M.V., Vol. 1, 122) (Scharf, Vol. 2,
1273)

CLAY, James. (Cpl.) Co. A, 7th Regiment Maryland
Infantry. (US) Age 27. Entered service at
Hagerstown, 12 August, 1862. Deserted at
Baltimore 2 September, 1862. (MSA-AGR, Vol. 1,
64) (MSA-AGR, Vol. 1, 63)

CLAYBURN, Thomas. (Pvt.) Co. I, 1st Regiment
"Russell's" Maryland Cavalry. (US) Enlisted at
Williamsport, 17 December, 1862. Discharged 28
February, 1863. (H.R.M.V., Vol. 1, page 732)
(MSA-AGR-S-936-38)

CLEGETT, Dr. Joseph Edward. (CSA) Rohrersville.
Unit unknown. He graduated from the medical
college of Winchester, Virginia, and attended
University of Maryland medical lectures. In
1861 he enlisted in the Army of Northern
Virginia and served until the war's end. He was

named chief surgeon, Forwarding and Receiving
Hospital, at Richmond. After the war he
practiced his profession in Richmond, and later
Baltimore. (Williams, Vol. 2, 804; Hartzler,
111; H.R.M.V., Part 1, 111).

CLEMENS, John. (Pvt.) Co. A, 45th Volunteers
(U.S.C.T.) (US) Williamsport. Served from
July, 1864 to September 1864. (1890-C)

CLEVINGER, Elias. (Pvt.) Co. H, 158th
Pennsylvania Infantry Regiment. (US) Hancock.
Served from 16 October, 1862 to 12 August,
1863. (1890-C)

CLINE, John. (Pvt.) Co. E, 1st Regiment Potomac
Home Brigade Infantry. (US) Age 19. Laborer.
Smithsburg. Served from 25 October, 1861 to 26
October, 1864. (H.R.M.V., Vol. 1, 506) (1890-
C) (MSA-S-936-23)

CLINE, Joseph H. (Pvt.) Co. E, 1st Regiment
Potomac Home Brigade Infantry. (US) Age 18.
Laborer. Smoketown. Served from 19 January,
1865 to 29 May, 1865. Transferred to Co. E,
13th Regiment Maryland Infantry. (H.R.M.V.,
Vol. 1, 444) (1890-C) (MSA-S-936-23)

CLINE, Levi. (Pvt.) Co. E., 1st Regiment Potomac
Home Brigade Infantry. (US) Washington Co.
Served from 25 October, 1861 to 20 July, 1863.
Buried in the Welty Church of the Brethren
Cemetery, near Greensburg. (H.R.M.V., Vol. 1,
506) (WCCR, Vol. 4, 114) (1890-C)

CLINE, William H. (Pvt.) Co. G, 1st Regiment
Potomac Home Brigade "Cole's" Cavalry. (US) Age
19. Laborer. Leitersburg. Served from 20
February, 1864 to 28 June, 1865. (H.R.M.V.,
Vol. 1, 671) (MSA-AGR-S-936-38) (1890-C)

CLIPP, Hirem O. (Pvt.) Unit unknown. (CSA)
Farmer. Sharpsburg. Left his birthplace on a
farm in Jefferson County, Va., to settle in
Sharpsburg, in 1861, at age 18. The following
year he joined the Confederate army. Not long

after that he was discharged due to a serious illness. Returning to the Sharpsburg area he obtained work on the Noah Rohrback and later David Wolf farms, the latter near Tilghmanton. Still later he tried his hand as a merchant by opening a small store in Sharpsburg, but the lure of farm work was too strong. During the fighting at Sharpsburg his family resided on the Sherrick farm, near Burnside Bridge. Along with other families they escaped the battleground for the safety of several caves along the nearby Potomac River. For two days, until the Rebel army retreated, they collected food from area farms and slept on the ground. Mrs. Clipp's father became an indirect victim of the Battle of Antietam. In 1863 Jonathan Keplinger discovered an unexploded shell on his farm property, and while attempting to remove it to a safe area it exploded in his face, killing him. (Hartzler 114) (Williams, Vol. 2)

CLOPPER, John D. (Pvt.) Co. I, 1st Regiment Potomac Home Brigade Infantry. (US) Rohrersville. Served from 1 October, 1861 to 1 October, 1864. (H.R.M.V., Vol. 1, 530) (1890-C)

CLOWER, Paul. (Pvt.) Co. M, 1st Regiment Maryland Cavalry. (US) Hagerstown. Served from 16 February, 1864 to 5 June, 1865. (1890-C)

COFFEE, Michael. (Pvt.) Co. I, 7th Regiment Maryland Infantry. (US) Age 20. Enlisted at Hagerstown, 27 August, 1862. Deserted 13 September, 1862. (MSA-AGR, Vol. 1, page 66) (H.R.M.V., Vol. 1, page 297)

COFFMAN, James (Pvt.) H. Co. E, 1st Regiment Potomac Home Brigade Infantry. (US) Hagerstown. Served from 14 September, 1861 to 1 October, 1864. Buried in Rose Hill Cemetery, Hagerstown. (H.R.M.V., Vol. 1, 506) (1890-C) (WCCR, Vol. 7, 266)

COLBERT, Arch. (Pvt.) Co. M, 1st Regiment Potomac Home Brigade "Cole's" Cavalry. (US) Washington Co. Served from 25 February to 28 June, 1865.

Buried in Samples Manor Cemetery. (WCCR, Vol.
4, 60) (H.R.M.V., Vol. 1, 698)

COLBERT, William Frederick. (Cpl.) Co. A, 3rd
Regiment Maryland Infantry. (US) Hagerstown.
Served from 15 June, 1861 to 15 June, 1864.
(H.R.M.V., Vol. 1, 117) (1890-C)

COLE, Joseph. (Pvt.) Co. F, 2nd United States
Regiment. (U.S.C.T.) (US) Hagerstown. Served 11
August, 1863 to 5 January, 1868.(1890-C)

COLKLESSER, William H. (Capt.) Co. A, 7th
Regiment Maryland Infantry, (US) Hagerstown.
Age 29. Entered service as first lieutenant
and was promoted to captain 21 January, 1864.
The family operated a successful shoe making
business in Hagerstown, on North Potomac
Street. He died at Hagerstown, February, 1870,
at age 40. (Scharf, Vol. 1, 327; Vol. 2, 1047)
(H.R.M.V., Vol. 1, 278) (Dorrance collection:
letter 24 August, 1862); (Camper and Kirkley,
123, 305) (1860-C, page 9) (MSA-S 936-17)

CONYRA, Charles. (Pvt.) Co. D, 39th Regiment
Infantry. (U.S.C.T.) (US) Washington County.
Enlisted as a freed man 31 March, 1864.
Purchased his own gun and equipment for $6.
Discharged 4 December, 1865. (H.R.M.V., Vol. 2,
270) (MSA-S-936-50)

COOK, Alexander H. (Pvt.) Co. A, 1st Regiment
Potomac Home Brigade Infantry. (US) Washington
Co. Served from 15 August, 1861 to 27 August,
1864. Buried in Shiloh United Brethren Church
Cemetery near Fiddlersburg. (H.R.M.V., Vol. 1,
487) (WCCR, Vol. 7, 468)

COOK, Charles. (Cpl.) Co. D, 39th Regiment
Infantry. (U.S.C.T.) (US) Washington County.
Owned by George Jacques. Enlisted at Baltimore
31 March, 1864. Discharged 4 December, 1865.
(H.R.M.V., Vol. 2, 270) (MSA-S-936-51)

COOK, Roger E. (Col.) 1st Regiment Potomac Home
Brigade Infantry. (US) Age 54. Hagerstown.

Early in the war formed the "Sharpsburg
Rifles." Entered service as captain of Co. A,
promoted to major 6 February, 1863; lieutenant-
colonel 23 November, 1863, at Sandy Hook, Md.,
and to colonel 24 February, 1865. (Scharf,
327) (H.R.M.V., Vol. 1, 485) (1890-C)
(Williams, Vol. 1, 308) (MSA-AGR-S- 936-22)

COON, James L. (Pvt.) Co. A, 7th Regiment
Maryland Cavalry. (US) Hagerstown. Age 31.
Served from 18 August, 1862 to 3 June, 1865.
Taken prisoner 31 March, 1865 at White Oak
Road, Va. Discharged at Annapolis, Md.
(H.R.M.V., Vol. 1, 279) (Scharf, Vol. 1, 226)
(MSA-AGR, Vol. 1, page 34 and MSA-S-936-17)

COON, Nelson. (Pvt.) Musician Second Class, 1st
Brigade (Moxley's) Band. (U.S.C.T) (US)
Hagerstown. Enlisted at Hagerstown, mustered
in at Baltimore, 26 September, 1863.
Participated in band assignments in Maryland
until mid-1864. In Virginia assisted the army
in non-musical duties. Coon became ill while
working at Bermuda Hundred, developed
consumption and died in 1872 at a hospital in
Washington, D.C. (Mrs. Catherine T.
McConnell and Dr. Roland C. McConnell,
Journal of Afro-American Historical and
Genealogical Society, Vol. 12, No. 1 and 2,
pages 11-15)

CORBITT, Francis T. (Cpl.) Co. F, 2nd Regiment
Potomac Home Brigade Infantry. (US) Hancock.
Farmer. Enlisted at Hancock, Sept. 1861.
Mustered in at Cumberland, Md. Wounded in left
leg above the knee at Mechanick's Gap, and
later at Romney, Va. Hospitalized at New Creek,
Va., Feb. 2nd, 1864. Furloughed March 11, 1864
for twenty days, then returned to regiment.
Mustered out September 30, 1864, at Cumberland,
Md. (H.R.M.V., Vol. 1, 558) (Records held by
Mrs. Candy Gloyd, of Warfordsburg, Pa.)

CORBY, George. (Pvt.) Co. I, 1st Regiment
Maryland Infantry. (US) Williamsport. Served
from 3 September, 1861 to 3 September, 1864.

(H.R.M.V., Vol. 1, 732) (1890-C)

COSENS, Dr. John Henry. (DVS) (CSA) Hagerstown.
Served three years in the Army of Northern
Virginia treating the horses of its most famous
officers. On one occasion rode all night to
care for "Stonewall" Jackson's mount. Named
chief cattle inspector for Washington County
after the war. Member St. John's Lutheran
Church, Hagerstown. (Portrait and Biographical
Record of the Sixth Congressional District of
Maryland 166-67)

COSGROVE, Jesse D. (Pvt.) Co. E, 1st Regiment
Potomac Home Brigade Infantry. (US) Age 31.
Blacksmith. Hagerstown. Enlisted at
Hagerstown, 14 September, 1861. Transferred to
Co. E, 13th Maryland Infantry. Discharged 29
May, 1865. (H.R.M.V., Vol. 1, page 506) (MSA-
S-936-23)

COST, John D. (Lt.) Co. B, 11th Regiment Maryland
Infantry. (US) Hagerstown. Served from 15 June,
1864 to 29 September, 1864. (H.R.M.V., Vol. 1,
378) (1890-C)

COST, John L. (2nd Lt.) Co. B, 11th Regiment
Maryland Infantry. (US) Hagerstown. Farmer.
Entered the service 15 May, 1863. Participated
in the battle of Monocacy Junction. Also stood
guard along the Potomac against Rebel guerilla
raiders chasing the famous Col. Mosby. He
enlisted as a drummer boy and was later
promoted to second lieutenant, serving in that
capacity until the war's end. After the war he
served three years as second lieutenant in Co.
B, 1st Regiment of Maryland National Guards,
Washington County, under Col. Henry Kyd
Douglas. Mr. Cost was born on Paper Mill Road
and before the war worked as a farmer and also
served the government in several positions
including mail carrier. At one time he
operated a grocery store in Hagerstown's public
square. (Portrait and Biographical Record of
the Sixth Congressional District of Maryland,
1898, pages 796-97) (Williams, Vol. 2, 1138)

(H.R.M.V., Vol. 1, 378)

COULTER, William M. (Pvt.) Unit unknown. Served
from 1861 to 1863. (CSA) Brownsville. (1890-C)

COY, Frederick, (Pvt.) Co. E, 1st Regiment
Maryland Cavalry. (US) Age 22. Farmer.
Cavetown. Enlisted at Cavetown, 7 March, 1864.
Discharged 8 August, 1865. (H.R.M.V., Vol. 1,
page 720) (MSA-AGR-S-936-36)

COY, Henry. (Pvt.) Co. F, 3rd Regiment Potomac
Home Brigade Infantry. (US) Age 24. Laborer.
Beaver Creek. Enlisted at Hagerstown, 20
December, 1861. Veteran. Transferred to Co. F.
Discharged 29 May, 1865. (H.R.M.V., Vol. 1,
page 592) (Captain Maxwell's roster) (MSA-S-
936-23)

COX, Henry. (Pvt.) Co. C, 5th Regiment Maryland
Infantry. (US) Benevola. Served from 29
October, 1864 to 1 September, 1865. (H.R.M.V.,
Vol. 1, 191) (1890-C)

COX, Joseph. (Pvt.) Co. H, 1st Regiment Potomac
Home Brigade Infantry. (US) Age 23.
Carpenter. Sharpsburg. Enlisted 25 October,
1861, discharged 29 May, 1865. Transferred to
Co. H, 13th Maryland Infantry. Buried in
Mountain View Cemetery, Sharpsburg. (H.R.M.V.,
Vol. 1, 525) (WCCR Vol. 1, 39) (1890-C)
(Scharf, 5) (MSA-S-936-23)

CRAIG, Jacob. (Pvt.) Co. I, 7th Regiment Maryland
Infantry. (US) Washington Co. Age 33. Served
from 31 August, 1862 to 31 March, 1863.
Discharged for disability. Buried in Rose Hill
Cemetery, Hagerstown. (H.R.M.V., Vol. 1, 297)
(WCCR, Vol. 7, 219) (MSA-AGR, Vol. 1, page 66)

CRAIG, William B. (Pvt.) Co. D, 6th Regiment
Pennsylvania Infantry. (US) Conococheague.
Served from unknown date in 1861 to
February, 1863. Reported mini ball still in
left hip in 1890. (1890-C)

CRALEY, Jacob. (Pvt.) (Unit unknown) (US) Age 23.
Enlisted at Hagerstown, 19 September, 1863.
Discharged with physical disability 31 March,
1864. (MSA-AGR, Vol. 1, page 66)

CRALEY, John. (Pvt.) Co. I, 7th Regiment Maryland
Infantry. (US) Age 18. Enlisted at Hagerstown,
September, 1863. Served until 31 May, 1865.
(MSA-AGR, Vol. 1, page 66) (H.R.M.V., Vol. 1,
page 297)

CRALEY, Joseph. (or Cralley) (Pvt.) Co. I, 7th
Regiment Maryland Infantry. (US) Age 23.
Enlisted at Hagerstown, 19 August, 1862.
Discharged with disability 31 March, 1863.
(H.R.M.V., Vol. 1, page 297) (MSA-AGR, Vol. 1,
page 66)

CRAMER, Daniel M. (or Creamer) (Pvt.) Co. I, 8th
Regiment Maryland Infantry. (US) Hagerstown.
Served from 26 March, 1863 to 11 January, 1864.
(H.R.M.V., Vol. 1, 325) (1890-C)

CRAMER, Jacob. (or Creamer) (Pvt.) Co. I, First
Regiment "Russell's" Maryland Cavalry. (US)
Smoketown. Entered service 3 September, 1861.
Deserted 10 May, 1862. (H.R.M.V., Vol. 1, 732)
(1890-C)

CRAMER, John H. (Pvt.) Co. E, 1st Regiment
Potomac Home Brigade Infantry. (US) Age 23.
Wagon maker. Washington County. Enlisted at
Sandy Hook, Md., 14 September, 1861.
Transferred to Co. E, 13th Regiment Maryland
Infantry. Discharged 29 May, 1865. (H.R.M.V.,
Vol. 1, page 506) (MSA-S-936-23)

CRAWFORD, Samuel. (Pvt.) Co. I, 1st Regiment
"Russell's" Maryland Cavalry. (US) Hagerstown.
Enlisted at Williamsport, 3 September, 1861.
Killed in action at Deep Bottom, Va. 7, 16
August, 1864. (H.R.M.V., Vol. 1, 732)
(McClannahan papers, 4) (1890-C) (MSA-AGR-S-
936-38)

CREAGER, Francis M. (Capt.) Co. I, 1st Regiment

Maryland Cavalry. (US) Washington County.
Date of enlistment unknown. Killed in action 9
June, 1863, at Brandy Station, Va. (H.R.M.V.,
Vol. 1, 731) (McClannahan papers, 4)

CREAGER, John T. A. (Pvt.) Co. A, 7th Regiment
Maryland Infantry. (US) Tilghmanton. Age 25.
Entered service 11 August, 1862. Transferred
to brigade band, 1 May, 1863. (H.R.M.V., Vol.
1, 279) (1890-C) (MSA-AGR, Vol. 1, page 66 and
MSA-S-936-17)

CREAMER, Daniel. (Sgt.) Co. H, 3rd Regiment
Maryland Cavalry. (US) Sharpsburg. Served from
28 September, 1863 to 20 May, 1865. (H.R.M.V.,
Vol. 1, 775) (1890-C)

CREAMER, James. (Pvt.) Co. A, 1st Regiment
Potomac Home Brigade Infantry. (US) Sharpsburg.
Served from 25 October, 1861 to 25 October,
1864. Buried in Mountain View Cemetery,
Sharpsburg. (H.R.M.V., Vol. 1, 525) (WCCR 1,
29)

CREAMER, James S. (Pvt.) Co. D, 2nd Regiment
Maryland Infantry. (US) Hagerstown. Served from
23 June, 1864 to 17 July, 1865. (H.R.M.V.,
Vol. 1, 86) (1890-C)

CREEK, Charles W. (Pvt.) Co. F, 2nd Regiment
Potomac Home Brigade Infantry. (US) Age 27.
Farmer. Washington County. Enlisted 4
September, 1861. Transferred to Co. C.
Veteran. Discharged 29 May, 1865.(H.R.M.V.,
Vol. 1, 558)(MSA-S-936-24)

CRETIN, John H. (Pvt.) Co. C, 1st Maryland
Cavalry, (CSA) Hagerstown. (Hartzler, 121)
(Huntsberry, 85) (Goldsborough, 232)

CRISSENGER, George F. (Pvt.) Co. A, 7th Regiment
Maryland Infantry. (US) Washington County.
Age 20. Enlisted 11 August, 1862, discharged 26
June, 1865, at Annapolis, Md. Taken Prisoner
18 August, 1864, at Weldon Railroad, Va.
(H.R.M.V., Vol. 1, 279) Scharf, Vol. 1, 226)

(MSA-AGR, Vol. 1, page 66 and MSA-S-936-17)

CRISWELL, Joseph. (Pvt.) Musician. 1st Regiment
Maryland Infantry. (US) Hagerstown. Served from
29 September, 1861 to 25 August, 1862.
(H.R.M.V., Vol. 1, 18) (1890-C)

CRONISE, William N. (Capt.) Co. H, 1st Regiment
Potomac Home Brigade Infantry. (US) Sharpsburg.
Served from 10 September, 1861 to 29 April,
1862 when he resigned. At the beginning of the
war he left his general store business in
charge of a clerk to enlist and was chosen
captain. After brief service with his men near
Harper's Ferry, he returned to Frederick and
camp. During a battalion drill he was
seriously wounded and later discharged from the
service at Winchester, Va. He returned to
Sharpsburg and relocated his store across the
river to Shepherdstown where the Confederates
stole all of his merchandise and carried it to
Berryville, Va. Cronise enlisted the service
of a company of Federal cavalry, went to
Berryville and secured the goods. Then he moved
back to Sharpsburg where he operated a general
store for fifty-two years. (H.R.M.V., Vol. 1,
523) (1890-C) (Portrait and Biographical Record
of the Sixth Congressional District of
Maryland, 1898, 209) (M. F. D., 748)

CROSS, James H. (Pvt.) Co. C, 5th Regiment
Maryland Infantry. (US) Mapleville. Served from
29 October, 1864 to 1 September, 1865.
H.R.M.V., Vol. 1, 191 (1890-C)

CROSS, James W. (Pvt.) Co. B, 1st Tennessee
Infantry, (CSA) Hagerstown. (Hartzler, 122)

CROSS, John A. (Cpl.) Co. C, 3rd Regiment West
Virginia Cavalry. (US) Funkstown. Served from
23 June, 1864 to 30 June, 1865. (1890-C)

CRUM, Abraham. (Pvt.) Co. I, 1st Regiment
"Russell's" Maryland Cavalry. (US)
Leitersburg. Served from 2 December, 1861 to
28 December, 1862. (H.R.M.V., Vol. 1, 732)

(1890-C)

CUNNINGHAM, Michael. (Pvt.) Co. B, 2nd Cavalry.
(US) Hagerstown. Served from 31 May, 1860 to 9
July, 1862. Discharged for disability due to
double hernia. Member Independent Junior Fire
Company, of Hagerstown. (1890-C) (I.J.F.C.
roster) (Pension Records, 157)

CURLEY, David. (Pvt.) Co. B, 3rd Regiment Potomac
Home Brigade Infantry. (US) Age 18. Laborer.
Broadfording. Served from 4 September, 1861 to
29 May, 1865. Transferred to Co. F. Veteran.
(H.R.M.V., Vol. 1, 592) (1890-C) (Captain
Maxwell's roster) (MSA-S-936-23)

CURTIS, (Reverend) Charles J. (Pvt.) Co. E, 2nd
Virginia Infantry. (CSA) Lappins, Washington
County. (Hartzler, 123)

CURTIS, Isadore. (Pvt.) Co. B, 3rd Regiment
Potomac Home Brigade Infantry. (US) Hagerstown.
Enlisted 15 October, 1861. Discharged 15
October, 1864. (H.R.M.V., Vol. 1, page 576)
(Captain Maxwell's roster)

CURTIS, John S. (Pvt.) Co. I, 1st Regiment
"Russell's" Maryland Cavalry. (US) Enlisted at
Williamsport, 17 December, 1862. Discharged 8
August, 1865. (H.R.M.V., Vol. 1, page 732)
(MSA-AGR-S-936-38)

CYRUS, Thomas Henry. (Pvt.) Musician Second
Class. 1st Brigade (Moxley's) Band. (U.S.C.T.)
(US) Hagerstown. Enlisted at Hagerstown,
mustered in 26 September, 1863, at Baltimore.
Served in Maryland and Virginia. Band acted in
various capacities near Petersburg and
Richmond, Va., to assist army with war effort
in addition to playing for parades etc.
Mustered out 20 April, 1866, at Brownsville,
Texas. (Mrs. Catherine T. McConnell and Dr.
Roland C. McConnell, Journal of Afro-American
Historical and Genealogical Society, Vol. 12,
No. 1 and 2, pages 11-15)

DALL, Rash. (CSA) (Pvt.) Williamsport. (Hartzler, 124)

DANNER, Andrew. (Cpl.) Co. H, 1st Regiment Potomac Home Brigade "Cole's" Cavalry. (US) Williamsport. Served from 24 February, 1864 to 28 June, 1865. Transferred from Co. F. (H.R.M.V., Vol. 1, 684) (1890-C)

DANNER, Edward E. (Pvt.) Co. B, 7th Regiment Maryland Infantry. (US) Age 23. Enlisted at Williamsport 3 October, 1862. Served to 12 June, 1865. Duty in commissary. (H.R.M.V., Vol. 1, 278, 280) (MSA-AGR, Vol. 1, page 91)

DANNER, John. (Pvt.) Co. A, 13th Regiment Maryland Infantry. (US) Sharpsburg. Served from 12 August, 1862 to 29 May, 1865. (1890-C) (Scharf, 226)

DAUGHERTY, William. (Pvt.) Co. A, 13th Regiment Maryland Infantry. (US) Boonsboro. Served from 21 February, 1865 to 29 May, 1865. (H.R.M.V., Vol. 1, page 433) (1890-C)

DAVIDSON, John W. (Pvt.) Co. E, 1st Regiment Maryland Infantry. (US) Enlisted at Hagerstown, 14 February, 1864. Discharged 2 November, 1864. (MSA-AGR, Vol. 1, 80) (H.R.M.V., Vol. 1, 43)

DAVIS, Amos. (Cpl.) Co. H, 6th Regiment Maryland Infantry. (US) Age 19. Enlisted at Hagerstown 21 August, 1862. Wounded in action and taken prisoner 1 June, 1864, at Cold Harbor, Va. Discharged near Washington, D.C., 20 June, 1865. (H.R.M.V., Vol. 1, 241) (1890-C) (MSA-AGR, Vol. 1, 91 and (MSA-AGR-S-936-2))

DAVIS, Frisby J. (Pvt.) Co. D, 11th Regiment Maryland Infantry. (US) Boonsboro. Saw five months service including Battle of the Monocacy. Brother to Rev. Peter Sibert Davis. (Williams, Vol. 2, 1143)

DAVIS, Jacob N. (Pvt.) Co. A, 2nd Maryland
Infantry. (CSA) Clear Spring. (Hartzler, 126)
(Huntsberry, 71)

DAVIS, John. (Pvt.) Co. E, 1st Regiment Potomac
Home Brigade Infantry. (US) Age 18. Boonsboro.
Laborer\carpenter. Enlisted at Sandy Hook, Md.,
19 January, 1865. Transferred to Co. E, 13th
Maryland Infantry. (H.R.M.V., Vol. 1, 507)
(MSA-S-936-23) (M.F.D., 720)

DAVIS, John W. (Pvt.) Co. B, 3rd Regiment Potomac
Home Brigade Infantry. (US) (Pvt.) Age 24.
Farmer. Washington County. Enlisted 31
December, 1862. Discharged 29 May, 1865.
(H.R.M.V., Vol. 1, page 576) (MSA-S-936-23)

DAVIS, Joseph. (Pvt.) (US) Teamster. Indian
Springs. Unit and dates of service not shown
on census report. (1890-C)

DAVIS, Roland M. (Pvt.) Co. A, 13th Regiment
Maryland Infantry. (US) Downsville. Served from
15 February, 1865 to 29 May, 1865. (H.R.M.V.,
Vol. 1, 433) (1890-C)

DAVIS, Thomas H. (Sgt.) Captain Firey's Co. B,
1st Regiment Potomac Home Brigade "Cole's"
Cavalry. (US) Age 21. Farmer. Hagerstown.
Enlisted 7 January, 1862. Veteran. Reenlisted
17 February, 1864, at Boliver, Va. (H.R.M.V.,
Vol. 1, 671) (MSA-S-936-30)

DAWSON, Nathan. (Pvt.) Co. C, 17th Texas
Infantry, (CSA) Hancock. Other infornmation
N/A. (Hartzler, 127)

DAWSON, Thomas W. (Sgt.) Co. G, 1st South
Carolina Infantry, (CSA) Hancock. (Hartzler,
127)

DAYWALT, Martin. (Pvt.) Co. F, 3rd Regiment
Potomac Home Brigade Infantry. (US) Age 22.
Smithsburg. Enlisted at Hagerstown, 12 October,
1861. Veteran. Transferred to Co. F.
Discharged 29 May, 1865. (H.R.M.V., Vol. 1,

592) (Captain Maxwell's Roster) (MSA-S-936-23)

DEAN, James. (Pvt.) Co. E, 1st Regiment Maryland
Infantry. (US) Hagerstown. Entered 14 February,
1864. Discharged due to physical disability 21
August, 1864. (MSA-AGR-Vol. 1, 80)

DEAN, James W. (Pvt.) Co. E, 1st Regiment
Maryland Infantry. (US) Age 21. Enlisted at
Hagerstown, 20 May, 1861. Discharged with
disability 12 August, 1863. (H.R.M.V., Vol. 1,
43) (MSA-AGR, Vol. 1, 80)

DEENER (or Deaner), David H. (Pvt.) (Pvt.) Co. F,
1st Regiment Potomac Home Brigade Infantry.
(US) Age 20. Carpenter. Brownsville. Enlisted
at Sandy Hook, Md., 30 January, 1865.
Transferred to Co. F, 13th Regiment Maryland
Infantry. Discharged 29 May, 1865. (H.R.M.V.,
Vol. 1, 446) (1890-C) (MSA-S-936-23)

DENNIS, Cyrus. (Cpl.) Co. G, 1st Regiment
"Cole's" Federal Cavalry. (US) Clear Spring.
Enlisted 29 February, 1864, at Frederick.
Discharged 28 June, 1865, at Harper's Ferry.
(Windmills of Time," 1981, a publication of the
Clear Spring Alumni Association, Vol. 1, 686.
The History and Roster of Maryland Volunteers,
Vol. 1, for Co. G, lists Dennis mustering out
with the rank of corporal. The Alumni
Association publication contains a letter from
the late Ruben U. Darby, indicating Dennis was
discharged as captain)

DENNIS, Jeremiah. (Pvt.) Captain Firey's Co. B,
1st Regiment Potomac Home Brigade "Cole's"
Cavalry.(US) Age 19. Boatman, Sharpsburg.
Enlisted at Hagerstown, 4 September, 1861.
Veteran. Wounded in action. Reenlisted 9 April,
1864 at Boliver, Va., after being discharged.
(H.R.M.V., Vol. 1, 671) (MSA-S-936-30)

DIBERT, Hamilton V. (Pvt.) Co. G, 1st Potomac
Home Brigade "Cole's" Cavalry. (US) Age 25.
Laborer. Williamsport. Served from 20
February, 1864 to 28 June, 1865. (H.R.M.V.,

DELAMARTER, Lewis. (Pvt.) Co. H, 6th United States Cavalry. (US) Hagerstown. Served under Gen. Phil Sheridan, and in Brig. Gen. Wesley Merritt's Brigade of Gen. John Buford's 1st Federal Cavalry Division. Saw action at Culpeper, Second Bull Run, South Mountain, Antietam and Brandy Station. He participated in the pursuit of Lee's Rebel army as it withdrew from Gettysburg into Washington County, and was engaged at Williamsport, Boonsboro and Funkstown. Later engaged at the Wilderness and Spotsylvania, near Richmond. Wounded twice. After the war he returned to Hagerstown and entered the lumber business. (Williams, Vol. 2, 1164)

DELANEY, John F. (Pvt.) Co. (A) 1st Regiment Potomac Home Brigade Infantry. (US) Sharpsburg. Fifer. Served from 15 August, 1861 to 27 August, 1864. Buried in Mountain View Cemetery, Sharpsburg. (H.R.M.V., Vol. 1, 487)(WCCR, Vol. 1, 38)

DENNISON, John. (Pvt.) (Unit unknown) (US) Enlisted at Hagerstown, 14 February, 1864. Discharged due to disability 1 May, 1865. (MSA-AGR, Vol. 1, 80)

DICK, David. (Sgt.) Captain Firey's Co. B, 1st Regiment Potomac Home Brigade "Cole's" Cavalry. (US) Age 30. Boatman. Millstone. Served from 4 September, 1861 to 28 June, 1865. Veteran. (H.R.M.V., Vol. 1, 671) (1890-C) (MSA-S-936-30)

DICK, James. (Pvt.) Co. F, 1st Regiment Potomac Home Brigade Infantry. (US) Millstone. Served from 4 September, 1861 to 4 September, 1864. Wounded in right leg. (H.R.M.V., Vol. 1, 511) (1890-C)

DICK, Jacob. (Pvt.) Co. K, 13th Regiment Maryland Infantry. (US) Smoketown. Served from 16 January, 1865 to 29 May, 1865. (H.R.M.V., Vol.

1, 457) (1890-C)

DICKEL, Charles H. (Pvt.) Co. G, 174th Regiment
Pennsylvania Volunteers. (US) Ringgold. Served
from 2 September, 1864 to 16 June, 1865. Died
at Lincoln Hospital, Washington, D. C., from
chronic diarrhea. (1890-C)

DIEHL, Samuel M. (Pvt.) Co. G, 17th Regiment
Pennsylvania Cavalry. (US) Edgemont. Entered
service 4 September, 1864. Deserted May, 1865.
Dishonorable discharge. (1890-C)

DIELLEN, (?) William. (Pvt.) Co. A, 1st Regiment
Maryland Infantry. (US) Hancock. Served from 9
September, 1864 to 25 May, 1865. (1890-C)

DIETRICK, Lewis. (Pvt.) Co. F, 11th Regiment
Maryland Infantry. (US) Hagerstown. Served
from 22 September, 1864 to 15 June, 1865.
(H.R.M.V., Vol. 1, 406) (1890-C)

DIFFENBAUGHER, George. (Pvt.) (Spelled in military
records as Dieffenbacher) Co. E, 1st Regiment
Potomac Home Brigade Infantry. (US) Smithsburg.
Served from 25 October, 1861 to 26 October,
1864. Suffered from chronic rheumatism from
1862 to 1890. (H.R.M.V., Vol. 1, 507) (1890-C)

DIGGS, Isaac M. (Pvt.) Co. H, 1st Regiment
Potomac Home Brigade Infantry. (US) Boonsboro.
Served from 25 October, 1861 to 25 October,
1865. (H.R.M.V., Vol. 1, 525)

DIGGS, Jenningham. (Sgt.) Co. I, 38th Regiment
(U.S.C.T.) Maryland Volunteers. (US)
Williamsport. Served from 12 February, 1863 to
1 January, 1865. (1890-C)

DIGGUS (?), Hiram. (Pvt.) Co. H, 1st Regiment
Maryland Cavalry. (US) Hagerstown. Served from
24 February, 1862 to 5 June, 1865. (1890-C)

DILLEN, William. (Pvt.) Co. A, 1st Regiment
Potomac Home Brigade "Cole's Cavalry." (US) Age
21. Enlisted at Hagerstown, 21 August, 1862.

Deserted from Camp Parole, near Annapolis, Md.,
20 June, 1865. (MSA-AGR, Vol. 1, 91)
(H.R.M.V., Vol. 1, 667)

DIMON, George. (Pvt.) Co. B, 3rd Regiment Potomac
Home Brigade Infantry. (US) Age 24. Farmer.
Cavetown. Enlisted at Hagerstown, 9 December,
1861. Veteran. Discharged 29 May, 1865.
(H.R.M.V., Vol. 1, 592) (Captain Maxwell's
roster) (MSA-S-936-23)

DINSMORE, Alvin K. (Pvt.) Co. K, 1st Regiment
Potomac Home Brigade "Cole's" Cavalry. (US)
Beaver Creek. Served from 29 March, 1864 to 28
June, 1865. (H.R.M.V., Vol. 1, 694) (1890-C)

DITLOW, William. (Pvt.) Co. H, 6th Regiment
Maryland Infantry. (US) Age 22. Williamsport.
Entered service 21 August, 1862 at Hagerstown.
Deserted 1 November, 1863. (H.R.M.V., Vol. 1,
241) (1890-C) (MSA-AGR, 936-2)

DIXON, George. (Pvt.) Co. H. 1st Regiment Potomac
Home Brigade "Cole's Cavalry." (US) Washington
County. Entered service 29 Feb., 1864.
Deserted 26 June, 1864. Buried in Fairview
Cemetery, near Keedysville. (H.R.M.V., Vol. 1,
689) (WCCR, Vol. 5, 146)

DIXON, John L. (Pvt.) Co. A, 7th Regiment
Maryland Infantry. (US) Age 30. Entered service
14 February, 1864, at Hagerstown. Wounded in
action 18 August, 1864. Transferred to Co. E,
1st Maryland Infantry 1 June, 1865. (H.R.M.V.,
Vol. 1, 279) (MSA-AGR, Vol. 1, 80)

DIXON, William. (Pvt.) Co. K, 1st Regiment
Pennsylvania Infantry. (US) Hagerstown. Served
from 8 January, 1861 to 1864. (1890-C)

DOLAN, John. (Pvt.) Co. H, 13th Regiment Maryland
Infantry, and Co. F, 1st Regiment Maryland
Infantry. (US) Indian Springs. Served from
February, 1865 to 29 May, 1865. Well known in
Hagerstown as the proprietor of the Franklin
House Hotel, on North Potomac Street. (Where

the city parking deck is today) His parents
moved to Clear Spring when he was three. He
enlisted at age 18 and was honorably
discharged. After the war he worked for the C
& O Canal as an operator and later as owner-
operator of a shipping business. In 1894 he
moved to Hagerstown and associated with the
hotel. (H.R.M.V., Vol. 1, 452) (1890-C)
(Williams, Vol. 2, 715)

DONAHUE, William. (Cpl.) Co. A, 2nd Maryland
Infantry Regiment. (US) Enlisted at Hagerstown
10 February, 1862. Veteran. Discharged at
Alexandria, Va., 17 July, 1865. (H.R.M.V.,
Vol. 1, 75) (MSA-AGR, Vol. 1, 83)

DORRANCE, James R. (Pvt.) Co. A, 7th Regiment
Maryland Infantry. (US) Clear Spring. Age 19.
Served from 8 August, 1862 to 31 May, 1865.
Discharged at Arlington Heights, Va. (H.R.M.V.,
Vol. 1, 279) (Scharf, Vol. 1, 226; spelled with
"L") (MSA-AGR, Vol. 1, 91 and MSA-S-936-17)

DORSEY, Edward W. (Pvt.) Co. A, 2nd Virginia
Cavalry. (CSA) Williamsport/Downsville.
Service dates not available. Member of the
state militia prior to the war with the rank of
lieutenant. Served as part of the detachment
that guarded John Brown after his capture.
Entered the Confederate service in 1861 and was
wounded at First Bull Run when a bullet pierced
his leg. Surgeons found nine bullet holes in
his clothing after the fighting was over. He
was discharged later due to physical
disabilities and returned home. Before he
reaching home, soldiers raided his property and
made off with his horse and stock. He began
farming on the John Grove farm, at Sharpsburg,
and later retired to Downsville. (Williams,
Vol. 2, 1324) (Hartzler, 132) (1890-C)

DORSEY, Henry W. (Pvt.) Co. D, 4th Regiment
Infantry. (U.S.C.T.) (US) Hagerstown. Served
from 28 August, 1863 to 4 May, 1866. Suffered
gunshot wound to left thigh. Received pension
of $2 per month. (Pensions List, 157)

DOUGLAS, Henry Kyd. (Col.) Aide to Confederate General Stonewall Jackson, was born at Shepherdstown, Va., the son of Rev. Robert Douglas and Mary, daughter of Col. John Robertson. He later moved with his family across the Potomac River into Maryland. His home today, overlooking the Potomac River, opposite Shepherdstown, has been converted into the headquarters of the Chesapeake and Ohio Canal National Park. Douglas attended Franklin and Marshall College, studying law, and after graduation, in 1860, taught Latin and English at the old Hagerstown Academy on South Prospect Street. Later Douglas studied law at Judge Brockenborough's Law School, at Lexington, Va. He was admitted to the bar at Charlestown, Va. (now Charles Town, W. Va.) He entered the Confederate Army as a private at Harper's Ferry, 18 April, 1861, in the Shepherdstown Company of the 2nd Virginia Infantry, later a part of the famous "Stonewall Brigade." He was promoted first sergeant 5 June, 2nd lieutenant, 14 September and captain in 1862. On 13 June, 1863, he became major, as assistant adjutant general of the Stonewall brigade. From there he transferred to Jackson's staff as aide-de-camp, where, on occasion, he acted as adjutant general. After Jackson's death he served as A. G. to Major Generals Edward Johnson, John B. Gordon, and Jubal A. Early. Later Douglas was made colonel of the 13th and 14th Virginia Regiments when they were consolidated. He distinguished himself at Antietam and was wounded at Gettysburg. When Lee surrendered at Appomattox, Douglas was commander of the Light Brigade. His commission as a brigadier general was signed in Richmond at war's end but not effected. After the war Douglas returned to live in Hagerstown, practice law and serve as colonel of militia on the governor's staff. During the rail road strikes he commanded the Department of Maryland. On 22 November, 1880, Douglas was named captain of the Hagerstown Light Infantry, and on 29 May, 1886 he was

appointed colonel. He held the position of
Adjutant General of the State of Maryland for
four years. Douglas was successful in his law
practice with an office on West Washington
Street. His appointment as Circuit Court Judge
came in 1891. (Historical Material of
Washington County, 119) (Hartzler, 62)

DOUGLAS, William G. (Pvt.) Co. B, 3rd Regiment
Potomac Home Brigade Infantry. (US) Hagerstown.
Drummer. Enlisted at Hagerstown, 17 April,
1862. Discharged 17 April, 1865. (H.R.M.V.,
Vol. 1, 576) (Captain Maxwell's roster) (MSA-S-
936-23)

DOYLE, David. (Pvt.) Co. G, 3rd Regiment Maryland
Infantry. (US) Smoketown. Service dates not
available. Died in action or in prison.
Papers not available for census. (1890-C)

DOYLE, David. (Cpl.) Co. B, 3rd Regiment Potomac
Home Brigade Infantry.(US) Age 22. Beaver
Creek. Enlisted at Hagerstown 12 Nov., 1861.
Discharged 12 Nov. 1864. (H.R.M.V., Vol. 1,
577) (Captain Maxwell's roster) (MSA-S-936-24)

DOWNING, David. (Pvt.) Co. B, 2nd Regiment
Maryland Infantry. (US) Hancock. Entered
service 8 June, 1864. Killed 30 July, 1864,
near Petersburg, Va. (H.R.M.V., Vol. 1, 80)
(1890-C)

DRENNER, John W. (2nd Lt.) Co. H, 1st Regiment
Potomac Home Brigade Infantry. (US) Age 40.
Indian Springs District. Entered service 10
September, 1861 as a private. Later promoted to
first sergeant and to second lieutenant 1
November, 1863. (Scharf, 327) (H.R.M.V., Vol.
1, 523) (MSA-S-936-23)

DRENNER, Otha W. (Cpl.) Co. A, 7th Regiment
Maryland Infantry. (US) Sharpsburg. Age 19.
Enlisted at Williamsport 8 August, 1862.
Promoted corporal 22 October, 1863. Taken
prisoner 16 September, 1864, near Winchester,
Va. Discharged near Arlington Heights, Va., 31

May, 1865. (H.R.M.V., Vol. 1, 279) (Scharf, 226) (MSA-AGR, Vol. 1, 91 and MSA-S-936-17)

DUCKETT, Osborn. (Pvt.) Co. D, 30th Regiment Maryland Infantry. (US) (U.S.C.T.) Washington County. Owned by Jacob Snebley. Enlisted at Baltimore, 21 February, 1864. Discharged 24 May, 1865, due to wound. (H.R.M.V., Vol. 2, 243) (1890-C) (MSA-S-936-51)

DUNLAP, Dr. Albert. Assistant surgeon 3rd Regiment Maryland Infantry. (US) Boonsboro. After the war he returned to Boonsboro, opening practice in the summer of November, 1865. (Portrait and Biographical Record of the Sixth Congressional District of Maryland, 558)

DUNN, Benjamin F. (Pvt.) Co. E, 1st Maryland Cavalry. (CSA) Washington County. (Hartzler, 136)

DUNN, James R. (Pvt.) Virginia Infantry. (CSA) Keedysville. Service dates not listed. Taken prisoner. (1890-C)

-- E --

EAKLE, John C. (Pvt.) Co. H, 6th Regiment Maryland Infantry. (US) Age 24. Smithsburg. Served from 21 August, 1862 to 20 June, 1865. (H.R.M.V., Vol. 1, 241) (1890-C) (MSA-AGR-S-936-2)

EAKLE, Thomas. (Pvt.) Co. F, 1st Regiment Potomac Home Brigade Infantry. (US) Age 42. Farmer. Washington County. Enlisted at Sandy Hook, Md., 19 January, 1865. Transferred to Co. F, 13th Regiment Maryland Infantry. Discharged 29 May, 1865. (H.R.M.V., Vol. 1, 511) (MSA-S-936-23)

EARHART, William. (Pvt.) Co. A, 7th Regiment Maryland Infantry. (US) Age 21. Enlisted at Hagerstown, 11 August, 1862. Billed by U.S. Army $2.87 for loss of haversack and tent. Discharged 31 May, 1865. Member Independent

Junior Fire Company, of Hagerstown. (H.R.M.V., Vol. 1, 279) (MSA-AGR, Vol. 1, 101 and MSA-S-936-17) (I.J.F.C. roster)

EARNSHAW, James N. (Pvt.) Co. D, 1st Regiment Potomac Home Brigade "Cole's" Cavalry. (US) Hagerstown. Served from 19 August, 1864 to 8 Nov. 1864. (H.R.M.V., Vol. 1, 679) (1890-C)

EASTON, Daniel. (Pvt.) Co. I, 3rd Regiment Maryland Infantry. (US) Rohrersville. Buried in the Rohrersville Cemetery. (WCCR, Vol. 3, 126) (H.R.M.V., Vol. 1, 459) (1890-C)

EASTON, Elisha. (Pvt.) Co. E, 1st Regiment Potomac Home Brigade Infantry. (US) Age 41. Laborer. Enlisted at Hagerstown, 14 September, 1861. Reenlisted 23 February, 1864 at Sandy Hook, Md. Transferred to Co. E, 13th Maryland Infantry. Discharged 29 May, 1865. (H.R.M.V., Vol. 1, 507) (MSA-S-936-23)

EATON, James. (Pvt.) Drummer. Co. D, 1st Regiment Maryland Infantry (US) Age 18. Enlisted at Williamsport, 16 December, 1862. Transferred to Co. F, 8th Maryland Volunteers. Discharged 2 July, 1865. (MSA-AGR, Vol. 1, 94) (H.R.M.V., Vol. 1, 38)

EASTON, William E. (Pvt.) Co. E, 1st Regiment Potomac Home Brigade Infantry. (US) Age 18. Laborer. Washington County. Enlisted 12 December 1864. Transferred to Co. E, 13th Regiment Maryland Infantry. Discharged 29 May, 1865. (H.R.M.V., Vol. 1, 507) (MSA-S-936-23)

EBBERT, John. (Pvt.) Co. I, 1st Regiment Potomac Home Brigade "Cole's" Cavalry. (US) Age 42. Clerk. Hagerstown. Enlisted at Hagerstown, 26 August, 1864. Discharged 31 March, 1865. (H.R.M.V., Vol. 1, 690) (MSA-AGR-S-736-33)

EDELEN, Denton J. (Pvt.) Co. A, 11th Regiment Maryland Infantry. (US) Clear Spring. Served 24 May, 1864 to 1 October, 1864. Buried at St. Peter's Lutheran Cemetery, Clear Spring.

(H.R.M.V., Vol. 1, 377) (WCCR, Vol. 2, 37)

EDEMY, James R. (Pvt.) Co. K, 19th Regiment
Infantry. (U.S.C.T.) (US) Weverton. Served
from 15 June, 1864 to 28 July 1865. Discharged
due to disability. (H.R.M.V., Vol. 2, 231)
(1890-C)

EDWARDS, Henry. (Pvt.) Hospital chaplain United
States Volunteers. (US) Washington Co.
(Scharf, Vol. 1, 327)

EDWARDS, Henry. (Pvt.) Co. H, 1st Regiment New
York Cavalry. (US) Smithsburg. Served from
August, 1863 to September, 1863. (1890-C)

EICHELBERGER, Thomas H. (Pvt.) Co. F, 1st
Regiment Potomac Home Brigade. (US) Hagerstown.
(1890-C)

EICHELBERGER, William H. (Pvt.) Co. B, 3rd
Regiment Potomac Home Brigade Infantry. (US)
Age 23. Laborer. Hagerstown. Enlisted at
Hagerstown, 30 December, 1861. Veteran.
Transferred to Co. F. Discharged 29 May, 1865.
(H.R.M.V., Vol. 1, 592) (Captain Maxwell's
roster) (MSA-S-936-23)

EKES, Sibth (?) (Pvt.) Co. E, 1st Regiment
Maryland Cavalry. (US) Age 19. Boatman.
Williamsport. Enlisted at Williamsport, 22
February, 1864. Discharged 8 August, 1865.
(H.R.M.V., Vol. 1, 721) (MSA-AGR-S-736-33)

EMBLY, George F. (Pvt.) Co. G, 17th Regiment
Pennsylvania Cavalry. (US) Smithsburg. Served
from 2 September, 1864 to 26 June, 1865.
(1890-C)

EMBRY, Charles W. (2nd Lt.) Co. I, 1st Regiment
"Russell's" Maryland Cavalry. (US) Hagerstown.
Entered the service as a private 3 September,
1861; promoted to second lieutenant 9 October,
1863. Veteran. (William, Vol. 1, 327) (1890-C)
(H.R.M.V., Vol. 1, 731)

ENGLEBRIGHT, Michael W. (Pvt.) Co. F, 13th
Regiment Maryland Infantry. (US) Age 20.
Laborer. Hagerstown. Veteran. Served from 21
August, 1861 to 29 May, 1865. Buried in Rose
Hill Cemetery, Hagerstown. (H.R.M.V., Vol. 1,
446) (1890-C) (WCCR, Vol. 7, 264) (MSA-S-936-
23)

ENGLERTCH, Joseph. (Pvt.) Co. B, 3rd Regiment
Maryland Infantry. (US) Age 17. Enlisted at
Williamsport, 5 September, 1861. Transferred to
V.R.C. 1864. Discharged 31 July, 1865.
(H.R.M.V., Vol. 1, 123) (MSA-AGR, Vol. 1, 97)

ERNST, George. (1st Lt.) 3rd Regiment Maryland
Potomac Home Brigade. (US) Clear Spring. Age
24. Blacksmith. Entered service 1 December,
1861, as private in Co. D. Promoted sergeant,
first lieutenant 1 November, 1863. Discharged
26 June, 1864. Served on field staff as
Commissary sergeant. (H.R.M.V., Vol. 1, 115,
131) (U.S. National Archives, Record Group No.
110, 4th Election District)

EVANS, George M. (Pvt.) Co. A, 3rd Regiment
Maryland Infantry. (US) Age 40. Enlisted at
Williamsport, 15 June, 1861. Discharged 15
June, 1864. (H.R.M.V., Vol. 1, 118) (MSA-AGR,
Vol. 1, 98)

EVERHART, Henry. (Cpl.) Co. A, 7th Regiment
Maryland Infantry. (US) Conococheague. Age 31.
Served from 18 August, 1862 to 31 May, 1865.
Wounded in right hip by shell fragment at
Dabney's Mill, Va., 14 Nov., 1862. Corporal 1
October, 1864. Lost tent Lost haversack, billed
$2.87 by army. Discharged at Arlington
Heights. (H.R.M.V., Vol. 1, 279) (1890-C) (MSA-
AGR, Vol. 1, 101 and MSA-S-936-17)

EVERHART, William. (Cpl.) Co. A, 7th Regiment
Maryland Infantry. (US) Washington County.
Served from 11 August, 1862 to 21 May, 1865.
(H.R.M.V., Vol. 1, 279) (Scharf, 226)

EYSTER, Samuel. (Pvt.) Co. A, 7th Regiment

Maryland Infantry. (US) Washington County. Age
18. Began service 9 August, 1862. Deserted 14
November, 1862, at Williamsport. Md.
(H.R.M.V., Vol. 1, 279) (Scharf, Vol. 1, 226)
(MSA-AGR, Vol. 1, 101 and MSA-S-936-17)

-- F --

FAHEY, Thomas. (Pvt.) Co. B, 3rd Regiment
Maryland Infantry. (US) Age 18. Enlisted at
Williamsport, 12 August, 1861. Discharged 4
August, 1864. (H.R.M.V., Vol. 1, 123)
(MSA-AGR, Vol. 1, 115)

FAIRFAX, Donald MacNeill. (Rear Admiral) (USN)
Born in Virginia, he died at Hagerstown in
1894, at his residence "The Columns," at 163
South Prospect Street. Fairfax was the great-
grandson of Byron, eighth Baron Fairfax of
Virginia. Entering the naval service in 1837
he earned rapid promotion through hard work.
When the war began he had earned the rank of
lieutenant. From 1861 to 1862 Fairfax was in
charge of ordinance at Philadelphia. In May,
1862, he was ordered to command of Cuyan,
reporting to Admiral Farragut near New Orleans.
Commissioned as commander, 16 July, 1862 and
took command of the monitor Nantucket,
reporting to Admiral Samuel Francis DuPont, and
participated in all actions on the outer forts
of Charleston. In September, 1864 Fairfax was
named Commandant of Midshipmen at the Naval
Academy, New Port, R.I. Commissioned captain,
25 July, 1866 and commodore, 24 August, 1863.
He advanced to rear-admiral 11 July, 1880.
Fairfax was placed on the retired list, 30
September, 1881. He served his country twenty
years and four months at sea and fifteen on
shore. (Williams, Vol. 2, 926) (Walking Tour
of Historic South Prospect Street, Hagerstown,
Md., No. 12, Washington County Historical
Society) (Records of Living Officers of the

(United States Navy and Marine Corps, 5th
edition, 1894, pages 46-47)

FARLING, George T. (Pvt.) Co. A, 1st Regiment
Potomac Home Brigade Infantry. (US) Washington
Co. Age 55. Enlisted 28 August, 1862. Died 6
March, 1863. Buried in Samples Manor Cemetery.
(H.R.M.V., Vol. 1, 487) (WCCR, Vol. 4, 67)
(MSA-AGR, Vol. 1, 121)

FARLING, John J. (Pvt.) Co. A, 1st Regiment
Potomac Home Brigade Infantry. (US) Washington
Co. Enlisted 15 August, 1861. Killed in
action, 3 July, 1863, at Gettysburg. Buried in
Samples Manor Cemetery. (H.R.M.V., Vol. 1,
487) (WCCR, Vol. 4, 67)

FARROW, James. (Pvt.) Co. I, 7th Regiment
Maryland Infantry. (US) Age 36. Enlisted at
Hagerstown, 30 August, 1862. Missing in action
8 May, 1864 near Spotsylvania, Va.,
battlefield. No further record. (H.R.M.V.,
Vol. 1, 297) (MSA-AGR, Vol. 1, 123)

FARROW, John E. (Pvt.) Co. I, 1st Regiment
"Russell's" Maryland Cavalry. (US) Enlisted at
Williamsport, 17 December, 1862. Died 24
February, 1864. (H.R.M.V., Vol. 1, 732) (MSA-
AGR-S-936-38)

FARST, Jacob. (Pvt.) Co. A, 7th Regiment Maryland
Infantry. (US) Age 20. Enlisted at Hagerstown,
28 February, 1864. Discharged at Washington,
D.C., 9 June, 1865. (H.R.M.V., Vol. 1, 279)
(MSA-AGR, Vol. 1, 120)

FEIGLEY, George. (Pvt.) Co. A, 7th Regiment
Maryland Infantry. (US) Hagerstown. Served
beginning 14 August, 1862. Transferred to
V.R.C. 6 February, 1864. (H.R.M.V., Vol. 1.
279) (1890-C)

FEIGLEY, John. (Pvt.) Co. B, 3rd Regiment Potomac
Home Brigade Infantry. (US) Age 23.
Hagerstown. Member Independent Junior Fire
Company, of Hagerstown. Enlisted at
Hagerstown, 30 December, 1862. Transferred to
Co. F. Discharged 29 May, 1865. (H.R.M.V.,

Vol. 1, 576) (Captain Maxwell's roster) (MSA-S-936-23) (I.J.F.C. roster)

FERGUSON, William P. (Pvt.) Chaplain. 1st Regiment Potomac Home Brigade Infantry. (US) Washington County. Entered service 28 November, 1861. Resigned 28 February, 1862. (Scharf, 327) (H.R.M.V., part 1, 485)

FESSLER, John. (Pvt.) Co. E, 1st Regiment Potomac Home Brigade Infantry. (US) Age 19. Shoemaker. Funkstown. Served from January, 1861 to August, 1865. Reenlisted 23 February, 1864. Transferred to Co. E, 13th Maryland Infantry. (1890-C) (H.R.M.V., Vol. 1, 507) (MSA-S-936-23)

FIEGLEY, Edward. (Pvt.) Co. I, 1st Regiment "Russell's" Maryland Cavalry. (US) Hagerstown. Age 24. Served from 3 September, 1861 to 3 September, 1863. Suffered partial loss of hearing. Farm laborer. Member Independent Junior Fire Company, of Hagerstown. (H.R.M.V., Vol. 1, 733) (1890-C) (1860-C) (I.J.F.C.)

FIEGLEY, George. (Pvt.) Co. A, 7th Regiment Maryland Infantry. (US) Hagerstown. Age 52. Began service 14 August, 1862. Transferred to V.R.C. 6 February, 1864. (H.R.M.V., Vol. 1 278) (Scharf, Vol. 1, 226) (MSA-S-936-17)

FIEGLEY, John. (Pvt.) Co. F, 3rd Regiment Maryland Infantry. (US) Hagerstown. Served from 13 January 1861 to 31 January, 1864. (1890-C)

FIEGLEY, Samuel. (Pvt.) Co. M, 1st Regiment Maryland Cavalry. (US) Age 26. Laborer. Enlisted at Williamsport, 22 February, 1864. Died 29 October, 1864. (H.R.M.V., Vol. 1, 742) (MSA-AGR-S-736-33)

FILE, William H. (Sgt.) Co. A, 7th Regiment Maryland Infantry. (US) Washington County. Age 20. Enlisted at Hagerstown 15 August, 1862. Reported sick in hospital at Annapolis. Discharged 15 July, 1865, at Annapolis.

(H.R.M.V., Vol. 1, 279) (Scharf, 226) (MSA-AGR, Vol. 1, 121 and (MSA-S-926-17)

FINEGAN, James W. (Pvt.) Co. I, 1st Regiment "Russell's" Maryland Cavalry. (US) Hagerstown. Served from 3 September, 1861 to 8 August, 1865. (H.R.M.V., Vol. 1, 733) (1890-C)

FINK, Jacob. (Cpl.) Co. F, 1st Regiment Potomac Home Brigade Infantry. (US) Millstone. Served from 4 September, 1861 to 1 December, 1864. Injured in neck and shoulders. (H.R.M.V., Vol. 1, 512) (1890-C)

FIREY, William. (Capt.) Co. B, 1st Regiment Potomac Home Brigade "Cole's" Cavalry. (US) Clear Spring. Entered service 24 August, 1861. Functioned as a highly respected officer until 1864, when he failed to appear within the prescribed time for a hearing on charges of being absent without leave. He was dismissed from the service, 30 May, 1864. (Scharf, 327) (H.R.M.V., Vol. 1, 670) (MSA-S-0935-41- Special order No. 215)

FISHACK, George R. (Pvt.) Co. L, 1st Regiment Potomac Home Brigade "Cole's" Cavalry. Smithsburg. Served from 29 March, 1864 to 28 June, 1864. (H.R.M.V., Vol. 1, 696) (1890-C)

FISHACK, Henry F. (Pvt.) Co. H, 6th Regiment Maryland Infantry. (US) Age 19. Smithsburg. Served from 21 August, 1862 to 20 June, 1865. Discharged at Washington, D.C. Suffered right side gunshot wound in action 2 April, 1865. Taken prisoner. Reported ball still in side in 1890. (H.R.M.V., Vol. 1, 241) (1890-C) (MSA-AGR, Vol. 1, 120 and MSA-AGR-S-936-2)

FISHACK, Jeremiah. (Pvt.) Co. H, 6th Regiment Maryland Infantry. (US) Age 18. Edgemont. Enlisted at Hagerstown, 21 August, 1862. Taken prisoner in 1863. Due $10 for rations while in prison. Reduced in rank from corporal to private 3 February, 1865. Discharged 20 June, 1865, near Washington D.C. (H.R.M.V., Vol. 1,

241) (1890-C) (MSA-AGR, Vol. 1, 121, (MSA-AGR-S-936-2))

FISHER, Frisby F. (Cpl.) Co. H, 6th Regiment Maryland Infantry. (US) Age 17. Enlisted at Hagerstown 11 August, 1862. Promoted corporal 3 April, 1865. Discharged near Washington, D.C., 20 April, 1865. (H.R.M.V., Vol. 1, 241) (MSA-AGR, Vol. 1, 120)

FISHER, George L. (Pvt.) Co. A, 7th Regiment Maryland Infantry. (US) Hagerstown. Age 18. A native of Germany, moved with his family to this country at age 5. Entered service at Hagerstown, on 16 August, 1862. Spent a week at Richmond's Libby Prison without food. Another four weeks in an old tobacco warehouse, in Danville, Va. The following four months he was confined at Salisbury, N. C., with a daily diet consisting of corn-meal, cobs and all without salt. A companion in his prison listed total deaths in their compound of 5,800 over a four month period. He witnessed the death of forty men in a single night and watched as they were moved to the "death house" the next morning. When his release was obtained, the week-long march north to Union lines, with others, claimed many more lives. He was discharged at Arlington Heights, Va., 3 May, 1865. After the war he returned to Hagerstown where he became a member of the regular army enlisting in Co. A, 2nd Infantry Regiment as sergeant. Completing his service he returned to Hagerstown and went to work for the Cumberland Valley Railroad. (H.R.M.V., Vol. 1, 279) (1890-C) (Portrait and Biographical Record of the Sixth Congressional District of Maryland, 1898, pages 842-43) (MSA-AGR, Vol. 1, 121 and MSA-S-936-17)

FISHER, George W. (Pvt.) Co. I, 2nd (U.S.C.T.) (US) Eakle's Mill. Served from 15 September, 1863 to 16 January, 1866. (1890-C)

FISHER, John W. (Pvt.) Co. ? 2nd Regiment Infantry. (U.S.C.T.) (US) Enlisted. (MSA-S-936-45)

FISHER, John W. (Pvt.) Co. A, 1st Potomac Home Brigade Infantry. (US) Sharpsburg. Served from 15 August, 1861 to 27 August, 1864. (H.R.M.V., Vol. 1, 487) (1890-C)

FISHER, Joseph. (Pvt.) 22nd Pennsylvania Cavalry. Hancock. Died 21 July, 1864. Buried in Tonoloway Baptist Cemetery, north of Hancock at the state line, in Pennsylvania. (WCCR Vol. 2, 155)

FITZHUGH, C. D. (Pvt.) Co. C, 1st Maryland Cavalry. (CSA) Washington County. (Hartzler, 145)

FLECKENSTINE, John. (Pvt.) Co. H, 6th Regiment Maryland Infantry. (US) Age 18. Enlisted at Hagerstown, 21 August, 1862. Killed in action 19 September, 1864 at Winchester, Va. (H.R.M.V., Vol. 1, 241) (MSA-AGR, Vol. 1, 121 and 936-2)

FLEMMING, William. (Sgt.) 3rd Maryland Light Artillery, (CSA) Funkstown. (Hartzler, 145)

FLETCHER, William J. (Pvt.) Co. B, 1st Regiment Potomac Home Brigade Infantry. (US) Boonsboro. Served from 6 September, 1861 to 6 September, 1864. Hospitalized four months. Reenlisted. (H.R.M.V., Vol. 1, 494) (1890-C)

FLICK, Henry B. (Pvt.) Co. I, 158th Pennsylvania Volunteer Infantry. (US) Hancock. Buried in Tonoloway Baptist Church Cemetery, north of Hancock at the state line, in Pennsylvania. (WCCR, Vol. 2, 163)

FLORA, Berlin H. (Sgt.) Co. L, 1st Regiment Potomac Home Brigade "Cole's" Cavalry. (US) Williamsport. Served from 29 March, 1864 to 28 June, 1865. (H.R.M.V., Vol. 1, 698) (1890-C)

FLOREY, Alexander M. (Major) Co. B, 1st Regiment Potomac Home Brigade "Cole's Cavalry." (US) Four Locks. Entered service as 1st lieutenant of Co. B, 24 August, 1861; promoted major 20 April, on field staff of regiment, 1864; discharged 12 October, 1864. Buried in St. Peter's Lutheran Cemetery, Clear Spring. (WCCR, Vol. 2, 42) (Scharf, 327) (H.R.M.V., Vol. 1, 664) (1890-C)

FLORY, Benjamin. (Pvt.) Co. H, 6th Regiment Maryland Infantry. (US) Age 24. Enlisted at Hagerstown, 21 August, 1862. A prisoner of war. Discharged near Washington, D. C., 20 June, 1865. (H.R.M.V., Vol. 1, 241) (MSA-AGR, Vol. 1, 121 and 936-2)

FLORY, Columbus. (Cpl.) Co. H, 6th Regiment Maryland Infantry. (US) Age 23. Enlisted 21 August, 1861 at Williamsport. Deserted 13 months. Sentenced to forfeit all pay and bounty. Transferred to 1st Maryland Voluntary Infantry. Transferred to V.R.C. 2 June, 1865. Discharged 20 June, 1865. (H.R.M.V., Vol. 1, 241) (MSA-AGR, Vol. 1, 120 and 936-2)

FLORY, Daniel W. (Cpl.) Co. H, 6th Regiment Maryland Infantry. (US) Age 22. Enlisted at Hagerstown 21 August, 1862. Promoted corporal 18 May, 1865. Discharged near Washington, D.C., 20 June, 1865. (H.R.M.V., Vol. 1, 241) (MSA-AGR, Vol. 1, 120 and 936-2)

FLORY, John J. (Sgt.) Co. H, 6th Regiment Maryland Infantry. (US) Age 19. Enlisted at Hagerstown 21 August, 1862. Promoted to Sergeant 17 May, 1865. Discharged near Washington D.C. 20 May, 1865. (H.R.M.V., Vol. 1, 241) (MSA-AGR, Vol. 1, 120)

FLORY, Lewis. (Pvt.) Co. H, 6th Regiment Maryland Infantry. (US) Age 22. Enlisted at Hagerstown, 21 August, 1862. Deserted at Harper's Ferry, 18 January, 1863. (MSA-AGR, Vol. 1, 241) (MSA-AGR, Vol. 1, 121, 936-2)

FLOUGHER, John C. (Pvt.) Co. B, 3rd Regiment Potomac Home Brigade Infantry. (US) Age 36. Beaver Creek. Enlisted at Hagerstown, 12

November, 1861. Transferred to Co. F. Discharged 12 November, 1864. (H.R.M.V., Vol. 1,
576) (Captain Maxwell's roster) (MSA-S-936-23)

FLUCK, James P. (Pvt.) Co. D, 13th Regiment
Maryland Infantry. (US) Hagerstown. Served from
2 February, 1865 to 29 May, 1865. (H.R.M.V.,
Vol. 1, 442) (1890-C)

FOCKLER, Samuel. (Pvt.) Co. R, 12th Regiment
Pennsylvania Infantry. (US) Smithsburg. Served
from September, 1861 to September, 1862.
(1890-C)

FOGG, Charles E. (Pvt.) Co. B., 6th Virginia
Cavalry. (CSA) Washington Co. Buried in the
Ringgold Church Cemetery. (WCCR, Vol. 4, 93)

FOGLE, Elias. (Cpl.) Co. B, 7th Maryland Regiment
Maryland Infantry. (US) Age 21. Enlisted at
Hagerstown 18 August, 1862. Promoted corporal
1 July, 1864. Discharged 31 May, 1865.
(H.R.M.V., Vol. 1, 281) (MSA-AGR, Vol. 1, 120)

FOGLE, John W. Co. B, 7th Regiment Maryland
Infantry. (US) Age 31. Enlisted at Hagerstown,
12 August, 1862. Discharged 31 May, 1865.
(H.R.M.V., Vol. 1, 281) (MSA-AGR, Vol. 1, 120)

FOGLE, Martin L. (Pvt.) Co. B, 7th Regiment
Maryland Infantry. (US) Age 21. Enlisted at
Hagerstown, 9 August, 1862. Discharged 31 May,
1865. (H.R.M.V., Vol. 1, 281) (MSA-AGR, Vol.
1, 120)

FOGLER, George W. (Pvt.) Co. H, 6th Regiment
Maryland Infantry. (US) Age 23. Enlisted at
Hagerstown, 21 August, 1862. Died 24 May, 1864
from wounds in action at the Wilderness, Va.
(H.R.M.V., Vol. 1, 241) (MSA-AGR, Vol. 1, 121
and 936-2)

FOGLER, Luther. (Pvt.) Co. H, 6th Regiment
Maryland Infantry. (US) Age 36. Smithsburg.
Enlisted at Hagerstown, 21 April, 1862.
Wounded in action 21 September, 1864, at

Fisher's Hill, Va. Severely wounded 2 April,
1865 in assault on Rebel works at Petersburg,
Va. Died of wounds 21 April, 1865. Buried in
St. Paul's Cemetery, Smithsburg. (H.R.M.V.,
Vol. 1, 241) (MSA-AGR, Vol. 1, 121 and 936-2)
(Scharf, Vol. 2, 1273)

FOLTZ, Frederick F. (Cpl.) Co. E, 1st Regiment
Potomac Home Brigade Infantry. (US)
Williamsport. Served from 1 October, 1861 to
29 May, 1865. Transferred to Co. E, 13th
Maryland Infantry. (H.R.M.V., Vol. 1, 507)
(1890-C)

FORD, James P. (Pvt.) Co. D, 13th Regiment
Maryland Infantry. (US) Boonsboro. Served from
13 February. 1865 to 29 May, 1865. (H.R.M.V.,
Vol. 1, 442) (1890-C)

FOREMAN, William H. (1st Lt.) Co. A, 3rd Regiment
Potomac Home Brigade infantry. (US) Age 20.
Hagerstown. Entered the service as private in
Co. F, promoted sergeant in Co. B, second
lieutenant of Co. K, 2 May, 1864; first
lieutenant 9 May, 1865. Veteran. (Scharf, 327)
(H.R.M.V., 1, 572, 592) (Captain Maxwell's
roster) (MSA-S-936-24)

FORNESTA, John. (Pvt.) Co. B, 7th Regiment
Maryland Infantry. (US) Age 43. Enlisted at
Hagerstown, 18 August, 1862. Hospitalized with
illness at Fairfax, Va. Discharged 12 June
1865. (H.R.M.V., Vol. 1, 281) (MSA-AGR, Vol.
1, 120)

FORSYTHE, David. (Pvt.) Co. G, 1st Regiment
Potomac Home Brigade "Cole's" Cavalry. (US)
Indian Springs. Served from 24 December, 1864
to 28 June, 1865. Suffered from exposure.
(H.R.M.V., Vol. 1, 687) (1890-C)

FORSYTH, John, Jr. (Pvt.) Co. F, 13th Regiment
Maryland Infantry. (US) Indian Springs. Served
from 15 February, 1865 to 29 May, 1865.
(H.R.M.V., Vol. 1. 447) (1890-C)

FORSYTH, Joseph. (Pvt.) Co. L, 1st Regiment
Potomac Home Brigade "Cole's" Cavalry. (US)
Indian Springs. Entered service 31 March,
1864. Deserted 16 June, 1864. (H.R.M.V., Vol.
1, 696) (1890-C)

FORSYTHE, Joseph L. (2nd Lt.) Co. D, 3rd Regiment
Potomac Home Brigade Infantry. (US) Indian
Springs District. Entered service as private
10 May, 1862, promoted to first sergeant then
to second lieutenant 10 May, 1862. (Scharf,
327) (H.R.M.V., Vol. 1, 583)

FORTH, Jacob F. (also Farsht) (Pvt.) Co. C, 1st
Regiment Maryland Infantry. (US) Age 20.
Enlisted at Hagerstown, 24 February, 1864. In
hospital July and August, 1864. Trans-ferred
later to Co. D, 7th Regiment Maryland Infantry.
Discharged 31 June, 1865. (MSA-AGR, Vol. 1,
114) (H.R.M.V., Vol. 1, 32)

FOSTER, George. (Pvt.) Co. F, 2nd Maryland
Cavalry. (US) Hancock. Killed in action 18
Sept., 1863, at age 27. (Scharf, Vol. 1, 1253)

FOX, John W. (Sgt.) Co. L, 1st Regiment Potomac
Home Brigade "Cole's" Cavalry. (US) Green
Springs Furnace. Served from 21 March, 1864 to
28 June, 1865. (H.R.M.V., Vol. 1, 696) (1890-C)

FRANKS, John C. (Pvt.) Co. B, 3rd Regiment
Potomac Home Brigade Infantry. (US) Age 21.
Washington County. Enlisted 12 November, 1861.
Discharged 12 November, 1864. (H.R.M.V., Vol.
1, 576) (MSA-S-936-23)

FRALEY, Daniel. (or David) (Pvt.) Co. I, 1st
Regiment "Russell's" Maryland Cavalry. (US)
Sharpsburg. Served from 2 December, 1861 to 8
August, 1865. Wounded at White Post, VA.
(H.R.M.V., Vol. 1, 733) (McClannahan papers,
4) (1890-C)

FRANTZ, Alfred L. (Cpl.) Co. B, 2nd Regiment
Potomac Home Brigade Infantry. (US) Cearfoss.
Served from 31 October, 1861 to 29 May, 1865.

Veteran. Wounded in action 18 June, 1864, at
Lynchburg. (H.R.M.V., Vol. 1, 548)

FRANTZ, John W. (Cpl.) Co. B, 2nd Regiment
Potomac Home Brigade Infantry. (US) Cearfoss.
Served from 27 February, 1862 to 29 May, 1865.
(H.R.M.V., Vol. 1, 548)

FRANTZ, Joseph F. (Pvt.) Co. B, 2nd Regiment
Potomac Home Brigade Infantry. (US) Cearfoss.
Served from 17 March, 1862 to 26 March, 1865.
(H.R.M.V., Vol. 1, 547)

FRANTZ, Joseph H. (Pvt.) Co. B, 2nd Regiment
Potomac Home Brigade Infantry. (US) Cearfoss.
Served from 17 March, 1865 to 29 May, 1865.
(H.R.M.V., Vol. 1, 548)

FRANTZ, George D. (Pvt.) Co. B, 2nd Regiment
Potomac Home Brigade Infantry. (US) Indian
Springs. Served from 5 April, 1862 to 29 May,
1865. (H.R.M.V., Vol. 1, 548)

FRANTZ, Frederick J. (Pvt.) Co. H, 2nd Regiment
Potomac Home Brigade Infantry. (US) Washington
County. Enlisted 18 September, 1861, died 17
August, 1864. (H.R.M.V., Vol. 1, 563)

FRAVEL, George W. (Pvt.) Co. A, 7th Regiment
Maryland Infantry. (US) Washington County.
Age 22. Entered service at Hagerstown, 9
August, 1862. Died of disease 26 August, 1864,
at Army Hospital, David's Island, in New York
Harbor. (H.R.M.V., Vol. 1 279 Scharf, 226)
(MSA-AGR, Vol. 1, 121 and MSA-S-936-17)

FREANER, George. (CSA) (Major) Hagerstown. aide-
de-camp to J. E. B. Stuart. Educated at
Dickinson College, Carlisle, Pa., he entered
the Hagerstown Bar in 1853. A few years later
he moved to Oakland, Calif., where he opened a
law office and was active in politics. Before
the start of the war he returned to Hagerstown
and the practice of law with Robert Wilson and
George Smith, and was elected to the House of
Delegates in 1859. He entered the Confederate

Army in the autumn of 1861 as adjutant of the
1st Virginia Cavalry, commanded by Col. L.
Tiernan Brien. While serving as adjutant and
lieutenant of Co. K, he was wounded in the leg,
17 June, 1863, at Aldie, Va. Upon Stuart's
death, at Yellow Tavern, Va., he became Asst.
Adjutant General on the staff of Gen. Fitzhugh
Lee, commander of the 1st Brigade of
Confederate Cavalry, and later, he was
transferred to the staff of Wade Hampton.
After the war Freaner returned to Hagerstown to
continue his law work with Andrew K. Syester,
from his office at 60 West Washington Street.
He died in 1878. (Scharf, part 1, 366)
(Hartzler, 148) (Williams, Vol. 2, 308)
(S.H.S.P., Vol. IX, page 80, XXXVIII, page 179)
(M. F. D., 727)

FREBURGER, Columbus. (Pvt.) Co. A, 2nd Regiment
Maryland Infantry. (US) Age 21. Enlisted at
Maryland Heights, 10 February, 1864.
Discharged near Alexandria, Va., 17 July, 1865.
Veteran. (MSA-AGR, Vol. 1, 114) (H.R.M.V., Vol.
1, 76)

FREDERICK, David M. (Pvt.) Co. I, 17th
Pennsylvania Cavalry. (US) Washington Co.
Died 1 March, 1865, in Winchester, Va.,
Hospital. (WCCR, Vol. 3, 309)

FRUSH, George W. (Sgt.) Co. F, 1st Regiment
Potomac Home Brigade Infantry. (US) Age 21.
Farmer. Clear Spring. Enlisted 4 September,
1861. Reenlisted 28 February, 1864, at
Frederick, Md. Transferred to Co. F, 13th
Regiment Maryland Infantry. Discharged 10
June, 1865. (H.R.M.V., Vol. 1, 512) (MSA-S-936-
23) (1890-C)

FRUSH, John D. (Pvt.) Co. F, 13th Regiment
Maryland Infantry. (US) Age 19. Farmer.
Hagerstown. Served 21 August, 1861 to 26 June,
1865. Veteran. Taken prisoner 29 June, 1864
at Duffield, Va. (H.R.M.V., Vol. 1, 447) (1890-
C) (MSA-S-936-23)

FRUSH, Samuel. (Cpl.) Co. F, 1st Regiment Potomac
Home Brigade Infantry. (US)   Age 20.   Laborer.
Clear Spring.   Enlisted 4 September, 1861.
Reenlisted at Frederick, Md., 28 February,
1864.   Transferred to Co.   F, 13th Maryland
Infantry.   Discharged 29 May, 1865.   (H.R.M.V.,
Vol. 1, 512) (1890-C) (MSA-S-936-23)

FRY, Daniel. (Pvt.) Co. A, 1st Regiment Potomac
Home Brigade Infantry. (US) Age 25.   Carpenter.
Sharpsburg.   Enlisted at Sharpsburg, 15 August,
1861. Transferred to Co.   D, 13th Regiment
Maryland Infantry.   Discharged 27 August, 1864.
Buried at Mountain View Cemetery, Sharpsburg.
(H.R.M.V., Vol. 1, 487) (WCCR Vol. 1, 16)
(1890-C) (Scharf, 226) (MSA-AGR-S-936-22)

FRY, Martin L. (2nd Lt.) Co. H, 1st Regiment
Potomac Home Brigade Infantry. (US)   Washington
County.   Began service 10 September, 1861.
Resigned 29 April, 1862. (Scharf, 327)
(H.R.M.V., Vol. 1, 523)

FRY, Silas. (Pvt.) Co. E, 1st Regiment Potomac
Home Brigade Infantry. (US)   Age 20.   Laborer.
Washington County. Enlisted at Sandy Hook, Md.,
19 January, 1865. Transferred to Co. E, 13th
Regiment Maryland Infantry.   Discharged 29 May,
1865. (H.R.M.V., Vol. 1, 507) (MSA-S-936-23)

FULLER, (?) John. (Pvt.) Co. H, 3rd Regiment
Maryland Infantry. (US) Williamsport. Served 1
September, 1863 to 6 June, 1865. (1890-C)

FULTON, David. (Cpl.) Co. E, 1st Regiment Potomac
Home Brigade Infantry. (US) Beaver Creek.
Served from 1 October, 1861 to 1 October, 1864.
(H.R.M.V., Vol. 1, 507) (1890-C)

FUNKHOUSER, Sidney. (Pvt.) Co. K, 33rd Regiment
Virginia Infantry. (CSA) Indian Springs.
Served from 2 February, 1863 to 7 June, 1863.
(1890-C)

FURRY, Frederick S. (Pvt.) Co. I, 7th Regiment

Maryland Infantry. (US) Hagerstown. Age 23,
Enlisted at Hagerstown, 28 August, 1862. 1865.
Transferred to V.R.C., 7 September, 1863.
Discharged at Washington, D.C., 26 June, 1865.
(MSA-AGR, Vol. 1, 123)

FURRY, John E. (Pvt.) Co. K, 1st Regiment
Maryland Infantry. (US) Boonsboro. Served from
16 December, 1864 to 30 May, 1865. (1890-C)

FUTTENER, Charles M. (Sgt.) Co. A, 7th Regiment
Maryland Infantry. (US) Hagerstown. Served from
21 August, 1862 to 8 June, 1865. Contracted
typhoid, hospitalized Stanton U. S. Hospital,
Washington, D.C.(H.R.M.V., Vol. 1, 279)(1890-C)

FUTTERER, Joseph M. (Pvt.) Bugler. Co. L, 2nd
Regular Cavalry. (US) Hagerstown. Served from 2
May, 1865 to 2 May, 1868.(1890-C)(MSA-S-936-17)

--- G ---

GABRIEL, Richard H. (Pvt.) Co. F, 22nd Iowa
Infantry. (US) Williamsport. Born in the old
Conococheague District. In 1841 a disastrous
fire, caused by a pipe-smoking tutor, nearly
ended his life. Only the barking family dog
save the lives of the Gabriel family. In 1865
Richard and his brother went to Iowa to work in
a brickyard. Richard entered the service in
1861, serving with distinction until
discharged. Gabriel participated in the
battles of Port Gibson, Champion Hill,
Vicksburg, Winchester and Fisher's Hill. At
Cedar Creek he was wounded in the right foot
when a ball passed completely through it.
Another tore his cartridge belt off, but did
not strike him. He returned to Washington
County after the war to manage the family farm.
(Williams, Vol. 2, 775)

GAGLE, John H. (Pvt.) Co. B, 3rd Regiment
Maryland Infantry. (US) Leitersburg. Entered
service 23 July, 1861. Veteran. Discharged 31
July, 1865. (HRMV, Vol. 1, 123) (Bell, 67)

GAGLE, Solomon. (Pvt.) Co. A, 6th Regiment
Maryland Infantry. (US) Leitersburg. Enlisted
28 June, 1864. Deserted. (H.R.M.V., Vol. 1,
226) (Bell, 67)

Gaines, Dr. John M. (CSA) 19th Virginia Artillery
and the 8th Virginia Infantry. A native of
Locust Hill, Culpeper County, Va. Dr. Gaines
graduated in 1858 from the University of
Virginia with a degree in chemistry. After
finishing medical studies at Jefferson Medical
College in 1860, he went to work in Alexandria,
Virginia. Gaines entered the service of the
Southern states on 17 July, 1861, at Culpeper
Hospital, assigned to Dea's Maryland Artillery.
The battery enlisted for the duration as light
artillery in the Maryland Line. On 3 November,
they went to the defense of Richmond at Battery
8, as Company C, 19th Virginia Heavy Artillery.
After the battle of Antietam, Gaines was placed
in charge of the wounded, at Boonsboro. At
this time his orders were being addressed as
Surgeon Gaines. Assisting him with his work
was an attractive young lady, Helen Smith,
daughter of Dr. Otha J. Smith, of Boonsboro.
They immediately developed a deep friendship.
After the retreat from Gettysburg, in July,
1863, Gen. Lee again directed that he remain
with the wounded at Williamsport, and
Hagerstown. Later, as a prisoner, he moved to
Hagerstown where he remained for several months
until being exchanged in December, 1863.
Returning to military service at Petersburg,
Va., Gaines was assigned to the 8th Virginia
Infantry, Longstreet's 1st Army Corps, until
the war ended. Dr. Gaines returned briefly to
Alexandria after the war, but then moved to
Boonsboro where he married Helen Jeanette
Smith, his assistant of 1862. Dr. Gaines went
into medical practice with his father-in-law
until 1893 when he moved to Hagerstown and
retired. He was a valued member of the
Washington County Medical Society, and at the
time of his death resided in a mansion-type
home at 465 North Potomac Street. He is buried,

along with his wife, in section K, lot 10, of
Rose Hill Cemetery, in Hagerstown.

GALL, Charles E. (Cpl.) Co. I, 7th Regiment
Maryland Infantry. (US) Hagerstown. Age 22.
Enlisted at Hagerstown 8 September, 1862.
Taken prisoner 31 March, 1865, at White Oak
Road, Va. Discharged 31 May, 1865. Became a
Hagerstown policeman after the war and was
killed in the line of duty in 1866 by an angry
mob. Buried in Rose Hill Cemetery, Hagerstown.
(WCCR, Vol. 7, 240) (Moser, History of the
Hagerstown Police, chapter on "Officers Killed
in the Line Of Duty." (Chapters not numbered)
(MSA-AGR, Vol. 1, 139)

GALL, John M. (Pvt.) Co. H., 1st Regiment
Maryland Cavalry. (US) Age 22. Hagerstown.
Enlisted at Hagerstown, 13 February, 1864.
Died by suicide 22 June, 1864. (H.R.M.V., Vol.
1, 729) (MSA-AGR-S-736-33)

GALLAGHER, Thomas. (Pvt.) Co. I, 1st Regiment
"Russell's" Maryland Cavalry. (US) Enlisted
at Williamsport, 17 December, 1862. Discharged
8 August, 1865, at Alexandria, Va. (H.R.M.V.,
Vol. 1, 732) (MSA-AGR-S-936-38)

GANS, George W. (Pvt.) Co. H, 6th Regiment
Maryland Infantry. (US) Age 21. Enlisted at
Hagerstown, 21 August, 1863. Discharged near
Washington D.C., 20 June, 1865. (H.R.M.V.,
Vol. 1, 241) (MSA-AGR, Vol. 1, 132 and
S-936-2)

GARDENER, John B. (Pvt.) 1st Maryland Light
Artillery. (CSA) Smithsburg. (Hartzler, 150)
(Huntzberry, 96)

GARDNER, Jeremiah. (Pvt.) Co. F, 1st Regiment
Potomac Home Brigade Infantry. (US) Washington
Co. Entered service 1 October, 1861, died 3
December, 1862. Buried in St. Paul's Methodist
Church Cemetery, at Cavetown, Maryland.
(H.R.M.V., Vol. 1, 507) (WCCR, Vol. 3, 102)

GARLOCK, George. (Pvt.) Co. F, 3rd Regiment
Potomac Home Brigade Infantry. (US) Washington
County. Buried in Rose Hill Cemetery,
Hagerstown. (WCCR, Vol. 7, 243)

GARLOCK, Joseph. (Pvt.) Co. B, 25th United States
Regular Cavalry Regiment. (US) Hancock.
Served from 28 February, 1864 to 26 February,
1867. (1890-C)

GARRISH, Joseph H. (Pvt.) Co. H, 6th Regiment
Maryland Infantry. (US) Age 18. Williamsport.
Entered service 8 August, 1862 at Hagerstown.
Discharged near Washington, D.C., 20 June,
1865. (H.R.M.V., Vol. 1, 241) (1890-C) (MSA-
AGR, Vol. 1, 137 and S-936-2)

GARRITY, Peter. (Pvt.) Co. B, 3rd Regiment
Potomac Home Brigade Cavalry. (US) Musician.
Age 18. Washington County. Enlisted at
Hagerstown. Served from 30 December, 1862 to
29 May, 1865. Veteran. Transferred to Co. F.
(H.R.M.V., Vol. 1, 592) (Captain Maxwell's
roster) (MSA-S-936-23)

GARVER, Daniel. (Pvt.) Co. A, 7th Regiment
Maryland Infantry. (US) Washington County.
Age 23. Served from 18 August, 1863 to 18
August, 1865. Taken prisoner during fighting
at Weldon Rail Road, Va. (H.R.M.V., Vol. 1,
279) (Scharf, Vol. 1, 226) (MSA-AGR, Vol. 1,
138 and MSA-S-936-17)

GASPER, Cyrus C. (Pvt.) Co. K, 39th Regiment
Infantry, Maryland Volunteers. (U.S.C.T.) (US)
Washington County. Owned by George Feight.
Enlisted at Baltimore, 31 March, 1864. Absent
from hospital since 24 April, 1865. (H.R.M.V.,
Vol. 2, 284) (MSA-S-936-51)

GASSFORD, George F. (Pvt) Co. H, 6th Regiment
Maryland Infantry. (US) Age 23. Enlisted at
Hagerstown, 21 August, 1862. Deserted at
Harper's Ferry, 18 January, 1863. (H.R.M.V.,
Vol. 1, page 241) (MSA-AGR, Vol. 1, page 137)

GATES, William. (Pvt.) (CSA) Washington County.
Lost his parents before he was 18, drifted
about in the tri-state until settling into a
job as a canal boat operator. His education
was meager and his life was one of great
difficulty. At 19 he was employed by the
Baltimore and Ohio Rail Road as a track hand.
While in the Rebel army he was captured in
Mineral County, Virginia and sentenced to be
shot as a spy. However, the officer in charge
was killed in a skirmish before the execution
could be carried out, and his successor, who
knew Gates from the past, offered him a parole,
which he accepted. After the war he again was
employed by the B & O Rail Road, this time as a
supervisor for the Hagerstown branch.
(Williams, Vol. 2, 859)

GAUFF Daniel. (Pvt.) Co. E, 1st Regiment Potomac
Home Brigade Infantry. (US) Age 23. Farmer.
Washington County. Served from 30 January,
1865 to 29 May, 1865. Transferred to Co. E,
13th Regiment Maryland Infantry. Buried in
Lutheran Church Cemetery, at Locust Grove.
(H.R.M.V., Vol. 1, 444) (WCCR, Vol. 3, 163)
(MSA-S-936-23)

GAUTZ, Peter. (Pvt.) Co. E, 1st Regiment Potomac
Home Brigade Infantry. (US) Age 18. Cooper.
Washington County. Enlisted 19 January, 1865.
Transferred to Co. E, 13th Maryland Infantry.
Discharged 29 May, 1865. (H.R.M.V., Vol. 1,
page 507) (MSA-S-936-2377)

GEARHART (or GERHART), Miles. (Pvt.) Co. I, 6th
Regiment Maryland Infantry. (US) Age 23.
Enlisted at Hagerstown, 12 August, 1862.
Transferred to V.R.C. Mustered out near
Washington D.C., 29 June, 1865. (H.R.M.V., Vol.
1, page 243) (MSA-AGR, Vol. 1, page 137)

GEHR, Joseph M. (Pvt.) Co. E, 1st Regiment
Potomac Home Brigade Infantry. (US) Age 23.
Farmer. Indian Springs. Served from 30 January,
1865 to 29 May, 1865. Transferred to Co. F,
13th Regiment Maryland Infantry. (H.R.M.V.,

Vol. 1, 447) (1890-C) (MSA-S-936-23)

GEHR, William. (Pvt.) Co. G, 5th Regiment
Maryland Infantry. (US) Ernstville. Served from
2 November, 1864 to 1 September, 1865.
(H.R.M.V., Vol. 1, 207) (1890-C)

GELWICKS, John Luther. (Pvt.) Co. A, 7th Regiment
Maryland Infantry. (US) Hagerstown. Age 26.
Enlisted at Hagerstown, 12 August, 1862.
Wounded in right leg. Discharged at Arlington
Heights, Va., 31 May, 1865. He owed the army
$2.69 on discharge for losing a knapsack and
canteen. (H.R.M.V., Vol. 1, 279) (Scharf, Vol.
1, 226) (1890-C) (MSA-AGR, Vol. 1, page 138 and
MSA-S-936-17)

GERLACK, George W. (Cpl.) Co. B, 3rd Regiment
Potomac Home Brigade Infantry. (US) Age 24.
Hagerstown. Enlisted at Hagerstown 23
November, 1861. Discharged 23 November, 1864.
(H.R.M.V., Vol. 1, 576) (Captain Maxwell's
roster) (MSA-S-936-23)

GETTING, Edward H. (Sgt.) Co. G, 7th Regiment
Virginia Cavalry. (CSA) Brownsville. Served
from 12 April, 1863 to 1865. (1890-C)

GEYER, Henry A. (Cpl.) Co. A, 7th Regiment
Maryland Infantry. (US) Hagerstown. Age 25.
Entered service 13 August, 1862, at Hagerstown.
Killed in action at Weldon Railroad, near
Petersburg, Va., 21 August, 1864. Buried in
Rose Hill Cemetery, Hagerstown. (H.R.M.V., Vol.
1, 279) (Scharf, Vol. 1, 226; Vol. 2, 1101)
(WCCR, Vol.7, 388) (MSA-AGR, Vol. 1, 137 and
MSA-S-936-17)

GIBBS, Charles R. (Pvt.) (CSA) Unit unknown.
Buried in Rose Hill Cemetery, Hagerstown.
(WCCR, Vol. 7, 352)

GIFT, Augustus. (Pvt.) Co. A, 1st Maryland
Potomac Home Brigade Infantry. (US) Washington
Co. Entered service 15 August, 1861. Died 16
January, 1862. Buried in Lutheran Church

Cemetery at Locust Grove. (H.R.M.V., Vol. 1, 488) (WCCR, Vol. 3, 160)

GIFFIN, Peter. (Pvt.) Co. A, 3rd Regiment Maryland Infantry. (US) Washington Co. Age 19. Enlisted at Hagerstown, 15 June, 1861 for three years. Discharged 15 June, 1864. (H.R.M.V., Vol. 1, page 118) (MSA-AGR, Vol. 1, page 132)

GILLINGER (or Gillmeger, or Gillmyer) Louis. (Pvt.) Co. I, 7th Regiment Maryland Infantry. (US) Age 19. Enlisted at Hagerstown, 26 August, 1862. Hospitalized at Washington, D.C. Discharged 31 July, 1865. Member Independent Junior Fire Company, of Hagerstown. (H.R.M.V., Vol. 1, page 297) (MSA-AGR, Vol. 1, page 137) (I.J.F.C. roster)

GIMPLE, John C. (Cpl.) Co. I, 7th Regiment Maryland Infantry. (US) Chewsville. Age 26. Served from 28 August, 1862 to 31 May, 1865. (H.R.M.V., Vol. 1, 297) (1890-C) (MSA-AGR, Vol. 1, 137)

GLASS, Martin. (Pvt.) Co. H, 1st Regiment Potomac Home Brigade Infantry. (US) Age 20. Laborer. Enlisted at Hagerstown, 10 September, 1861. Discharged 25 October, 1864. (H.R.M.V., Vol. 1, page 525) (MSA-S-936-23)

GLASS, Peter. (Pvt.) Co. A, 1st Regiment Potomac Home Brigade Infantry. (US) Sharpsburg. Served from 15 August, 1861 to 27 August, 1864. (H.R.M.V., Vol. 1, 488) (WCCR Vol. 1, 24)

GLASS, William. (Pvt.) Co. A, 1st Regiment Potomac Home Brigade Infantry. (US) 32. A cooper. Enlisted at Sharpsburg, 15 August, 1861. Dishonorably discharged without pay or allowances at military prison, Wheeling, Va., 5 September, 1865. (H.R.M.V., Vol. 1, page 433) (MSA-AGR-S-936-22)

GLETNER, James D. (Pvt.) Bugler. Captain Firey's Co. B, 1st Regiment Potomac Home Brigade "Cole's" Cavalry. (US) Age 19. Boatman. Indian

Springs. Enlisted 4 September, 1861. Veteran. Reenlisted 14 February, 1864. (H.R.M.V., Vol. 1, page 671) (MSA-S-936-30)

GOLDEN, William. (Pvt.) Co. B, 3rd Regiment Potomac Home Brigade Infantry. (US) Age 29. Laborer. Boonsboro. Enlisted at Hagerstown, 28 December, 1861. Transferred to Co. F and V.R.C. 30 July, 1864. (Discharge date NA) (H.R.M.V., Vol. 1, page 592) (Captain Maxwell's roster) (MSA-S-936-23)

GOOD, William. (Pvt.) 7th Regiment Virginia Infantry. (CSA) Broadfording. Served from April, 1863 to May, 1864. (1890-C)

GORDON, Alexander. (Pvt.) (CSA) Brownsville. Service dates unknown. (1890-C)

GORDON, James. (Pvt.) (CSA) Brownsville. Service dates unknown. (1890-C)

GOODRICH, Matthew. (Pvt.) Co. B, 3rd Regiment Potomac Home Brigade Infantry. (US) Age 43. Williamsport. Enlisted at Hagerstown, 1 March, 1865. Transferred to Co. F. Discharged 29 May, 1865. (H.R.M.V., Vol. 1, page 592) (Captain Maxwell's roster) (MSA-S-936-23)

GOSSARD, George F. (Pvt.) Co. H, 6th Regiment Maryland Infantry. (US) Age 23. Enlisted at Hagerstown, 21 August, 1862. Deserted 18 January, 1863. (H.R.M.V., Vol. 1, page 241) (MSA-AGR, S-936-2)

GOUFF, Jacob. (Pvt.) Co. E, 3rd Regiment Potomac Home Brigade Infantry. (US) Rohrersville. Entered service 28 March, 1864. Discharged 29 May, 1865. (H.R.M.V., Vol. 1, 589)

GOUFF, John. (Pvt.) Co. I, 1st Regiment Potomac Home Brigade Infantry. (US) Rohrersville. Enlisted 14 September, 1861. Died 6 March, 1865, at Andersonville, Ga. Prison of chronic dairrhoea. Grave No. 12735. (H.R.M.V., Vol. 1, 531) (The Soldier's Story, 294)

GOUKER, Elias. (Pvt.) Co. H, 6th Regiment
Maryland Infantry. (US) Age 19. Enlisted at
Hagerstown, 21 August, 1862. Wounded by
exploding ball 25 March, 1865, in assault on
Rebel picket line near Petersburg, Va. Taken
prisoner. Exchanged. Discharged with
disability near Washington, D.C., 20 June,
1865. (H.R.M.V., Vol. 1, page 241) (MSA-AGR,
Vol. 1, page 137 and S-936-2))

GOUKER, Joseph W. (Pvt.) Co. H, 6th Regiment
Maryland Infantry. (US) Age 22. Enlisted at
Hagerstown, 21 August, 1862. Discharged with
physical disability 10 November, 1863.
(H.R.M.V., Vol. 1, page 241) (MSA-AGR, Vol. 1,
page 137 and S-936-2)

GOWER, Jacob. (Pvt.) Co. I, 1st Regiment
"Russell's Maryland Cavalry. (US) Enlisted at
Williamsport, 17 December, 1862. Discharged 8
August, 1865. (H.R.M.V., Vol. 1, page 732)
(MSA-AGR-S-936-38)

GRAVES, Charles. (Pvt.) Co. F, 2nd Regiment
Potomac Home Brigade Infantry. (US) Age 19.
Farmer. Washington County. Enlisted 5
September, 1861. Transferred to Co. C.
Veteran. Discharged 29 May, 1865. (H.R.M.V.,
Vol. 1, 558) (MSA-S-936-24)

GRAY, Daniel Peter. (Pvt.) Co. F, 3rd Regiment
Potomac Home Brigade Infantry. (US) Blacksmith.
Age 19. Beaver Creek. Raised on Cool Hollow
Road. Enlisted at Hagerstown, 19 August, 1862.
Taken prisoner at Harper's Ferry, September,
1862 and also at Monocacy Junction, Md., 9
July, 1864. Spent seven months in prison at
Danville, Va. Suffered from smallpox in spring
of 1864. Worked as regimental hospital nurse.
Discharged 29 May, 1865. (H.R.M.V., Vol. 1,
page 592) (Captain Maxwell's roster) (W.C.H.S.,
Civil War Letters file)

GRAY, George. (Pvt.) Co. B, 7th Virginia
Infantry. (CSA) Eakle's Mill. Served for

three years. (1890-C)

GRAY, John F. (Pvt.) Co. H, 3rd Regiment Maryland
Cavalry. (US) Beaver Creek. Served from 28
September, 1863 to 5 September, 1865.
(H.R.M.V., Vol. 1, 775) (1890-C)

GRAY, John W. (Pvt.) Co. A, 1st Regiment Potomac
Home Brigade Infantry. (US) Sharpsburg. Served
from 15 August, 1861 to 27 August, 1864.
Buried in Lutheran graveyard, Main Street,
Sharpsburg. (H.R.M.V., Vol. 1, 489) (WCCR Vol.
1, 73) (1890-C) (Scharf, Vol. 1, 226)

GRAY, Moses. (Pvt.) Co. I, 4th Regiment Infantry
(U.S.C.T.) Maryland Volunteers. (US)Hagerstown.
Service dates not available. (1890-C)

GREEN, David.(Pvt.) Musician Third Class Number
One Brigade (Moxley's) Band. (U.S.C.T.) (US)
Hagerstown. Enlisted at Hagerstown, mustered in
26 September, 1863, at Baltimore. Served in
Maryland until mid-1864 when the band went
south to Virginia. It assisted the army with
non-musical duties in front of Petersburg and
Richmond. Mustered out 20 April, 1866, at
Brownsville, Texas. Buried in Beautiful View
Cemetery, near State Line, Pa. (WCCR, Vol. 6,
60) (Mrs. Catherine T. McConnell and Dr.Roland
C. McConnell, Journal of Afro-American
Historical and Genealogical Society, Vol. 12,
No. 1 and 2, pages 11-15)

GREEN, James. (Pvt.) Co. F, 2nd Regiment,
(U.S.C.T.) Maryland Volunteers. (US) Washington
Co. Buried in Beautiful View Cemetery, near
State Line. (WCCR, Vol. 6, 60)

GREEN, Joseph. (Pvt.) The Stonewall Brigade,
(CSA) Hagerstown. A body servant to Gen.
Stonewall Jackson. Died at Williamsport in 1925
at age 88. (Hartzler, 158) (Confederate Veteran
Magazine, Vol. XXXIII, page 468.)

GREEN, William. (Sgt.) Battery K, 3rd U. S.
Regular Artillery. (US) Edgemont. Served

beginning 11 September, 1861 to the end and
remained in the service for the next 16
years.(1890-C)

GREENWALT, Andrew J. (Pvt.) Co. B, 3rd Regiment
Potomac Home Brigade Infantry.(US) Age 21.
Laborer. Boonsboro. Enlisted at Hagerstown, 14
Jan. 1862. Transferred to Co. F. Veteran.
Discharged 29 May, 1865. (H.R.M.V., Vol. 1,
page 592)(Capt. Maxwell's roster)(MSA-S-936-23)

GREENWALT, Martin. (Pvt.) Co. B, 3rd Regiment
Potomac Home Brigade Infantry. (US) Age 20.
Farmer. Boonsboro. Enlisted at Hagerstown, 3
December, 1861. Veteran. Transferred to Co. F.
Discharged 29 May, 1865. (H.R.M.V., Vol. 1,
page 592)(Capt. Maxwell's roster)(MSA-S-936-23)

GRESSER, William. (Cpl.) Co. B, 3rd Regiment
Potomac Home Brigade Infantry. (US) Age 32.
Hagerstown. Enlisted at Hagerstown 12
November, 1861. Discharged 12 November, 1864.
(H.R.M.V., Vol. 1, 576) (Captain Maxwell's
roster) (MSA-S-936-23)

GRIFFEY, Jacob H. (Pvt.) Co. C, 1st Regiment
Maryland Cavalry. (US) Age 24. Hagerstown.
Blacksmith. Entered service at Hagerstown, 7
March, 1864. Killed at Petersburg, Va., 16
August, 1864. (H.R.M.V., Vol. 1, 714) (1890-C)
(MSA-S 936-36)

GRIM. Eli R. (Pvt.) Co. H, 1st Regiment Potomac
Home Brigade Infantry. (US) Washington County.
Entered service 14 September, 1861. Transferred
to Co. H, 13th Maryland Infantry. Discharged
29 May, 1865. (H.R.M.V., Vol. 1, 525)

GRIM, Josiah C. (Pvt.) Co. H, 1st Regiment
Potomac Home Brigade Infantry. (US) Locktender.
Washington County. Age 23. Entered service 25
October, 1861. Discharged 25 October, 1864.
Died 1871 of illness related to service.
(H.R.M.V., Vol. 1, 525)

GRIMES, William H. (Cpl.) Co. I, 1st Regiment

Maryland "Russell's" Cavalry. (US)Williamsport.
Served from 3 September, 1861 to 8 August,
1865. (H.R.M.V., Vol. 1, 733) (1890-C)

GRIMM, David H. (Pvt.) Co. H, 13th Regiment
Maryland Infantry. (US) Boonsboro. Served from
8 February, 1865 to 29 May, 1865. (H.R.M.V.,
Vol. 1. 452) (1890-C)

GRIMM, George W. (Pvt.) Co. H, 6th Regiment
Maryland Infantry. (US) Age 21. Hagerstown.
Enlisted at Hagerstown, 14 August, 1862. A
prisoner of war. Exchanged. Discharged near
Washington, D.C., 20 June, 1865. Member
Independent Junior Fire Company, of Hagerstown.
(H.R.M.V., Vol. 1, page 241) (MSA-AGR, Vol. 1,
page 137 and S-936-2) (I.J.F.C. roster)

GRIMM, John M. (Pvt.) Co. F, 1st Regiment
Maryland Infantry. (US) Age 21. Baker.
Sharpsburg. Enlisted 4 September, 1861.
Reenlisted 28 February, 1864, at Frederick, Md.
Transferred to Co. F, 13th Regiment Maryland
Infantry. Discharged to 28 June, 1865. (1890-
C) (H.R.M.V., Vol. 1, page 512) (MSA-S-936-23)

GRIMM, Nathaniel. (Pvt.) Musician. Co. G, 13th
Regiment Maryland Infantry. (US) Brownsville.
Served from 2 February, 1865 to 29 May, 1865.
(H.R.M.V., Vol. 1, 447) (1890-C)

GROFF, Isaac. (Pvt.) Co. B, 3rd Regiment Potomac
Home Brigade Infantry. (US) Washington
County. Enlisted at Hagerstown, 30 January,
1862. Transferred to Co. F. Discharged 29
May, 1865. (H.R.M.V., Vol. 1, page 592)
(Captain Maxwell's roster) (MSA-S-936-23)

GROOMS, John. (Pvt.) (US) Indian Springs.
Teamster. Other information N/A. (1890-C)

GROVE, Abraham. (Pvt.) Co. H, 6th Regiment
Maryland Infantry. (US) Age 35. Enlisted at
Hagerstown, 14 August, 1862. Transferred to Co.
H, 24th Regular V.R.C. 15 April, 1865.
Discharged 19 July, 1865. (H.R.M.V., Vol. 1,

page 241)(MSA-AGR, Vol. 1, page 137/ S-936-2))

GROVE, Daniel S. (Pvt.) Co. H, 15th Regiment Illinois Infantry. (US) Served from 25 February, 1865 to August, 1865. Discharge lost. (1890-C)

GROVE, Francis Thomas. (Pvt.) Co. F, 1st Virginia Cavalry, (CSA) Sharpsburg. (Hartzler, 161)

GROVE, William F. (Pvt.) Co. E, 13th Regiment Maryland Infantry. (US) Smithsburg. Served from 7 February, 1865 to 29 May, 1865. (H.R.M.V., Vol. 1, 444) (1890-C)

GROVE, William H. (Pvt.) Breathed's Battery, Stuart's Horse Artillery. (CSA) Sharpsburg. (1890-C)

GUMBERT, William E. Drummer. (Pvt.) Co. A, 7th Regiment Maryland Infantry. (US) Hagerstown. Age 16. Enlisted at Hagerstown, 18 August, 1862. Discharged at Arlington Heights, Va., 31 May, 1865. (H.R.M.V., Vol. 1, 279) (Scharf, Vol. 1, 226) (1890-C) (MSA-AGR, Vol. 1, page 138 and MSA-S-936-17)

GYSER (Geyser ?) Philip. (Pvt.) Potomac Home Brigade. Company and regiment unknown. (US) Age 22. Clear Spring. Cabinet maker. (U.S. National Archives, Record Group No. 110, 4th Election District)

-- H --

HAGAMAN, Charles. Musician. (Pvt.) Co. C, 1st Regiment Maryland Infantry. (US) Age 15. Enlisted at Hagerstown, 12 March, 1864. Transferred to Co. A, 7th Regiment Maryland Infantry, 31 May, 1865. (MSA-AGR, Vol. 1, page 144) (H.R.M.V., Vol. 1, page 32)

HAGAN, Franklin T. (Pvt.) Co. A, 1st Virginia Cavalry. (CSA) Eakle's Mill. Served from 30 August, 1862 to December, 1864. (1890-C)

93

HAGAN, John. (Pvt.) Co. F, 1st Maryland Infantry, (CSA) Washington County. (Hartzler, 162) (Huntsberry, 65)

HAGENBERGER, Frisby. (Pvt.) Co. I, 7th Regiment Maryland Infantry. (US) Age 16. Enlisted at Hagerstown, 29 August, 1862. Killed in action 8 May, 1864 near Spotsylvania, Va. (H.R.M.V., Vol. 1, page 297) (MSA-AGR, Vol. 1, page 168)

HAGER, David R. (Cpl.) Co. I, 21st Pennsylvania Cavalry. (US) Hagerstown/Antrim Township. Enlisted in 1863 and served until the end of the war. Fought at Cold Harbor, Petersburg, Five Forks, Yellow Tavern, Farmville and Appamattox Court House. Mustered out of service 16 July, 1865, at Harrisonburg, Va. David had three brothers who also were participants in the war: John, who was with an Ohio regiment; Samuel, in a western company under Gen. U. S. Grant and Jerome, who served initially in an Ohio infantry company and later enlisted in the heavy artillery. Before he could see action with his new outfit John was stricken with a serious illness and died. David returned to Washington County after the war and in 1898 became superintendent of the Washington County Almes House for one year. Then returned to farming. (Williams, Vol. 2, 633) (WCCR Vol. 7, 236)

HAGERMAN, Andrew. (Pvt.) Co. B, 3rd Regiment Potomac Home Brigade Infantry. (US) Age 43. Merchant. Hagerstown. Enlisted at Hagerstown, 14 October, 1861. Transferred to Co. F. Discharged 14 October, 1864. (H.R.M.V., Vol. 1, page 577) (Captain Maxwell's roster) (MSA-S-936-23)

HAGERMAN, Charles. (Pvt.) Co. I, 7th Regiment Maryland Infantry. (US) Drummer. Age 15. Enlisted at Hagerstown, 12 April, 1864. Transferred to Co. C, 1st Regiment Maryland Infantry. Discharged 2 July, 1865. (H.R.M.V., Vol. 1, page 297) (MSA-AGR, Vol. 1, page 168)

HAILEY, James H. (Pvt.) Co. E, 1st Regiment
Maryland Infantry. (US) Age 18. Enlisted at
Hagerstown. Transferred to Co. E, 8th Regiment
Maryland Infantry. (MSA-AGR, Vol. 1, page 145)

HAINES, James R. (Pvt.) Co. B, 1st Regiment
Pennsylvania Cavalry. (US) Age 45. Green
Springs Furnace. Served from 10 June, 1863 to
20 August, 1863. Discharged with broken right
arm. (1890-C) (H.R.M.V., Vol. 1, page 241)
(MSA-AGR, S-936-2)

HALE, George G. (Pvt.) (unit unknown) Son of Rev.
John Hale, of Geneva, New York. Buried in 1862
in Zion Reformed Church Cemetery, Hagerstown.
(Church Records).

HALE, George W. (Pvt.) Co. B, 3rd Maryland
Regiment Potomac Home Brigade. (US) Age 24.
Upholsterer. Hagerstown. Served from 30
October, 1861 to 29 May, 1865. Veteran.
Transferred to Co. F. Buried in Rose Hill
Cemetery, Hagerstown. (H.R.M.V., Vol. 1, 577)
(WCCR, Vol. 7, 232) (Captain Maxwell's roster)
(MSA-S-936-23)

HALL, David D. (Pvt.) Co. F, 1st Regiment Potomac
Home Brigade Infantry. (US) Age 41.
Blacksmith. Washington County. Enlisted 4
September, 1861. Transferred to Co. A, 1st
Potomac Home Brigade Cavalry. Discharged 25
May, 1863. (H.R.M.V., Vol. 1, page 512) (MSA-
S-936-23)

HALL, James William. (Pvt.) Co. B, 3rd Regiment
Potomac Home Brigade Infantry. (US) Age 18.
Clear Spring. Enlisted 18 November, 1862.
Discharged 11 December, 1864. Buried in St.
Peter's Lutheran Cemetery, Clear Spring.
(H.R.M.V., Vol. 1, 143) (WCCR, Vol. 2) (MSA-S-
936-23)

HALLEY, Tacitus N. (Capt.) Co. F, 1st Maryland
Potomac Home Brigade Infantry. (US) Washington
County. Served from 21 August, 1861 to 18

March, 1862. (Scharf, 327) (H.R.M.V., Vol. 1, 510)

HALMON, Henry. (Pvt.) Co. B, 3rd Regiment Potomac Home Brigade Infantry. (US) Age 29. Cooper. Washington County. Enlisted 14 October, 1861. Veteran. Discharged 29 May, 1865.(H.R.M.V., Vol. 1, page 577)(MSA-S-936-23)

HAMMOND, Elias. (Pvt.) Co. A, 7th Regiment Maryland Infantry. (US) Washington County. (Scharf, Vol. 1, 226)

HAMMOND, Thomas B. (Pvt.) Co. H, 1st Regiment Potomac Home Brigade Infantry. (US) Age 20. Laborer. Washington County. Enlisted 2 July, 1864. Discharged 3 December, 1864. (H.R.M.V., Vol. 1, page 525) (MSA-S-936-23)

HANES, G. W. (Pvt.) Co. H., 1st Maryland Potomac Home Brigade Infantry. (US) Harper's Ferry. Served from 25 October, 1861 to 11 August, 1862. Buried in the Sandy Hook Cemetery. (WCCR, Vol. 4, 77)

HANES, H. F. (Pvt.) Co. B, Loudoun Rangers, West Virginia Volunteers. Buried in Samples Manor Cemetery. (WCCR, Vol. 4, 65)

HANES, James. (Pvt.) Co. H, 6th Regiment Maryland Infantry. (US) Washington Co. Age 48. Served from 11 August, 1862 to 20 June, 1865. Buried in Samples Manor Cemetery. (H.R.M.V., Vol. 1, 241) (WCCR, Vol. 4, 65) (MSA-AGR, Vol. 1, page 163)

HANEY, Thomas. (Pvt.) Co. A, 7th Regiment Maryland Infantry. (US) Washington County. Age 18. Entered service 12 August, 1862, at Hagerstown. Deserted 1 February, 1863, at Maryland Heights. (Scharf, Vol. 1, 226) (H.R.M.V., Vol. 1, 279) (MSA-AGR, Vol. 1, page 166 and MSA-S-936-17))

HANSON, John. (Pvt.) Co. B, 8th Regiment Maryland Infantry. (US) Hagerstown. Served from 16

October, 1862 to 1 July, 1863. Shot in the leg.
(1890-C)

HARBAUGH, Alexus J. (Pvt.) Co. I, 1st Regiment
Potomac Home Brigade Infantry. (US) Hagerstown.
Served from 27 February, 1865 to 29 May, 1865.
Transferred to Co. I, 13th Maryland Infantry.
(H.R.M.V., Vol. 1, 531) (1890-C)

HARBAUGH, Ignatious. (Major) Staff of Gen. J. E.
B. Stuart. (CSA) Smithsburg. (Hartzler, 166)

HARRIS, John. (Pvt.) (US) (U.S.C.T.) Hagerstown.
Served from June, 1863 to October, 1865.
(1890-C)

HARRIS, William B. (Pvt.) Co. A, 7th Regiment
Maryland Infantry. (US) Washington County.
Age 19. Served from 8 August, 1862 to 31 May,
1865. (H.R.M.V., Vol. 1, 279) (Scharf, Vol. 1,
226 and MSA-S-936-17)

HARRISON, Andrew. (Pvt.) Co. D, 13th Regiment
Potomac Home Brigade Infantry. (US) Age 21.
Boatman. Weverton. Enlisted 18 September,
1861. Veteran. Transferred to Co. D, 13th
Regiment Maryland Infantry. (H.R.M.V., Vol. 1,
page 503) (MSA-AGR-S-936-22)

HARRISON, James H. (Pvt.) Co. H, 1st Regiment
Potomac Home Brigade Infantry. (US) Weverton.
Age 22. Served from 14 August, 1862 to 29 May,
1865. Transferred to Co. H, 13th Maryland
Infantry. Discharged at Arlington Heights, Va.
(H.R.M.V., Vol. 1, 525) (1890-C) (MSA-AGR, Vol.
1, page 164)

HARRISON, John T. (Pvt.) Co. I, 1st Regiment
"Russell's" Maryland Cavalry. (US) Enlisted at
Williamsport, 17 December, 1862. Discharged 8
August, 1865. (H.R.M.V., Vol. 1, page 732)
(MSA-AGR-S-936-38)

HARRISON, Richard.(Pvt.) Co. G, 1st Regiment
(U.S.) Cavalry. (U.S.C.T.) Hagerstown. Served
from 5 Jan., 1865 to 15 March, 1866. (1890-C)

HARRY, George Albert. (Pvt.) Co. C, 1st Maryland Cavalry, (CSA) Hagerstown. (Hartzler, 168) (Huntsberry, 85) (Goldsboro, 232)

HARTMAN, Pard. (Pvt.) Co. A, 7th Regiment Maryland Infantry. (US) (Scharf, Vol. 1, 226)

HATFIELD, Robert. (Pvt.) Co. A, 7th Regiment Maryland Infantry. (US) Hagerstown. Age 19. Served beginning 16 August, 1862. Discharged with disability 20 March, 1863.(Scharf, Vol. 1, 226) (H.R.M.V., Vol. 1, 279 and MSA-S-936-17)

HARDY, George W. (Pvt.) Co. B, 5th Regiment Maryland Infantry. (US) Washington Co. Served from 25 September, 1864 to 10 October, 1864. Discharged due to disability. Buried in Samples Manor Cemetery. (H.R.M.V., Vol. 1, 188) (WCCR, Vol. 4, 71)

HARMAN, Hewitt. (Pvt.) Co. B, 3rd Regiment Maryland Infantry. (US) Age 21. Enlisted at Williamsport, 22 June, 1861. Wounded in action near Chancellorsville, Va., 3 May, 1863. Discharged 22 June, 1864. (H.R.M.V., Vol. 1, page 123) (MSA-AGR, Vol. 1, page 153)

HARMAN (or Harmon), John. (Cpl.) Co. H, 1st Regiment Potomac Home Brigade "Cole's" Cavalry. (US) Funkstown. Entered service 25 March, 1864. Killed in action at Kernstown, Va., 25 July, 1864. (H.R.M.V., Vol. 1, 689) (1890-C)

HARNE, James H. (Pvt.) Co. H, 6th Regiment Maryland Infantry. (US) Age 28. Printer. Enlisted at Hagerstown, 21 August, 1862. General court marshall 25 April, 1864. Sentenced to forfeit all pay and allowances and to serve 13 extra months on his original term of enlistment. Transferred to 1st Maryland Volunteers 20 June, 1865. Discharged 2 July, 1865. (H.R.M.V., Vol. 1, page 241) (MSA-AGR, Vol. 1, page 163 and S-936-2)

HATFIELD, Robert. (Pvt.) Co. A, 7th Regiment
Maryland Infantry. (US) Age 20. Enlisted at
Hagerstown, 16 August, 1862. Discharged 20
March, 1863, with surgeon's certificate of
disability. (H.R.M.V., Vol. 1, page 279) (MSA-
AGR, Vol. 1, page 164)

HAWKEN, James E. (Sgt.) (Unit unknown) (CSA)
Williamsport. (Hartzler, 169)

HAYNES, John. (Pvt.) Co. C, 11th Regiment
Maryland Infantry. (US) Ringgold. Served from 5
June, 1864 to 29 April, 1865. (1890-C)

HAYS, James A. (Pvt.) 11th U.S. Signal Corps.
(US) Leitersburg. Served from 21 March, 1864 to
11 August, 1865. (1890-C)

HEBB, Edward. (Pvt.) Co. H, 1st Regiment Maryland
Potomac Home Brigade Infantry. (US) Sharpsburg.
Served from 8 Feb., 1865 to 29 May, 1865.
Transferred to 13th Maryland Infantry.
(H.R.M.V., Vol. 1, 452 and 525) (1890-C)

HEBB, Richard H. (Pvt.) Co. A, 1st Regiment
Potomac Home Brigade Infantry. (US) Served
from 15 August, 1861 to 27 August, 1864.
Buried in Mountain View Cemetery, Sharpsburg.
(H.R.M.V., Vol. 1, 488) (WCCR Vol. 1, 49)
(1890-C)

HECK, Jacob. (Pvt.) Co. G, 2nd Maryland Infantry,
(CSA) Boonsboro. (Hartzler, 171) (Huntsberry,
76)

HECK, Jeremiah H. (Pvt.) Captain Firey's Co. B,
1st Regiment Potomac Home Brigade "Cole's"
Cavalry. (US) Age 24. Boatman. Sharpsburg.
Enlisted 2 June, 1862 at Hagerstown. Veteran.
Reenlisted 14 February, 1864, at Boliver, Va.
(H.R.M.V., Vol. 1, page 671) (MSA-S-936-30)

HECK, John. (Pvt.) Co. I, 1st Regiment Potomac
Home Brigade "Cole's" Cavalry. (US) Boonsboro.
Served August 19, 1864 to 28 June, 1865. John,
and his brother Jacob, above, were reunited

during the fighting near Boonsboro, in September, 1862. Jake paid a visit to his mother and sister Sally, and was at the breakfast table when John, who had to pass through enemy lines, came to the door to see his family. After breakfast John crossed the lines again and went back to his unit. The two were reconciled after the war. (H.R.M.V., Vol. 1, 692) (Doug Bast in Vol. 20, No. 6, the Maryland Cracker Barrel, page 26.)

HECK, Robert A. (Pvt.) Co. C, 19th Virginia Heavy Artillery, (CSA) Boonsboro. (Hartzler-171)

HEIDLER, John A. (Pvt.) Co. I, 1st Regiment "Russell's" Maryland Cavalry. Enlisted at Williamsport, 17 December, 1863. Discharged 8 August, 1865. (H. R.M.V., Vol. 1, page 732) (MSA-AGR-S-936-38)

HELFERSTAY, Charles Luther. (Pvt.) Co. A, 7th Regiment Maryland Infantry. (US) Hagerstown. Age 27. Entered service 16 August, 1862, at Hagerstown. Killed in action. Shot in the neck, 1 April, 1865, at Five Forks, Va. (Scharf, Vol. 1, 226) (H.R.M.V., Vol. 1, 279) (1890-C) (MSA-AGR, Vol. 1, page 164 and MSA-S-936-17)

HELLANE, Henry. (Cpl.) Co. I, 7th Regiment Maryland Infantry. (US) Age 27. Enlisted at Hagerstown 21 August, 1862. Promoted corporal 1 January, 1865. Discharged 31 May, 1865. (H.R.M.V., Vol. 1, 297) (MSA-AGR, Vol. 1, 168)

HEMPHILL, Henry. (Pvt.) Co. D, 1st Regiment Potomac Home Brigade Infantry. Age 22. Laborer. Enlisted at Sharpsburg, 15 August, 1861. Veteran. Transferred to Co. D, 13th Regiment Maryland Infantry. Discharged 29 May, 1865. (H.R.M.V., Vol. 1, page 503) (MSA-AGR-S-936-22)

HENNEBERGER, George. (Pvt.) Co. I, 1st Regiment "Russell's" Maryland Cavalry. (US) Hagerstown. A cabinet maker before entering the service at age 22. The son of cabinet maker John

Henneberger. Served from 21 October, 1861 to 3
September, 1864. (H.R.M.V., Vol. 1, 733) (1890-
C) (1860-C, 28)

HENRY, John. (Pvt.) Musician Third Class Moxley's
Number One Brigade Band. (U.S.C.T.) (US)
Hagerstown. Enlisted at Hagerstown, mustered in
at Baltimore 26 September, 1863. Served in
Maryland until mid-1864 when the band went
south to Virginia. Assisted the army in many
non-musical duties in front of Petersburg and
Richmond. Mustered out 20 April, 1866, at
Brownsville, Texas. (Mrs. Catherine T.
McConnell and Dr. Roland C. McConnell, Journal
of Afro-American Historical and Genealogical
Society, Vol. 12, No. 1 and 2, pages 11-15)

HENRY, Thomas E. I. (Pvt.) Musician Second Class
Moxley's Number One Brigade Band. (U.S.C.T.)
(US) Hagerstown. Enlisted at Hagerstown,
mustered in at Baltimore, 26 September, 1863.
Served in Maryland until mid-1864. Assisted
army with non-musical duties near Petersburg
and Richmond. Mustered out 20 April, 1866, at
Brownsville, Texas. (1890-C) (Mrs. Catherine
T. McConnell and Dr. Roland C. McConnell,
Journal of Afro-American Historical and
Genealogical Society, Vol. 12, No. 1, 2, pages
11-15)

HERBERT, F. D. (Pvt.) Paymaster. (US) Washington
County Volunteer service. (Scharf, 324)

HERBERT, Stewart. (Pvt.) Co A, 7th Regiment
Maryland Infantry. (US) Fairview Village. Age
18. Served from 14 August, 1862 to 31 May,
1865. (H.R.M.V., Vol. 1 278) Herbert enlisted
at 21 years-of-age and served as a drummer boy
until he was blinded for life on the
battlefield. At time of discharge the army
billed his 67C for a lost haversack. (local
and MSA-AGR, Vol. 1, page 164 and MSA-S-936-17)

HERBERT, William H. (Pvt.) Co. C, 12th Virginia
Cavalry, The Laurel Brigade. (CSA) Born at
Hagerstown, later resided at Clear Spring.

Enlisted 1 January, 1862. Served as a scout. (Hartzler, 173) (CVM, Vol. 14, 276)

HERR, Edgar Green Williams. (Pvt.) Co. D, 12th Virginia Cavalry, (CSA) Williamsport. His company served as scouts and couriers for the commanding officers of the second army corps. Died after the war at his home in Shepherdstown, W. Va. (Hartzler, 173) (CVM, Vol. 9, 175)

HERR, Samuel. (Pvt.) Co. I, 7th Regiment Maryland Infantry. (US) Age 33. Enlisted at Hagerstown, 10 September, 1862. Discharged 31 May, 1865. (H.R.M.V., Vol. 1, page 297) (MSA-AGR, Vol. 1, page 168)

HERSHBERGER, Elder Joseph C. (Pvt.) Co. D, 8th Regiment Maryland Infantry. (US) Conococheague. Served from 21 May, 1864 to 2 July, 1865. Wounded in action, 21 August, 1864. Transferred to Co. D, 1st Maryland Infantry. Buried in Bethel Church of God Cemetery, near Broadfording. (H.R.M.V., Vol. 1, 316) (WCCR, Vol. 3, 278) (1890-C)

HESS, John W. (Pvt.) Co. B, 3rd Regiment Maryland Infantry. (US) Age 19. Enlisted as a substitute, at Williamsport, 19 November, 1863. Deserted near Baltimore, 13 July, 1864. (H.R.M.V., Vol. 1, page 123) (MSA-AGR, Vol. 1, page 153)

HEWITT, Daniel, (Pvt.) Co. A, 1st Regiment Potomac Home Brigade Infantry. (US) Sharpsburg. Served from 15 August, 1861 to 27 August, 1864. (H.R.M.V., Vol. 1, 488) (1890-C)

HEWITT, Jacob. (Capt.) Co. A, 1st Potomac Home Brigade Infantry. (US) Washington County. Entered service 15 August, 1861 as first lieutenant, promoted captain 9 February, 1863. Mustered out 27 August, 1864. (Scharf, 328) (H.R.M.V., Vol. 1, 486)

HICKMAN, Freeland. (Pvt.) Co. H, 6th Regiment

Maryland Infantry. (US) Age 19. Enlisted at
Hagerstown, 21 August, 1862. Died at Harper's
Ferry, 8 April, 1862, of chronic diarrhea.
(H.R.M.V., Vol. 1, page 241) (MSA-AGR, Vol. 1,
page 163 and S-936-2))

HICKS, John M. (Pvt.) Co. A, 1st Regiment
Maryland Infantry. (US) Age 21. Hagerstown.
Entered service 10 August, 1862, at Hagerstown.
Deserted 7 March, 1863, at Maryland Heights.
(Member Independent Junior Fire Company of
Hagerstown. (H.R.M.V., Vol. 1, 279) (Dorrance
collection: letter of 16 February, 1863) (MSA-
AGR, Vol. 1, page 166 and MSA-S-936-17)
(I.J.F.C. roster)

HIGGS, Thomas B. (Pvt.) Co. A, 3rd Regiment
Maryland Infantry. (US) Age 23. Enlisted at
Hagerstown, 15 June, 1861. Discharged 15 June,
1864. (H.R. M.V., Vol. 1, page 118) (MSA-AGR,
Vol. 1, 153)

HIGHBARGER, Alfred. (Sgt.) Co. A, 1st Regiment
Potomac Home Brigade Infantry. (US) Sharpsburg.
Served from 15 August, 1861 to 27 August, 1864.
Buried in Mountain View Cemetery, Sharpsburg.
(H.R.M.V., Vol. 1, 488) (WCCR, Vol. 1, 17)
(1890-C)

HIGMAN, William. (Pvt.) Co. A, 13th Regiment
Maryland Infantry. (US) Downsville. Served
from 15 February, 1865 to 29 May, 1865.
(H.R.M.V., Vol. 1, 433) (1890-C)

HILL, James. (Pvt.) Musician Third Class Moxley's
Number One Brigade Band. (U.S.C.T.) (US)
Hagerstown. Enlisted at Hagerstown, mustered
in at Baltimore 26 September, 1863. Served in
Maryland until mid-1864 when the band went
south to Virginia. It assisted the army in non-
musical duties in front of Richmond and
Petersburg. Discharged 20 April, 1866 at
Brownsville, Texas. (Mrs. Catherine T.
McConnell and Dr. Roland C. McConnell, Journal
of Afro-American Historical and Genealogical
Society, Vol. 12, No. 1 and 2, pages 11-15)

HILL, Samuel. (Pvt.) Co. H, 45th Regiment
(U.S.C.T.) Maryland Volunteers. (US) Washington
Co. Buried in Beautiful View Cemetery, near
State Line. (WCCR, Vol. 6, 61)

HILLARD, Thomas Elliot. (Pvt.) (CSA) Washington
Co. Unit unknown. Served as Register of Wills
for Washington County. Buried in Rose Hill
Cemetery, Hagerstown. (WCCR, Vol. 6, 216)

HILTEBRIDLE, George W. (Pvt.) Co. F, 13th
Regiment Maryland Infantry. (US) Chewsville.
Served from 8 August, 1864 to 29 May, 1865.
(H.R.M.V., Vol. 1. 447) (1890-C)

HIMES, John P. (Pvt.) Co. A, 7th Regiment
Maryland Infantry. (US) Hagerstown. Age 27.
Son of carpenter Samuel Himes. Served from 9
August, 1862 to 31 May, 1865. Discharged at
Arlington Heights, Va. (Scharf, Vol. 1, 226)
(H.R.M.V., Vol. 1, 279) (1860-C, page 53) (MSA-
AGR, Vol. 1, page 153 and MSA-S-936-17)

HINES, J. (1st Sgt.) Co. B, 3rd Regiment Maryland
Infantry. (US) Weaverton. Served from 1861 to
1864. (1890-C)

HINES, Jeremiah. (Pvt.) Co. H, 1st Maryland
Potomac Home Brigade Infantry. (US) Washington
Co. Served from 14 September, 1861 to 29 May,
1864. Buried in Samples Manor Cemetery.
(H.R.M.V., Vol. 1, 525) (WCCR, Vol. 4, 77)

HITESHEW, Daniel C. (1st Lt.) Co. H, 1st Regiment
Maryland Cavalry. (US) Washington County.
Entered service as private in Co. H, 1st
Virginia Union Cavalry; promoted second
lieutenant, then first lieutenant 25 April,
1862. Mortally wounded in action, 13 September,
1862, at Maryland Heights. Died 26 October,
1862. (Scharf, 328) (H.R.M.V., Vol. 1, 728)

HITESHEW, Philip L. (Capt.) Co. I, 1st Regiment
Maryland Cavalry. (US) Age 23. Washington

County. Entered as private 3 September, 1861.
Promoted sergeant 28 August, 1863; captain 29
October, 1864. Acting A. A. general, Evan's
Brigade, Kantz's Division, Army of the James.
Severely wounded 13 September, 1862, at
Harper's Ferry. Mustered out 8 August, 1866.
(Scharf, 328) (H.R.M.V., Vol. 1, 731) (MSA-AGR-
S-936-38) (McClannahan papers, 4)

HOEFLICH, John F.   Saddler. (Pvt.) Captain
   Firey's Co. B, 1st Regiment Potomac Home
   Brigade "Cole's" Cavalry. (US)   Age 24.
   Trimmer. Clear Spring. Enlisted 4 September,
   1861. Veteran. Reenlisted 14 February, 1864.
   (H.R.M.V., Vol. 1, page 673) (MSA-S-936-30)

HOFFER, John. (Pvt.) Co. B, 3rd Regiment Potomac
   Home Brigade Infantry. (US) Age 20. Cooper.
   Broadfording. Enlisted at Hagerstown, 5
   November, 1861. Transferred to Co. F. Veteran.
   Discharged 29 May, 1865. (H.R.M.V., Vol. 1,
   page 592) (Captain Maxwell's roster) (MSA-S-
   936-23)

HOFFER, Michael. (Cpl.) Co. B, 3rd Regiment
   Potomac Home Brigade Infantry. (US) Age 22.
   Broadfording. Enlisted at Hagerstown 30 April,
   1861. Discharged 30 October, 1864. (H.R.M.V.,
   Vol. 1, 577) (Captain Maxwell's roster) (MSA-
   S-936-23)

HOFFMAN, George H. (Pvt.) Co. B, 12th Regiment
   Maryland Infantry. (US) Smoketown. Served
   from 18 June, 1864 to 6 November, 1864.
   (H.R.M.V., Vol. 1, 424) (1890-C)

HOFFMAN, John M. (Pvt.) Co. A, 3rd Regiment
   Maryland Infantry. (US) Boonsboro. Age 31.
   Enlisted at Hancock, 9 February, 1865. Deserted
   5 December, 1864. Arrested and returned to unit
   18 February, 1865. Deserted again on 23 June,
   1865. Forfeited all wages and allowances and
   sentenced to make good the time lost.
   (H.R.M.V., Vol. 1, 433) (1890-C) (MSA-AGR,
   Vol. 1, page 153)

HOFFMASTER, Franklin. (Pvt.) Co. H, 6th Regiment Maryland Infantry. (US) Hagerstown. Served from 14 August, 1862 to (?). (1890-C)

HOFFMASTER, Livinston. (Pvt.) Virginia artillery battery. (CSA) Eakle's Mill. Service dates unknown. (1890-C)

HOFFMASTER, Samuel. (Pvt.) 7th Virginia Cavalry. Sharpsburg. (1890-C)

HOLBERT, James. (Pvt.) Teamster, Co. G, 1st Regiment Potomac Home Brigade "Cole's" Cavalry. (US) Clear Spring. Served from 25, February, 1864 to 28 June, 1865. Buried in St. Peter's Lutheran Church Cemetery, Clear Spring. (H.R.M.V., Vol. 1, 687)

HOLLAND, Daniel Ringgold. (Pvt.) Co. B, 1st Regiment Potomac Home Brigade "Cole's" Cavalry. (US) Millstone. Enlisted at Clear Spring, 24 August, 1861. to 15 September, 1864. Captured the following year near Hancock and sent to Libby Prison, at Richmond, for two weeks and then exchanged. In the thick of action at Brandy Station, in 1863, he was captured again, this time by Mosby's guerillas, and held for two and one-half months. Holland fought at first and second Winchester and his reputation was such that the Rebels offered him $2,000 to change sides. After the war he worked for the C & O Canal and later opened a store at Lappan's Crossroads. His brother Joseph, served in the U.S. Army, was captured and jailed at Libby Prison, where he died. (1890-C) (Williams, Vol. 2, 954)

HOLLAND, Joseph L. (Cpl.) Co. B, 1st Regiment Potomac Home Brigade "Cole's" Cavalry. (US) Indian Spring. Entered service 24 August, 1861. Taken prisoner in October, 1863. Died 23 March, 1864 of disease contracted in Libby Prison, at Richmond, Va. (H.R.M.V., Vol. 1, 672) (1890-C)

HOLLYDAY, William H. (Pvt.) Co. A, 2nd Maryland

Infantry, (CSA) Hagerstown. (Hartzler, 178)
(Huntsberry, 71)

HOLMES, Bartley. (Pvt.) Co. D, 39th Regiment
Infantry. (U.S.C.T.) (US) Hagerstown.
Served from 24 June, 1864 to 27 May, 1865.
(H.R.M.V., Vol. 2, 270) (1890-C)

HOLMES, Henry C. (Pvt.) Co. D, 1st Regiment
Potomac Home Brigade "Cole's" Cavalry. (US)
Trego. Served from 23 February, 1863 to 28
June, 1865. (H.R.M.V., Vol. 1, 679) (1890-C)

HOLZPFEL (also spelled Holtzapple and Hulsapple)
Henry. (Pvt.) Co. I, 7th Regiment Maryland
Infantry. (US) Hagerstown. Age 23. Served from
1 September, 1862 to 31 May, 1865. After the
war he returned to Washington County and took
up farming. Buried in Rose Hill Cemetery,
Hagerstown. (H.R.M.V., Vol. 1, 297) (1890-C)
(WCCR, Vol. 7, 377) (Williams, Vol. 2, 1250)
(MSA-AGR, Vol. 1, page 168)

HOOVER, Henry. (Pvt.) Co. G, 209th Pennsylvania
Volunteer Infantry. (US) Hagerstown. Served
from 2 September, 1864 to 31 May, 1865.(1890-C)

HOOVER, William H. (Pvt.) Co. E, 1st Regiment
Potomac Home Brigade Infantry. (US) Hagerstown.
Age 23. Mustered in 14 September, 1861, at
Frederick, Md. Sick in regimental hospital July
through December, 1864. Mustered out 1 October,
1864. (H.R.M.V., Vol. 1, 508) (records
provided by Justin Mayhue, a relative, of
Hagerstown, Md.)

HOPEWOOD, John W. (Cpl.) Co. A, 3rd Regiment
Maryland Infantry. (US) Age 28. Enlisted at
Williamsport, 15 June, 1861. Discharged 15
June, 1865. (MSA-AGR, Vol. 1, 153) (H.R.M.V.,
Vol. 1, 118)

HORINE, William H. H. (2nd Lt.) Co. A, 7th
Regiment Maryland Infantry. (US) Hagerstown.
Age 25. Entered service as private, 8 August,
1862. Promoted corporal, sergeant, then second

lieutenant 10 November, 1864. His commanding
officer, Major Edward Mobley, once wrote Mrs.
Horine describing her husband to be "As brave a
man as there is in the army." (Scharf, 328)
(H.R.M.V., Vol. 1, 278 and MSA-S-936-17)
(Mobley letter dated 19 February, 1865, from
Headquarters, 7th Maryland Volunteers)

HORN, James H. (Pvt.) Co. A, 1st Regiment
Maryland Infantry. (US) Age 28. Enlisted at
Hagerstown, 21 August, 1862. Absent with out
leave. Returned to make up time with extended
enlistment. Transferred to 6th Regiment
Maryland Infantry. Discharged 6 April, 1864.
(MSA-AGR, Vol. 1, page 143)

HORNSBY, Reuben Andrew Jackson. Confederate
Navy, (CSA) CSS Virginia. Williamsport. The
last survivor of the great naval battle between
the Virginia and the Monitor. Hornsby was
nearly drowned when an explosion blew him into
the water. He was rescued by an unknown
sailor. (Hartzler, 178) (Confederate Veteran
Magazine, Vol. XXXIII, page 468)

HOUCK, Albert H. (Cpl.) Co. A, 7th Regiment
Maryland Infantry. (US) Clear Spring. Age 18.
Enlisted at Hagerstown 16 August, 1862. Killed
in action 5 May, 1864, at the Wilderness.
(Scharf, Vol. 1, 226) (H.R.M.V., Vol. 1, 275)
(MSA-AGR, Vol. 1, 164 and MSA-S-936-17)

HOUCK, Benjamin F. (Capt.) Co. H, 1st Regiment
Potomac Home Brigade "Cole's Cavalry." (US)
Clear Spring. Enlisted 29 February, 1864.
Killed in action 22 August, 1864, at Charles
Town, Va. (Scharf, 328) (H.R.M.V., Vol. 1, 688)

HOUSE, Lawson. (Pvt.) Co. H, 1st Regiment Potomac
Home Brigade Infantry. (US) Knoxville. Served
from 21 August, 1862 to 29 May, 1865.
(H.R.M.V., Vol. 1, 526) (1890-C)

HOUSER, Aaron. (Pvt.) Co. H., 1st Regiment
Potomac Home Brigade Infantry. (US) Washington
Co. Served from 25 October, 1861 until 25

October, 1864. Buried in a graveyard near
Samples Manor, on the William Nichols farm.
(H.R.M.V., Vol. 1, 526) (WCCR, Vol. 4, 80)

HOUSER, Samuel. (Cpl.) Co. H, 6th Regiment
Maryland Infantry. (US) Cavetown. Age 31.
Enlisted at Hagerstown 21 August, 1862.
Participated in hard fighting at Winchester,
the Wilderness, Spotsylvania and Fisher's Hill.
He was present for the surrender of Gen. Lee.
Discharged 20 June, 1865, near Washington, D.C.
(Williams, Vol. 2, 796) (H.R.M.V., Vol. 1, 241)
(1890-C) (MSA-AGR, Vol. 1, 163 and S-936-2)

HOVIS, Jacob. (Pvt.) Co. H, 6th Regiment Maryland
Infantry. (US) Age 30. Enlisted at Hagerstown,
21 August, 1862. Discharged near Washington
D.C., 20 June, 1865. (H.R.M.V., Vol. 1, page
241) (MSA-AGR, Vol. 1, page 163 and S-936-2))

HOWARD, James. (Pvt.) Musician Third Class
Moxley's Number One Brigade Band. (U.S.C.T.)
(US) Hagerstown. Enlisted at Hagerstown,
mustered in at Baltimore 26 September, 1863.
Served in Maryland until mid-1864. Afterwards,
in Virginia, along with other band members
assisted the army with non-musical duties.
Mustered out 20 April, 1866, at Brownsville,
Texas. (Mrs. Catherine T. McConnell and Dr.
Roland C. McConnell, Journal of Afro-American
Historical and Genealogical Society, Vol. 12,
No. 1, 2, 1991, pages 11-15)

HUBBARD, John L. (Pvt.) Co. F, 2nd Maryland
Infantry, (CSA) Hagerstown. (Hartzler, 181)
(Huntsberry, 75)

HUFF, William. (Pvt.) Co. B, 7th Regiment
Virginia Infantry. (CSA) Ringgold. Served from
June of 1861 to June of 1863. (1890-C)

HUFFER, Jonas Q. (Pvt.) Co. A, 7th Regiment
Maryland Infantry. (US) Chewsville. Age 22.
Served from 16 August, 1862 to 18 July, 1865.
Transferred to V.R.C. 15 January, 1865.
(H.R.M.V., Vol. 1, 279) (1890-C) (MSA-AGR, Vol.

1, page 164 and MSA-S-936-17)

HUGHES, Edward. (Pvt.) Co. B, 39th Regiment
Infantry. (U.S.C.T.) Maryland Volunteers.
(US) Hancock. Entered service in 1864.
Discharge papers not available for census.
(1890-C)

HUGHES, Joseph L. (Pvt.) Co. F, 1st Regiment
Potomac Home Brigade Infantry. (US) Age 20.
Plasterer. Washington County. Enlisted 4
September, 1861. Reenlisted 28 February, 1864,
at Frederick, Md. Transferred to Co. F, 13th
Regiment Maryland Infantry. Discharged 29 May,
1865. (H.R.M.V., Vol. 1, page 513) (MSA-S-936-
23)

HUGHES, Lewis. (Pvt.) Co. H, 7th Regiment
Maryland Infantry. (US) Age 20. Enlisted at
Hagerstown, 15 August, 1862. Discharged 15
August, 1865. (H.R.M.V., Vol. 1, 297) (MSA-
AGR, Vol. 1, 168)

HUGHES, Thomas. (Pvt.) Co. G, 1st Regiment
Potomac Home Brigade "Cole's Cavalry." (US) Age
45. Carpenter. Leitersburg. Enlisted at
Hagerstown, 20 February, 1864. Discharged 30
May, 1865 with physical disability. (H.R.M.V.,
Vol. 1, page 687) (MSA-AGR-S-936-38)

HULL, Henry. (Pvt.) Co. H, 13th Regiment Maryland
Infantry. (US) Clear Spring. Entered service 28
February, 1865. Deserted 5 May, 1865.
(H.R.M.V., Vol. 1, 453) (1890-C)

HULL, Michael. (Pvt.) Co. I, 7th Regiment
Maryland Infantry. (US) Age 46. Enlisted at
Hagerstown, 31 August, 1862. Died of disease
contracted in service 3 Oct., 1863. (H.R.M.V.,
Vol. 1, page 297) (MSA-AGR, Vol. 1, 168)

HULL, Napoleon B. Jr. (Pvt.) Co. H, 14th Virginia
Cavalry. (CSA) Clear Spring. Age 23. Fought at
Chancellorsville where he was killed and his
body discovered, on the field, by his father, a
member of the Union army. (Williams, Vol. 2,

1023) (Hartzler, 181)

HULL, Napoleon, B. Sr. (Pvt.) (US) Co. A, 3rd
Regiment Maryland Infantry. Clear Spring.
Wounded in action and captured 3 May, 1863 at
Chancellorsville where he discovered his
namesake son, in the Rebel Cavalry, dead on the
field. Discharged 15 June, 1864. The senior
Hull is buried in Hagerstown's Rose Hill
Cemetery. The Clear Spring District Historical
Society has an undated copy of a picture
showing Hull holding the horse of General
Robert E. Lee. The original picture is held at
the Stonewall Jackson Museum, in Lexington, Va.
(Hartzler, 181) (WCCR, Vol. 6, 125) (MSA-AGR,
Vol. 1, 153.

HULL, Peter. (US) (Pvt.) Indian Springs.
Teamster. Unit and dates of service not shown
on census report. (1890-C)

HURD, Joseph. (Pvt.) Musician, 1st Alabama
Infantry. (CSA) Williamsport. Hurd was the
father of a later, popular druggist at
Williamsport, George W. Hurd. Joseph's
regiment fought and was captured at Vicksburg.
Among the Union soldiers taking him prisoner
was his brother Byram P. Hurd, with Gen.
Sheridan's Command. Each man was not aware of
the other's presence on the ield. Byram was
killed later at Egypt Station, Mo. Joseph
survived the war and graduated with honors from
the University of Maryland School of Pharmacy,
in Baltimore. Initially, he went into business
in Clear Spring purchasing the business of Drs.
G. A. and R. S. Richardson. Afterwards he
opened a second store in Williamsport.
(Williams, Vol. 2, 1245) (Hartzler, 182)

HURLEY, Benjamin Franklin Morgan. (Col.) Born at
Chewsville, he was educated at the old Academy,
on Prospect Street, in Hagerstown and at
Franklin and Marshall College. He worked as a
surveyor in Kansas, and then returned to
Maryland when Kansas became a state. Hurley
completed his studies at the Columbia Law

School in 1859. In 1863 he was named state
military agent (US) and was later appointed
auditor of the United States Treasury. He
served as ambassador to Holland for one term,
returning to the United States in 1865. He was
at Ford's Theater the night President Lincoln
was assassinated. (Williams, Vol. 2, 1245)

HURLEY, Otha J. (Pvt.) Co. K, 1st Virginia
Cavalry, (CSA) Hagerstown. (Hartzler, 181)

HUTZLER, John E. (Pvt.) Co. I, 1st Regiment
"Russell's" Maryland Cavalry. (US) Enlisted at
Williamsport, 17 December, 1862. Discharged 8
August, 1865. (H.R.M.V., Vol. 1, page 732)
(MSA-AGR-S-936-38)

-- I --

INGLES, Alexander. (Pvt.) Co. K, 1st Regiment
Potomac Home Brigade Infantry. (US) Hagerstown.
Served 13 December, 1861 to 17 December, 1864.
(H.R.M.V., Vol. 1, page 537) (1890-C)

INGRAM, John W. (Pvt.) Co. D, 1st Regiment
Potomac Home Brigade Infantry. (US) Age 21.
Laborer. Enlisted at Sharpsburg, 18 September,
1861. Veteran. Transferred to Co. D, 13th
Maryland Regiment. (H.R.M.V., Vol. 1, page 503)
(MSA-AGR-S-936-22)

IRVIN, Hezakiah. (Pvt.) Co. H, 6th Regiment
Maryland Infantry. (US) Age 30. Enlisted at
Hagerstown, 20 August, 1862. Discharged 20
June, 1865. (H.R.M.V., Vol. 1, 241) (MSA-AGR-S-
936-2)

IRVIN, Joseph. (Pvt.) Co. E, 13th Regiment
Maryland Infantry. (US) Smoketown. Served from
2 February, 1865 to 29 May, 1865. (H.R.M.V.,
Vol. 1, 444) (1890-C)

IRVIN, William H. (1st Lt.) Co. I, 1st Regiment
"Russell's" Maryland Cavalry. (US)
Williamsport. Entered service as corporal;

promoted second lieutenant 9 September, 1862;
first lieutenant 29 December, 1862; died 9
April, 1863 of disease contracted in service.
Buried in Williamsport Cemetery. (Scharf, Vol.
1, 328, Vol. 2, 1221) (H.R.M.V., Vol. 1, 731)

-- J --

JACKSON, Daniel. (Pvt.) Co. H, 6th Regiment
Maryland Infantry. (US) Age 22. Hagerstown.
Enlisted at Hagerstown, 14 August, 1862.
Deserted 1 November, 1863, from Camp Parole,
near Annapolis, Md. (H.R.M.V., Vol. 1, 241)
(MSA- AGR, Vol. 1, 181 and S-936-2)

JACOBS, Emanuel. (Pvt.) Co. D, 1st Regiment
Maryland Volunteers. (US) Washington Co. Buried
in Bakersville, Md. Cemetery, near Eakle's
Crossroads. (WCCR, Vol. 5, 82)

JAMES, Edwin. (Sgt.) Also quartermaster, Co. H,
1st Virginia Infantry, (CSA) Washington County.
(Hartzler, 184)

JAMES, Isaac N. (Pvt.) Co. A, 7th Regiment
Maryland Infantry. (US) Benevola. Age 21.
Enlisted 19 August, 1862. Serious gunshot wound
to left leg in action 5, May, 1864, at
Wilderness. Transferred to N. W. Department, 13
September, 1864. Received pension of $6 per
month. (Pensions List, 156) (Scharf, Vol. 1,
226) (H.R.M.V., Vol. 1, 279) (1890-C) (MSA-AGR,
Vol. 1, 182 and MSA-S-936-17)

JAMES, John. (Pvt.) Co. A, 1st Regiment Maryland
Potomac Home Brigade Infantry. (US) Age 18.
Boatman. Sharpsburg. Served from 8 Dec. 1861
to 18 June, 1864. (1890-C) (MSA-AGR-S-936-22)

JAMISON, John Vincent. (Pvt.) (CSA) Unit unknown.
Buried in Rose Hill Cemetery, Hagerstown.
(WCCR, Vol. 6, 216)

JEFFERS, Franklin. (2nd Lt.) Co. B, 3rd Regiment
Potomac Home Brigade Infantry. (US) Age 20.
Enlisted 12 December, 1861, as private in Co.

F.   Promoted hospital steward; second
lieutenant (not mustered), 3 May, 1865.
Veteran.   (H.R.M.V., Vol. 1, 571, 577) (MSA-S-
936-23)

JENKINS, Edward. (Pvt.) Co. K, 4th Regiment
Infantry, (U.S.C.T.) Maryland Volunteers. (US)
Hagerstown.   Served from 1 September, 1863 to
25 May, 1865. Discharged due to dis-ability.
(H.R.M.V., Vol. 2, 153) (1890-C)

JENNINGS, George. (1st Sgt.) Co. H, 6th Regiment
Maryland Infantry. (US) Age 21. Enlisted at
Hagerstown 14 August, 1862. Discharged 20 June,
1865. (H.R.M.V., Vol. 1, 241) (MSA-AGR-S-936-2)

JENNINGS, Patrick H.(Sgt.) Co. H, 6th Regiment
Maryland Infantry. (US) Age 21. Brownsville.
Served 14 August, 1862 to 21 June, 1865.
Promoted sergeant 21 Jan. 1865. Wounded 6
April, 1865, near Saylers Creek, Va.(H.R.M.V.,
Vol. 1, 242) (1890-C) (MSA-AGR-S-936-2)

JOHNSON, Barnett Walter. (Pvt.) Co. A, 7th
Regiment Maryland Infantry.   (US)   West Beaver
Creek.   Served between 13 August, 1862 and 31
May, 1865. Injuries to right hand and leg from
bursting shell.   Discharge papers lost.   (1890-
C) (MSA-S-936-17)

JOHNSON, Jacob F. (Pvt.) Co. A, 7th Regiment
Maryland Infantry.   (US)   Washington County.
Age 24.   Enlisted at Hagerstown, 11 August,
1862.   Deserted 14 November, 1862.   Returned to
service 8 February, 1864 to complete time.
Wounded in action 8 May, 1864.   Transferred to
1st Maryland Infantry.   (Scharf, Vol. 1, 226)
(H.R.M.V., Vol. 1, 279) (MSA-AGR, Vol. 1, 182
and MSA-S-936-17)

JOHNSON, John. (Pvt.) Co. E, 19th Regiment
Infantry.   (U.S.C.T.) (US)   Knoxville. Served
from 25 August, 1864 to 15 January, 1867.
(H.R.M.V., Vol. 1, 219) (1890-C) (1860-C)

JOHNSON, John H. (Pvt.) Co. I, 2nd Regiment

Infantry. (U.S.C.T.) (US) Funkstown. (MSA-S-936-45)

JOHNSON, John H. (Pvt.) Co. D, 1st Potomac Home Brigade Infantry. (US) Age 20. Laborer. Sharpsburg. Enlisted Sharpsburg, 15 August, 1861. Veteran. Transferred to Co. D, 13th Regiment Maryland Infantry. Discharged 29 May, 1865.(H.R.M.V., Vol. 1, 503) (MSA-AGR-S-936-22)

JOHNSON, John P. (Pvt.) Co. A, 1st Regiment Potomac Home Brigade Infantry. (US) Age 18. Hagerstown. Served from 15 August, 1861 to 27 August, 1864. Buried in Samples Manor Cemetery. (H.R.M.V., Vol. 1, 489) (WCCR, Vol. 4, 71)

JOHNSON, Levi.(Pvt.) Co. I, 2nd Regiment Infantry. (U.S.C.T.) (US) Hagerstown. (MSA-S-936-45)

JOHNSON, Walter. (Pvt.) Co. A, 7th Regiment Maryland Infantry. (US) Washington County. Age 29. Served from 13 August, 1862 to 31 May, 1865. Discharged at Arlington Heights, Va. (Scharf, Vol. 1, 226) (H.R.M.V., Vol. 1, 279.) (MSA-AGR, Vol. 1, 182)

JOHNSON, William H. (Pvt.) Battery G, 112th Pennsylvania Heavy Artillery. (US) Hagerstown. Served from 1861 to 1863. Other dates not available. (1890-C)

JONES, Dr. David W. Co. I, 7th Maryland Infantry Regiment. (US) Hagerstown. A specialist in chronic and nervous disorders, Dr. Jones was born near Hagerstown in 1827. He completed his education at the Hagerstown Academy where one of his classmates was future Governor William T. Hamilton. He studied under Samuel Funk, of Washington County, and at the Cincinnati Eclectic Medical Institute, and later the Pennsylvania Eclectic Medical College, of Philadelphia. On August 28, 1862 he enlisted in the 7th Maryland Infantry and was appointed hospital steward for his regiment. On April 13, 1864, just before his term was to expire, he

was disabled with a serious heart disorder and
transferred to the Volunteer Reserve Corps. On
discharge he received a pension of $8 per
month. (1890-C) (Pensions List, 157)
(H.R.M.V., Vol. 1, 296) (The 7th Maryland
Infantry defended Williamsport in September,
1862 and later was stationed around Hagerstown.
It also participated in the attack on Maryland
Heights, on 7 July, 1863, and in light action
around Funkstown on 12 and 13 July. The 7th was
composed of many Western Marylanders, especially
in Company I. Company A, recruited in
Hagerstown, included Major Edward Mobley and
Capt. William Colklesser, both of Hagerstown.

JONES, George. (Pvt.) Co. E, 1st Regiment Potomac
Home Brigade Infantry. (US)   Age 22.
Fencemaker.   Enlisted 14 September, 1861.
Reenlisted 23 February, 1864.   Transferred to
Co. E, 13th Maryland Infantry.   Discharged 28
May, 1863.(H.R.M.V., Vol. 1, 508)(MSA-S-936-23)

JONES, Nicholas. (Pvt.) Co. L, 6th Regiment New
York Cavalry. (US)   Funkstown.   Served from 15
November, 1862 to 15 August, 1865. (1890-C)
(MSA-AGR, Vol. 1, 182)

JONES, Thomas. (Pvt.) Co. C, 1st Regiment
Maryland Infantry. (US) Age 23.   Hagerstown.
Musician.   Enlisted at Hagerstown, 20 August,
1862. Discharged 31 May, 1865, near
Washington, D.C.   Member Independent Junior
Fire Company, of Hagerstown.   (H.R.M.V., Vol.
1, 279) (MSA-AGR, Vol. 1, 182) (I.J.F.C.
roster)

JONES, William. (Pvt.) Co. H, 6th Regiment
Maryland Infantry.   (US)   Age 31. Cavetown.
Served from 20 August, 1862 to 26 December,
1863.   Transferred to V. R. C. Discharged with
physical disability. (H.R.M.V., Vol. 1, 242)
(1890-C) (MSA-AGR, Vol. 1, 181 and 936-2)

JONES, William H. (Pvt.) Co. C, 1st Regiment
Potomac Home Brigade "Cole's" Cavalry.   (US)
Hagerstown.   Served from 23 February, 1865 to

30 June, 1865. (H.R.M.V., Vol. 1, 676) (1890-C)

JONES, William M. (Pvt.) Co. G, 1st Regiment
Potomac Home Brigade Infantry. (US)
Sharpsburg. Served from 27 March, 1865 to 29
May, 1865. Transferred to Co. G, 13th Regiment
Maryland Infantry. (1890-C) (H.R.M.V., Vol. 1,
520)

JUSTICE, John J. B. (Pvt.) Co. H, 6th Regiment
Maryland Infantry. (US) Age 27. Smoketown.
Served from 20 August, 1862 to 26 December,
1863. Discharged with physical disability.
(H.R.M.V., Vol. 1, 242) (1890-C) (MSA-AGR, Vol.
1, 181)

-- K --

KAUFFMAN, Henry. (Pvt.) Co. B, 1st Regiment
Potomac Home Brigade Infantry. (US) Hagerstown.
Served from 6 September, 1861 to 10 January,
1862. (H.R.M.V., Vol. 1, 495) (1890-C)

KEADLE, Abraham L. (Sgt.) Co. H, 13th Maryland
Volunteer Infantry. (US) Washington Co.
Veteran. Served from 1 Oct., 1861 to 29 May,
1865. Buried in St. Paul's Cemetery, Clear
Spring. (H.R.M.V., Vol. 1, 444) (WCCR, Vol.
5, 255)

KEIZER, Peter E. (Cpl.) Co. H, 6th Regiment
Maryland Infantry. (US) Age 42. Enlisted at
Hagerstown 21 August, 1862. Discharged with
physical disability 29 April, 1864. (H.R.M.V.,
Vol. 1, 242) (MSA-AGR-Vol. 1, 201 and S-936-2)

KELLEY, Jacob R. (Pvt.) (US) Washington Co. Unit
unknown. Buried in St John's Episcopal Church
Cemetery, Hagerstown. (WCCR, Vol. 7, 456)

KELLY, Michael. (Pvt.) Co. C, 1st Regiment
Maryland Infantry. (US) Age 36. Enlisted at
Hagerstown, 11 March, 1864. Reported absent
from Camp Parole, near Annapolis, Md., March,
1864. Taken prisoner 19 August, 1864 at Weldon
Railroad, Va. Transferred to Co. A, 7th

Maryland Regiment 31 May, 1865. No further
record. (H.R.M.V., Vol. 1, 33) (MSA-AGR, Vol.
1, 191)

KELLY, Upton. (Pvt.) Co. C, 1st Regiment Maryland
Infantry. (US) Age 21. Enlisted as a
substitute at Hagerstown, 6 February, 1864.
(MSA-AGR, Vol. 1, 191) (H.R.M.V., Vol. 1, 33)

KEMP, Lorenzo A. (Sgt.) Co. B, (?) Regiment
Maryland Infantry. (US) Funkstown. Served from
16 August, 1861 to 15 September, 15 September,
1864. (1890-C)

KENNEDY, Samuel. (Cpl.) Co. C, 5th Regiment
Maryland Infantry. (US) Boonsboro. Served from
29 October, 1864 to 1 Sept. 1865. (H.R.M.V.,
Vol. 1, 192) (1890-C)

KENNEDY, Thomas. (Pvt.) Co. C, 3rd U.S. Infantry.
Hagerstown. Service dates not available.
(1890-C)

KENNEDY, William B. (Major) Co. A, 3rd Regiment
Maryland Infantry. (US) Williamsport. Formed
the "Union Guards" of Williamsport at the
outset of the war. Entered service 15 June,
1861, as captain, 1st Virginia Union Infantry,
then transferred to 3rd Maryland Infantry, 16
February, 1862; promoted major 7 May, 1862.
Killed in action at Cedar Mountain, 9 August,
1862. (Scharf, 328) (H.R.M.V., Vol. 1, 113-116)
(Williams, Vol. 2, 308)

KEPLINGER, Jacob M. (Pvt.) Battery M, 4th U.S.
Artillery. (US) Keedysville. Served from 13
June, 1861 to 31 June, 1867. (1890-C)

KERSHNER, Andrew J. (1st Lt.) Co. B, 1st Regiment
Potomac Home Brigade "Cole's" Cavalry." (US)
Clear Spring. Served from 24 August, 1861 to
30 March, 1863. Contracted typhoid fever and
was discharged by the regimental surgeon Samuel
Smith, due to disability. (H.R.M.V., Vol. 1,
672) (GSA/NA records 314-10, 19859)

KERSHNER, Dr. Edward. Medical Inspector. U.S. Navy. Clear Spring. Dr. Kershner attained the position of United States Medical Inspector near the end of a distinguished naval career. He was born in Clear Spring District in 1839, the son of Gustavus Kershner. His home was along the Conococheague Creek, east of Wilson's, where his grandfather, Jacob, Jr., operated a tavern along the National Pike. Dr. Kershner's early education was received in a local one-room school. In 1858-59 he "read" medicine under the preceptorship of Dr. William Fiery, of Clear Spring. Graduating from the University of the City of New York in 1861, he entered the U.S. Navy on 2 September of that year as an assistant surgeon. His first active duty was on the sloop-of-war Cumberland, at Hampton Roads, Virginia, an assignment that almost ended his brief career. On 8 March, 1862, it was sunk by the Confederate Ironclad *Virginia* (Merrimac) in a thirty-minute battle. Two of Cumberland's guns were disabled when their muzzles were shot off. One anchor, the smokestack and the steam-pipes were also shot away. The continual pounding proved too much and Cumberland slowly sank into a watery grave. One-third of the crew was entombed in her hull and drowned as she went to the bottom in nearly nine fathoms of water. Kershner went down with the ship and was, by some miracle, rescued in unconscious condition by an unidentified marine. After service at the Washington Navy Yard he was assigned to the *New Ironsides* and was aboard in April 1863, during the attack on Charleston Harbor. Kershner served on several ships in the North Atlantic Squadron and after the war, in 1872, achieved the rank of surgeon and then medical inspector in 1890. Dr. Kershner also distinguished himself with service to China, and Japan at the time of the great cholera epidemics. When his naval service ended he served an extended term as professor of hygiene, and emeritus professor in the New York Post-Graduate Medical School and Hospital. Many other honors were attended to him before he retired to Hagerstown in 1902. This, after a dispute with superior offices over the use of drinking water during an outbreak of yellow fever in the Windward Islands. His home was at 503 North Potomac Street. He was a member of Zion Reformed Church, Hagerstown, and is buried in the family lot in St. Paul's Cemetery, near Clear Spring. (10)

KERSHNER, George Monroe. (Capt.) Co. G, 1st Regiment Potomac Home Brigade "Cole's Cavalry." (US) Indian Springs. Entered service 7 March, 1864, mustered out 28 June, 1865. (Scharf, 328) (H.R.M.V., Vol. 2, 686)

KERSHNER, Joseph H. (Pvt.) Co. B, 1st Regiment Potomac Home Brigade, "Cole's" Cavalry. (US) Clear Spring. Served from 24 August, 1861 to 30 March, 1863. He furnished his own horse and equipment and was not paid for them until the last muster. Discharged with disability by regimental surgeon Samuel Smith. (H.R.M.V., Vol. 1, 672) (GSA/NA Record 4579-314-10)

KEY, Henry. (Sgt.) 25th Regiment Pennsylvania Infantry. (US) (U.S.C.T.) Hagerstown. Service dates not available. Shot in the foot. (1890-C)

KEYS, Jonas. (Pvt.) Co. H, 30th Regiment Infantry. (U.S.C.T.) (US) Washington County. Enlisted at Baltimore, 31 March, 1864. Deserted from hospital on unknown date. (H.R.M.V., Vol. 2, 255) (MSA-S-936-50)

KEYS, Singleton. (Pvt.) Co. A, 19th Regiment (U.S.C.T.) Maryland Volunteers. (US) Age 33. Washington Co. Enlisted at Baltimore, 10, December 1863. Served to 15 January, 1867. Buried in Beautiful View Cemetery, at State Line. (H.R.M.V., Vol. 2, 210) (WCCR, Vol. 6, 61) (1890-C) (MSA-S-936-49)

KIMBEL, William A. (Pvt.) Co. I, 1st Regiment "Russell's" Maryland Cavalry. (US) Williamsport. Served from 17 December, 1862 to 8 August, 1865. (H.R.M.V., Vol. 1, 753) (1890-C)

KIMBLE, Robert J. (2nd Lt.) Co. I, 1st Regiment
Maryland Cavalry. (US) Washington County.
Entered service 3 December, 1861 as private in
Co. H; promoted second lieutenant 29 December,
1862. (Scharf, 328) (H.R.M.V., Vol. 1, 731)

KINDLE, John. (Pvt.) Co. F, 13th Regiment
Maryland Infantry. (US) Smithsburg. Served from
28 February, 1865 to 29 May, 1865. (H.R.M.V.,
Vol. 1, 447) (1890-C)

KINDLE, John. (Pvt.) Co. H, 1st Regiment Maryland
Cavalry. (US) Hagerstown. Served from 11
December, 1862 to 8 August, 1865. (H.R.M.V.,
Vol. 1, 729) (1890-C)

KINDLE, Simon. (Pvt.) Co. H, 1st Maryland
Cavalry. (US) Washington County. Served from
11, Dec, 1862 to 8 Aug. 1865. Buried at
Bakersville Cemetery, near Eakle's Cross Roads.
(WCCR, Vol. 5, 72.) (H.R.M.V., Vol. 1, 729.)

KINDLE, William R. (Pvt.) Co. F. 5th Regiment
Maryland Infantry. (US) Smithsburg. Entered
service 27 August, 1864. Deserted 5 June, 1865.
(H.R.M.V., Vol. 1, 200) (1890-C)

KING, Andrew J. (Pvt.) Co. E, 3rd Regiment
Maryland Infantry. (US) Boonsboro. Served
from 14 December, 1861 to 13 May, 1865.
Veteran. Gunshot wound to left arm and
shoulder. Earned pansion of $6 per month.
After war suffered from sore leg from military
service. (H.R.M.V., Vol. 1, 590) (1890-C)
(Pensions List, 157)

KING, David. (Pvt.) Co. G, 1st Potomac Home
Brigade "Cole's" Cavalry. (US) Clear Spring.
Served from 9 March, 1865 to 28 June, 1865.
(H.R.M.V., Vol. 1, 687) (1890-C)

KING, Harrison E. (1st Lt.) Co. E, 1st Regiment
Potomac Home Brigade Cavalry. (US) Washington
County. Entered service as a private 1 August,
1861, promoted to corporal, then first

lieutenant 1 March, 1865. Veteran volunteer. Transferred to Co. E, 13th Maryland Infantry. (Scharf, 328) (H.R.M.V., Vol. 1, 443, 505)

KING, Hiram. (Pvt.) Co. C, 1st Regiment Potomac Home Brigade "Cole's" Cavalry. (US) Hagerstown. Served from 5 September, 1861 to 5 September, 1864. Wounded left leg. Received a monthly pension of $6. (Pensions List, 17) (H.R.M.V., Vol. 1, 676) (1890-C)

KING, John R. (Sgt.) Co. H, 6th Regiment Maryland Infantry. (US) Age 18. Enlisted at Hagerstown 21 August, 1862. Discharged from Frederick Maryland General Hospital 16 May, 1865, with physical disability. (H.R.M.V., Vol. 1, 242) (MSA-AGR, Vol. 1, 201)

KING, Patrick. (Pvt.) Co. H, 6th Regiment Maryland Infantry. (US) Age 19. Enlisted at Hagerstown, 7 April, 1862. Deserted 2 September, 1862, at Baltimore. (H.R.M.V., Vol. 1, 242) (MSA-AGR, Vol. 1, 201)

KING, William H. (Pvt.) Co. H, 6th Regiment Maryland Infantry. (US) Age 24. Hagerstown. Enlisted at Hagerstown, 14 August, 1862. Wounded in action at Five Forks, Va., 2 April, 1865. Shot in the foot, and taken prisoner. Discharged near Washington, D. C., 20 August, 1865. Member Independent Junior Fire Company, of Hagerstown. (H.R.M.V., Vol. 1, 242) (1890-C) (MSA-AGR, Vol. 1, 201 and 936-2) (I.J.F.C. roster)

KINSEL, Martin. (Pvt.) Co. F, 1st Regiment Potomac Home Brigade Infantry. (US) Age 20. Laborer. Millstone. Served from 4 September, 1861, to 29 May, 1865. Transferred to Co. F, 13th Maryland Infantry. Veteran. (H.R.M.V., Vol. 1, 513) (1890-C) (MSA-S-936-23)

KINSEY, John F. (Pvt.) Co. E, 1st Regiment Potomac Home Brigade Infantry. (US) Age 18. Laborer. Smoketown. Enlisted 19 January, 1865. Transferred to Co. E, 13th Regiment Maryland

Infantry. Discharged 29 May, 1865. (H.R.M.V.,
Vol. 1, 444) (1890-C) (MSA-S-936-23)

KIPE, James W. (Sgt.) Co.'s A, E and H, 2nd and
126 Pennsylvania cavalry and infantry. (US)
Eakle's Mill. Served from 2 April, 1862 to 7
August, 1865. (1890-C)

KISSNER, William. (or Kisner) (Pvt.) Co. A, 3rd
Regiment Maryland Infantry. (US) Age 34.
Enlisted at Williamsport, 15 July, 1861.
Discharged 15 July, 1865. (MSA-AGR, Vol. 1,
196) (H.R.M.V., Vol. 1, 119)

KITZMILLER, Frisby. (Cpl.) Co. A, 2nd Regiment
Maryland Infantry. (US) Keedysville. Served
from 9 June, 1864 to 17 July, 1865. Suffered
facial wound in action 30 September, 1864, at
Petersburg, Va. (H.R.M.V., Vol. 1, 76) (1890-C)

KLINE, Jacob H. (Pvt.) Co. A, 7th Regiment
Maryland Infantry. (US) Age 20. Enlisted at
Hagerstown, 28 February, 1864. Wounded 1 April,
1865 at Five Forks, Va. Patient at Lincoln
Hospital. Transferred to Co. C, 1st Maryland
Regiment, 21 May, 1865. Mustered out while a
patient in Salterlee U.S. Army General
Hospital, West Philadelphia, Pa., 10 July,
1865. (H.R.M.V., Vol. 1, 279) (MSA-AGR, Vol.
1, 191, 201)

KLINE, John. (Pvt.) Co. B, 11th Regiment Maryland
Infantry. (US) Boonsboro. Served from 26 May,
1864 to 29 September, 1864. Discharged due to
medical affliction. (1890-C)

KLINE, Samuel. (Pvt.) Co. D, 12th Regiment
Maryland Infantry. (US) Leitersburg. Entered
service 25 July, 1864. Discharged 6 November,
1864. (H.R.M.V., Vol. 1, 427) (Bell, 67)

KLINE, William. (Pvt.) Co. B, 1st Regiment
Maryland Cavalry. (US) Leitersburg. Entered
service 17 February, 1863. Deserted 21 Sept.,
1863.(H.R.M.V., Vol. 1, 710)(Bell, 67)

KNEPPER, William D. (2nd Lt.) Co. F, 1st Regiment
Potomac Home Brigade Infantry. (US) Age 19.
Tinner. Washington County. Enlisted 4
September, 1861. Promoted sergeant, second
lieutenant. Transferred to Co. F, 13th Regiment
Maryland Infantry. Veteran. Discharged 29 May,
1865.(H.R.M.V., Vol. 1, 447, 513)(MSA-S-936-23)

KNIGHT, William A. (Pvt.) Co. B, 1st Maryland
"Snow's" Light Artillery, Battery B. (US)
Washington Co. Served from 14 September, 1861,
to 30 June, 1864. Buried in Samples Manor
Cemetery. (H.R.M.V., Vol. 1, 807) (WCCR, Vol.
4, 65)

KNIGHT, William T. (Pvt.) Co. D, 7th Regiment
Virginia Cavalry. (CSA) Williamsport. Served
from 6 June, 1861 to June, 1864. (1890-C)

KNODE, Artimus O. (Pvt.) Co. I, 42nd Regiment
Ohio Infantry. (US) Downsville. Served from 14
September, 1861, to 2 December, 1864. Suffered
wounds of the head. Sent to Libby Prison in
Richmond. (1890-C)

KNODLE, Charles S. (2nd Lt.) Co. I, 7th Regiment
Maryland Infantry. (US) Washington County.
Served 5 September, 1862 to 31 May, 1865.
(Scharf 328) (H.R.M.V., Vol. 1, 297)

KOOGLE, Jacob. (1st Lt.) Unit unknown.
Chewsville. (CSA) Entered the Confederate Army
in 1862 and served to the end of the war.
Awarded a bronze medal for bravery in rushing a
breastwork and capturing an enemy flag.
Participated in 23 battles and skirmishes
without being wounded. (Williams, Vol. 2, 826)

KOONTZ, Silas A. (Pvt.) Co. E, 1st Regiment
Potomac Home Brigade Infantry. (US)
Rohrersville. Served from 7 February, 1865 to
29 May, 1865. Transferred to Co. E, 13th
Maryland Regiment. (H.R.M.V., Vol. 1, 508)
(1890-C)

KOONTZ, Thomas E. (Sgt.) Co. H, 6th Regiment

Maryland Infantry. (US) Brownsville. Age 21.
Entered service 8 August, 1862. Died 20
November, 1862, at Brownsville, Md., from
typhoid fever, contracted in service.
(H.R.M.V., Vol. 1, 242) (1890-C) (MSA-AGR, Vol.
1, 201 and S-936-2))

KOPPISCH, Charles E. H. (Pvt.) Co. B, 1st
Regiment Potomac Home Brigade "Cole's Cavalry."
(US) Leitersburg. Entered service 4 August,
1861. Taken prisoner 13 May, 1864, at
Spotsylvania, Va. Discharged 15 September,
1864. (H.R.M.V., Vol. 1, 672) (Bell, 67)

KOUGH, George. (Pvt.) Co. H, 6th Regiment
Maryland Infantry. (US) Age 24. Enlisted at
Hagerstown, 20 August, 1862. Deserted 20 May,
1865. (H.R.M.V., Vol. 1, 242) (MSA-AGR-S-936-2)

KREPS, Benjamin F. (Pvt.) Co. F, 1st Regiment
Potomac Home Brigade Infantry. (US) Clear
Spring. Served from 4 September, 1861 to 4
September, 1864.(H.R.M.V., Vol. 1, 513)(1890-C)

KREPS, John M. (Pvt.) Co. I. 1st Regiment
"Russell's" Maryland Cavalry. (US) Clear
Spring. Served from 17 December, 1862 to 8
August, 1865. (H.R.M.V., Vol. 1, 733) (1890-C)

KREPS, Samuel D. (Pvt.) Co. F, 13th Regiment
Maryland Infantry. (US) Clear Spring. Served
from 7 February, 1865 to 29 May, 1865.
(H.R.M.V., Vol. 1, 447) (1890-C)

KRETZER, David. (Pvt.) Co. H, 1st Regiment
Maryland Cavalry. (US) Keedysville. Served
from 17 March, 1864 to 28 June, 1865. Received
rupture from riding horseback. (1890-C)

KRETZER, Hiram. (Pvt.) Co. A, 1st Maryland
Infantry, (CSA) Funkstown. (Hartzler, 197)
(Huntsberry, 56)

KROUSE, George. (Pvt.) Co. A, 7th Regiment
Maryland Infantry. (US) Washington County.
Age 34. Served from 10 August, 1862 to 31 May,

1865. Taken prisoner 16 September, 1864, at
Weldon Railroad, Va. (Scharf, Vol. 1 226)
(H.R.M.V., Vol. 1, 279. (MSA-AGR, Vol. 1, 201
and MSA-S-936-17)

KRUNKLETON, John W. (Pvt.) Co. B, 3rd Regiment
Potomac Home Brigade Infantry. (US) Age 24.
Washington County. Enlisted 21 December, 1861.
Veteran. Discharged 29 May, 1865. (H.R.M.V.,
Vol. 1, 577) (MSA-S-936-24)

KUHN, Daniel. (Pvt.) Co. B, 3rd Regiment Potomac
Home Brigade Infantry. (US) Age 45. Enlisted
26 October, 1861. Discharged 26 October, 1864.
(H.R.M.V., Vol. 1, 577) (MSA-S-936-23)

KUHN, James S. (Pvt.) Co. A, 7th Regiment
Maryland Infantry. (US) Hagerstown. Served
from 18 August, 1862 to 9 June, 1865. Member
Independent Junior Fire Company, of Hagerstown.
(1890-C) (I.J.F.C. roster)

KUHN, John. (Pvt.) Co. A, 1st Regiment Potomac
Home Brigade Infantry. Later Co. A, 13th
Regiment Maryland Infantry. (US) Near Sandy
Hook. Laborer in a stone quarry. Entered
service at Frederick Md., 12 August, 1861, at
age 48. Captured and paroled at Harpers Ferry,
15 September, 1862. Listed as a deserter
November, 1862. Reduced in rank from sergeant
to private. (AWOL) Returned to service 30 July,
1863. Discharged 27 August, 1864, at Berlin
(Brunswick) Md. Migrated to Kansas with wife,
a daughter and her husband. Applied for land
under the Homestead Act of 20 May, 1862 and
received 162 acres and remained there as
farmer. Died 1886. Buried, along with wife
Lois, in Walnut Grove (Wolff) Cemetery,
Pleasant Valley Township, Saline, Kansas.
(H.R.M.V., Vol. 1, 487) (Major portion provided
by Mrs. Helen C. Dingler, of Enterprise, Kansas
through Mr. and Mrs. Richard Smith, of
Hagerstown.

KUHN, Leander H. (Capt.) Co. D, 13th Regiment
Maryland Infantry. (US) Hancock. Entered

service 18 September, 1861 as private in Co. D,
1st Potomac Home Brigade Infantry: promoted to
sergeant; second lieutenant, 26 November, 1864;
first lieutenant 2 March, 1865; captain 20
March, 1865. Served to 29 May, 1865.
Participated in fighting at Gettysburg under
Gen. Slocum, where he suffered a gunshot wound
to the foot. Surgeons insisted on an
amputation, but Kuhn refused. Thereafter it
caused him great misery and suffering for the
next forty years until it was removed in 1903
at Johns Hopkins Hospital, in Baltimore. Upon
his discharge he was presented with a fine
sword by the members of his company. His great
demeanor throughout the war earned for him the
rank of captain. (H.R.M.V., Vol. 1, 441)
(Portrait and Biographical Record of the Sixth
Congressional District, of Maryland, 1898,
pages 402-05) (1890-C) (H.R.M.V., Vol. 1, 502)

-- L --

LAKENS, John W. (Pvt.) Co. L. 1st Regiment
Potomac Home Brigade "Cole's" Cavalry. (US) Age
17. Boonsboro. Laborer. Entered service 31
March, 1864. Discharged 28 June, 1865, at
Harper's Ferry. (H.R.M.V., Vol. 1, 696)
(Official discharge papers)

LAMKIN, S. L. (Pvt.) (Co. ?) 40th Virginia
Infantry (CSA)Regiment. Age 17. Hagerstown.
Died 24 December, 1914. (CVM VOL XXVI, 161)

LANCASTER, Jacob. (Pvt.) Co. I, 7th Regiment
Maryland Infantry. (US) Age 22. Enlisted at
Hagerstown, 25 August, 1862. Discharged 25
August, 1865. (MSA-AGR, Vol. 1, 219)
(H.R.M.V., Vol. 1, 298)

LANCASTER, St. Clair. (Pvt.) Co. 1, 7th Regiment
Maryland Infantry. (US) Age 21. Enlisted at
Hagerstown, 28 August, 1862. Discharged 28
August, 1865. (MSA-AGR, Vol. 1, 219)
(H.R.M.V., Vol. 1, 298)

LANEY, Jacob H. (Pvt.) Co. A, 7th Regiment

Maryland Infantry. (US) Washington County.
Age 26. Served from 14 August, 1862 to 20
July, 1865. Wounded at Gravel Run, Va., 31
March, 1865. Confined to Finley Army Hospital,
Washington, D.C. (Scharf, Vol. 1, 226)
(H.R.M.V., Vol. 1, 279) (MSA-AGR, Vol. 1, 218
and MSA-S-936-17)

LANT, John. (Pvt.) Co. I, 7th Regiment Maryland
Infantry. (US) Age 24. Enlisted at
Hagerstown, 27 August, 1862. Deserted at
Williamsport, Md., November, 1862. (MSA-AGR,
Vol. 1, 219) (H.R.M.V., Vol. 1, 298)

LANTZ, Samuel T. (Pvt.) Co. H, 1st Regiment
Potomac Home Brigade "Cole's" Cavalry. (US)
Keedysville. Served from 17 March, 1864 to 28
June, 1864. Taken prisoner 6 July, 1865.
Imprisoned at Andersonville, Ga. (H.R.M.V.,
Vol. 1, 690) (1890-C)

LANTZ, William H. (Pvt.) 1st Regiment of Maryland
Volunteer Infantry. (US) Washington County.
Buried in Fairview Cemetery, near Keedysville.
(WCCR, Vol. 5, 144)

LARSHBAUGH, Jacob. (Pvt.) Co. H, 1st Regiment
Maryland Cavalry. (US) Hagerstown. Served
from 22 February, 1864 to 8 August, 1865.
(H.R.M.V., Vol. 1, 730) (1890-C)

LATE, Jacob. (Pvt.) Co. A, 7th Regiment Maryland
Infantry. (US) Hagerstown. Age 18. Member
Junior Independent Fire Company of Hagerstown.
Served from 14 March, 1862 to 31 March, 1865.
(Scharf, Vol. 1, 226) (H.R.M.V., Vol. 1, 279)
(1890-C) (MSA-AGR, Vol. 1, 218 and MSA-S-936-
17) (I.J.F.C. roster)

LAW, JAMES, William. (Pvt.) Co. E, 1st Regiment
Potomac Home Brigade Infantry. (US) Cavetown.
Served from 1 October, 1861, to 1 October,
1864. (1890-C)

LAWSON, Morgan. (Pvt.) Co. A, 1st Maryland
Potomac Home Brigade Infantry. (US) Washington

Co. Buried in Samples Manor Cemetery. (WCCR, Vol. 4, 65)

LAWVER, Elliot J. (Pvt.) Co. E, 1st Regiment Potomac Home Brigade Infantry. (US) Hagerstown. Served from 1 October, 1861, to 1 October, 1864. (H.R.M.V., Vol. 1, 508) (1890-C)

LEARY, William L. (Pvt.) Co. I, 1st Regiment "Russell's" Maryland Cavalry. Enlisted at Williamsport, 17 December, 1862. Discharged 8 August, 1865. (H.R.M.V., Vol. 1, 732) (MSA-AGR-S-936-38)

LEEVY, Daniel. (Pvt.) Co B, 2nd Pennsylvania Artillery. (US) Clear Spring. Buried in St. Peter's Lutheran Cemetery, Clear Spring. (WCCR, Vol. 2, 69)

LEFEVRE, James. (Pvt.) Co. I, 7th Regiment Maryland Infantry. (US) Age 23. Enlisted at Hagerstown, 28 August, 1862. Deserted at Williamsport, Md., September, 1862. (MSA-AGR, Vol. 1, 219) (H.R.M.V., Vol. 1, 298)

LEGGETT, John F. (Pvt.) Co. E, 13th Regiment Maryland Infantry. (US) Hagerstown. Served from 2 February, 1865 to 29 May, 1865. (H.R.M.V., Vol. 1, 445) (1890-C)

LEGGETT, Joseph N. (Pvt.) Co. E, 13th Regiment Maryland Infantry. (US) Hagerstown. Served from 2 February, 1865 to 29 May, 1865. (H.R.M.V., Vol. 1, 445) (1890-C)

LEGGETT, William H. (Pvt.) Co. E, 3rd Regiment Potomac Home Brigade Infantry. (US) Boonsboro. Served from 12 April, 1862 to 29 May, 1865. (H.R.M.V., Vol. 1, 590) (1890-C)

LEMON, Jacob F. (Pvt.) Co. H, 1st Maryland Cavalry Regiment. (US) Washington Co. Served from 3 December, 1861 to 3 December, 1864. Buried in Rose Hill Cemetery, Hagerstown. (H.R.M.V., Vol. 1, 730) (WCCR, Vol. 6, 208)

LEMON, Peter L. (Pvt.) Co. I, 1st Regiment "Russell's" Maryland Cavalry. (US) Williamsport. Served from 3 September, 1861 to 3 September, 1864. Educated in the schools of Williamsport and later opened a grocery store in 1867. Enlisted in the spring of 1861 for three years service. Saw action at Brandy Station and Gettysburg and on many other battlefields. In 1864 he was detached to provost duty in Baltimore, and mustered out in September of that year. He also served on the Williamsport town council. (H.R.M.V., Vol. 1, 733) (1890-C)

LEMON, Thomas J. (Pvt.) Co. I, 1st Regiment "Russell's" Maryland Cavalry. (US) Williamsport. Served from 3 September, 1861 to 3 September, 1864. (H.R.M.V., Vol. 1, 733) (1890-C)

LEOPOLE, Andrew T. (Lt.) Co. D, 12th Regiment Virginia Cavalry. (CSA) Sharpsburg. Enlisted 20 April, 1861, in Co. F, 1st Virginia Cavalry. Served as regimental color bearer. Transferred to 12th Virginia and promoted to lieutenant. Reported absent, then returned. Captured at Shepherdstown 28 November, 1862. Exchanged 6 January, 1863. Captured again at Shepherdstown 22, April, 1863. Imprisoned at Fort McHenry, at Baltimore. Court Marshalled for shooting a Union sympathizer and hanged 12 May, 1864. Buried in Elmwood Cemetery, Shepherdstown. On 25 April, 1863, Leopole, while in irons, gave the following statement to the staff of Gen. Robert H. Milroy at Winchester, Va. Hometown, Sharpsburg, Md. Enlisted in Confederate service two years ago in 1st Regiment Virginia (Rebel) Cavalry and remained in that regiment until (J.E.B.) Stuart's appointment as brigadier. About a month after the Battle of First Manassas became ensign of the brigade, continued until last May (1862) when transferred to (12th) Virginia Cavalry as third lieutenant. Continued until after the Battle of Sharpsburg when promoted to first lieutenant of Co. D. Captured 24 November at

Shepherdstown. Remained prisoner until 6
January, 1863 when exchanged. Reported to
Gen. Stuart and until 13 January acting as
chief of couriers. On 14 January left for
Castleman's Ferry in command of 70 men and
remained until captured with six of my men.
My business was to observe the movement of
Federal forces and report to Gen. Fitzhugh
Lee. Am tired of fighting and wish to take the
oath of allegiance and retire to Ohio. I have
always stood high with General Stuart, enjoyed
his confidence, and when at his headquarters
ate at his table. Andrew T. Leopole.
(The statement transmitted to Maj. Gen. Robert
C. Schenck, in Baltimore. Official Records,
Series 1, Vol. 25, Part 2, pages 252-53)

LEOPOLD, John H. (Pvt.) Co. K, 13th Regiment
Maryland Infantry. (US) Knoxville. Served from
14 January, 1865 to 29 May, 1865. (H.R.M.V.,
Vol. 1, 458) (1890-C)

LEWIS, John. (Pvt.) Battery K, 5th New York Heavy
Artillery. (US) Trego. Served from 9 August,
1861 to 5 June, 1865. Damage to eyes reported.
(1890-C)

LIAMBAUGH, William C. (Pvt.) (CSA) Hagerstown.
(Hartzler, 203)

LINEBAUGH, Daniel. (Pvt.) Co. A, 7th Regiment
Maryland Infantry. (US) Washington County.
Age 27. Served from 18 August, 1862 to 5 July,
1865. Deserted 13 June, 1863. Returned to
service 16 November, 1863. Taken prisoner 16
September, 1864 at Weldon Railroad, Va.
Transferred to Co. C, 1st Maryland Infantry,
(MSA-AGR, Vol. 1, 218) (Scharf, Vol. 1, 226)
(H.R.M.V., Vol. 1, 279 and MSA-S-936-17)

LINEBAUGH, Henry. (Pvt.) Co. A, 7th Regiment
Maryland Infantry. (US) Washington County.
Age 19. Entered service 18 August, 1862 at
Hagerstown. Deserted 19 November, 1862, at
Williamsport, Md. (Scharf, Vol. 1, 226)
(H.R.M.V., Vol. 1, 279) (MSA-S-936-17)

LINN, Noah. (Pvt.) Co. B, 3rd Regiment Potomac Home Brigade Infantry. (US) Age 23. Hancock. Enlisted 9 March, 1864. Discharged 29 May, 1865. (H.R.M.V., Vol. 1, 577) (MSA-S-936-24)

LITTLE, Charles F. (Pvt.) Co. A, 7th Regiment Maryland Infantry. (US) Hagerstown. Age 24. Served 8 August, 1862 to 8 May, 1865. (Scharf, Vol. 1, 226) (H.R.M.V., Vol. 1, 279) (1890-C) (MSA-S-936-17)

LITTON, Thomas D. (Pvt.) Co. B, 3rd Regiment Potomac Home Brigade Infantry. (US) Age 23. Hancock. Enlisted 29 February, 1864. Discharged 29 May, 1865. (H.R.M.V., Vol. 1, 577) (MSA-S-936-24)

LITTLE, William H. (Cpl.) Co. A, 7th Regiment Maryland Infantry. (US) Hagerstown. Age 22. Served from 8 August, 1862 to 2 June, 1865. Wounded in action 18 August, 1864. Hospitalized at Frederick, Md. Appointed corporal 20 August, 1864. Buried in Rose Hill Cemetery, Hagerstown. (Sharf, 226) (H.R.M.V., Vol. 1, 279 and MSA-S-936-17) (WCCR, Vol.7, 398)

LITTLE. Daniel, Jr. (Pvt.) Maryland Guerrilla Zouaves. (US) Hagerstown. Fatally wounded at the Battle of Lookout Mountain, Tenn., 15 December, 1863. Buried in Zion Reformed Church Cemetery, Hagerstown. (Church Records) (Hartzler, 204) (WCCR, Vol. 6, 35)

LITTON, Anthony. (Cpl.) Captain Firey's Co. B, 1st Regiment Potomac Home Brigade "Cole's" Cavalry. (US) Age 24. Farmer. Clear Spring. Enlisted 4 September, 1861. Veteran. Reenlisted 14 January, 1864, at Boliver, Va. (H.R.M.V., Vol. 1, 678) (MSA-S-936-30)

LITTON, Upton, L. (Pvt.) Co. B, 1st Regiment Potomac Home Brigade "Cole's" Cavalry. (US) Millstone. Served from 1 December, 1862 to 15 September, 1864. Taken prisoner 18 June, 1863.

Sent to Libby Prison in Richmond. Exchanged. (H.R.M.V., Vol. 1, 672) (1890-C)

LIZER, Henry. (Pvt.) Co. B, 3rd Regiment Potomac Home Brigade Infantry. (US) Age 26. Laborer. Beaver Creek. Enlisted at Hagerstown, 31 December, 1861. Transferred to Co. F. Veteran. Discharged 29 May, 1865. (H.R.M.V., Vol. 1, 592) (Captain Maxwell's roster) (MSA-S-936-23)

LIZER, John. (Pvt.) Co. E, 1st Regiment Potomac Home Brigade Infantry. (US) Age 25. Laborer. Smithsburg. Enlisted at Hagerstown, 1 October, 1861. Reenlisted 23 February, 1864, at Sandy Hook, Md. Transferred to Co. E, 13th Maryland. Discharged 29 May, 1865. (H.R.M.V., Vol. 1. 508) (1890-C) (MSA-S-936-23)

LIZER, Simon. (Pvt.) Co. E, 1st Regiment Potomac Home Brigade Infantry. (US) Age 18. Laborer. Washington County. Enlisted 2 February, 1865. Transferred to Co. E, 13th Regiment Maryland Infantry. Discharged 29 May, 1865. (H.R.M.V., Vol. 1, 508) (MSA-S-936-23)

LONG, Daniel. (Pvt.) Co. A, 7th Regiment Maryland Infantry. (US) Hagerstown. Age 18. Farm laborer. Enlisted 18 August, 1862, at Hagerstown. Wounded in action 8 May, 1864, at Laurel Hill, Va. Taken prisoner 31 March, 1865. Discharged 3 June, 1865, at Annapolis, Md. (Scharf, Vol. 1, 226) (H.R.M.V., Vol. 1, 279) (1860-C) (MSA-AGR, Vol. 1, 218 and MSA-S-936-17)

LONG, John Davenport. (Pvt.) Co. I, 1st Regiment "Russell's" Maryland Cavalry. (US) Williamsport. Served from 3 September, 1861 to 3 September, 1864. Originally from Martinsburg, W.Va., the family moved to Williamsport before the war, and he eventually became one of the town's outstanding citizens. The family made no secret of their sympathy for the Southern cause. On one occasion when his sister Sally visited a friend in Virginia, her return to Williamsport was barred by a blockade

of Federal soldiers. Appealing to the
soldiers, she was informed that the only way to
reach her Maryland home was to ride to
Washington, D.C., where she must take the oath
of allegiance. She agreed, and eventually
returned home. Before the war began, John Long
started the Pilot newspaper which later became
The Leader. When the war started he went
against his parents' feelings and enlisted in
Capt. Charles Russell's Williamsport company
of Federal cavalry and also served in the
commissary department as a clerk. Returning
home after the war he learned that his wife had
given his only two good shirts to several
Confederate soldiers who then destroyed his
newspaper office. (Williams, Vol. 2, 671)
(H.R.M.V., Vol. 1, 731) (1890-C)

LONG, Samuel W. (Pvt.)   Co. I, 1st Regiment
    "Russell's" Maryland Cavalry. (US)
    Williamsport. A farmer, enlisted 3 September,
    1861, at age 21. Wounded at Brandy Station, 9
    June, 1863. Killed in action at Deep Bottom,
    Va., 16 August, 1864. (H.R.M.V., Vol. 1, 733)
    (McClannahan papers, 4) (1860-C, 85)

LOPP, George. (Pvt.) Co. E, 13th Regiment
    Maryland Infantry. (US)   Age 33.   Cooper.
    Boonsboro.   Served from 14 September, 1861 to
    29 May, 1865.   Veteran.   Transferred to Co. E,
    13th Maryland Infantry. Lost his hearing in the
    war.   (H.R.M.V., Vol. 1, 445) (1890-C) (MSA-S-
    936-23)

LOUDENSLAGER, Everhart. (Pvt.) Co. I, 7th
    Regiment Maryland Infantry. (US)   Hagerstown.
    Age 35.   Served from 16 August, 1862 to 31 May,
    1865.   (H.R.M.V., Vol. 1, 298) (1890-C) (MSA-
    AGR, Vol. 1, 219)

LOVELL, Albert G. (Pvt.) Co. E, 12th Regiment
    Maryland Infantry. (US) Benevola.   He was
    educated at the Bellevue Hospital Medical
    College in New York. He enlisted 6 August,
    1862, and served nine months. Discharged 18
    May, 1863. Dr. Lovell participated in heavy

fighting at both Chancellorsville, and
Fredericksburg. (Williams, Vol. 2, 744)(1890-C)

LOWE, Robert W. (Pvt.) Co. E, 18th Regiment
Pennsylvania Cavalry. (US) Hagerstown. Served
8 September, 1862 to 16 June, 1865. (1890-C)

LOWRY, Charles A. (Pvt.) Co. H, 6th Maryland
Volunteer Infantry. (US) Age 19. Boonsboro.
Entered service 19 August, 1862 at Hagerstown.
Captured at Winchester, Va., 15 June, 1863.
Confined at Richmond and then paroled at City
Point, Va., 23 June, 1863. After the fall of
Richmond he was a patient in a City Point, Va.,
hospital, for acute diarrhea. While there he
shook the hand of President Lincoln, who was
touring hospitals of that area. Transferred
from Columbia U.S.A. Hospital in June and was
mustered out at Mt. Pleasant Hospital,
Washington, D.C., 29 June, 1865. (H.R.M.V.,
Vol. 1, 242) (WCCR, Vol. 7,352) (MSA-AGR,
Vol. 1, 218 and 936-2) (D. L. Griffith in
extract from Lowry's wartime diary, Washington
County Historical Society, Civil War Letters
File) (this file was expanded from one in book)

LOWERY, James M. (Pvt.) Co. H, 6th Regiment
Maryland Infantry. (US) Hagerstown. Enlisted at
Hagerstown, 19 August, 1862. Reported sick in
Mt. Pleasant Hospital, 10 June, 1865.
Discharged 26 June, 1865. (H.R.M.V., Vol. 1,
242) (MSA-AGR-S-936-2)

LOWMAN, Charles W. (Pvt.) Co. A, 7th Regiment
Maryland Infantry. (US) Washington County.
Age 22. Enlisted at Hagerstown, 14 August,
1862. Missed time when struck by disease.
Patient in Jarvis Hospital, Baltimore.
Discharged 31 May, 1865. (Scharf, Vol. 1 226)
(H.R.M.V., Vol. 1, 279) (MSA-AGR, Vol. 1, 218
and MSA-S-936-17)

LOWMAN, George U. (Pvt.) Co. B, 3rd Potomac Home
Brigade Cavalry. (US) Leitersburg. Served from
24 August, 1861 to 12 February, 1864. (1890-C)

LOWMAN, George W. (Cpl.) Captain Firey's Co. B,
1st Regiment Potomac Home Brigade "Cole's"
Cavalry. (US) Age 20. Farmer, Leitersburg.
Enlisted 4 September, 1861. Veteran.
Reenlisted 14 February, 1864, at Boliver, Va.
Discharged 28 June, 1865. (H.R.M.V., Vol. 1,
673) (MSA-S-936-30)

LOWMAN, Jacob F. (Pvt.) Co. G, 1st Regiment
Potomac Home Brigade Infantry. (US) Clear
Spring. Served from 21 August, 1861 to 4
September, 1864. (1890-C)

LOWMAN, Jacob F. (Cpl.) Co. G, 1st Potomac Home
Brigade "Cole's Cavalry." (US) Age 26. A
laborer. Leitersburg. Enlisted at Hagerstown
20 February, 1864. Discharged 28 June, 1865.
(H.R.M.V., Vol. 1, 687) (MSA-AGR-S-936-38)

LOWRY, Charles A.(Pvt.) Co. H, 6th Maryland
Volunteer Infantry. (US) Age 19. Washington Co.
Served from 19 August, 1862 to 20 June, 1865.
Discharged near Washington, D.C. (H.R.M.V.,
Vol. 1, 242) (WCCR, Vol. 7,352) (MSA-AGR, Vol.
1, 218 and 936-2)

LOWRY, James M. (Pvt.) Co. H, 6th Regiment
Maryland Infantry. (US) Age 30. Rohrersville.
Enlisted at Hagerstown, 19 August, 1862.
Discharged from Columbia U.S. Army Hospital,
Washington, D.C., 26 June, 1865, with rupture.
(H.R.M.V., Vol. 1, 242) (1890-C) (MSA-AGR, Vol.
1, 218 and 936-2)

LUCAS, Daniel. (Pvt.) Co. C, 13th Regiment
Maryland Infantry. (US) Millstone. Served from
March, 1864 to May, 1865. (1890-C)

LUCAS, James Buchanan. (Pvt.) Co. B, 2nd Maryland
Cavalry, (CSA) Washington County. (Hartzler,
207)

LUGENBEL, Henry. (Sgt.) Co. B, 7th Regiment
Maryland Infantry. (US) Age 32. Enlisted at
Hagerstown 14 August, 1862. Promoted
commissary sergeant 16 July, 1863. Discharged

31 May, 1865. (MSA-AGR, Vol. 1, 218)
(H.R.M.V., Vol. 1, 282)

LULLY, William F. (or Lilly) (Pvt.) Musician.
Co. C, 7th Regiment Maryland Infantry. (US)
Age 16. Enlisted at Hagerstown, 29 August,
1862. Discharged 31 May, 1865. (MSA-AGR, Vol.
1, 218) (H.R.M.V., Vol. 1, 284)

LYNCH, James. (Pvt.) Co. I, 7th Regiment Maryland
Infantry. (US) Age 29. Enlisted at Hagerstown,
22 August, 1862. Deserted one month later at
Williamsport, Md. (MSA-AGR, Vol. 1, 219)
(H.R.M.V., Vol. 1, 298)

LYNCH, John W. (Pvt.) Co. A, 13th Regiment
Maryland Infantry. (US) Boonsboro. Age 19.
Served from 10 February, 1865 to 29 May, 1865.
Hospitalized sick at Camp Parole, near
Annapolis, Md. (H.R.M.V., Vol. 1, 434) (1890-C)
(MSA-AGR, Vol. 1, 218)

LYNCH, W.E. (Pvt.) Co. D, 13th Regiment Maryland
Infantry. (US) Boonsboro. Served from 13
February 29 July, 1865. (1890-C)

LYNCH, William E. (Pvt.) Co. C, 7th Regiment
Maryland Infantry. (US) Age 16. Enlisted at
Hagerstown, 18 August, 1862. Wounded in action
8 May, 1864, at Spotsylvania Va., taken
prisoner 16 September, 1864, near Winchester,
Va. Hospitalized with illness at Camp Parole,
near Annapolis. Discharged at Annapolis, 9
June, 1865. (MSA-AGR, Vol. 1, 218) (H.R.M.V.,
Vol. 1, 284)

LYNE, John. (Pvt.) Unit unknown. (CSA)
Sharpsburg. (Hartzler, 208)

MACE, George W. (Pvt.) Co. L, 1st Regiment
Potomac Home Brigade "Cole's" Cavalry. (US)
Hagerstown. Served from 2 February, 1865 to 28
June, 1865. (H.R.M.V., Vol. 1, 697) (1890-C)

MACGILL, Dr. Charles. (Pvt.) (CSA) Hagerstown.
Reared and educated in Baltimore, Dr. Charles

MacGill graduated from the University of Maryland in the spring of 1827, opened his practice at Martinsburg, Va., (now West Virginia) and relocated to Hagerstown in 1833. He became one of the leading physicians of the area, and assisted in starting the *Hagerstown Mail* and *Martinsburg Republican* newspapers. At the outbreak of the Civil War, Dr. MacGill received a commission as a colonel in the 24th Maryland Militia. Later he was promoted to the rank of major general. His Hagerstown home was on South Potomac Street, near Antietam Street. He was very outspoken about his feelings for the South. In September, 1861, a Federal cavalry squad of 65 soldiers, on orders of Col. John R. Kenley (1st Maryland Regiment)arrested him at his home, alleging authority of the secretary of state. As the two sides discussed the merits of this action MacGill asked to visit his sick wife in an upstairs bedroom. As he moved to the stairs he was challenged by two privates. MacGill turned and with one swing knocked the pair down the steps, precipitating a brief struggle. Dr. Charles MacGill Jr., went to his father's aid as did a daughter who struck out at the soldiers with a riding whip. Young Dr. MacGill received a saber cut in the neck as the incident concluded with a show of force by the military. Officers and soldiers drew their swords and guns, pushing the rebellious MacGills against a wall. Father and son were arrested and removed to Camp Banks, near Williamsport, for a hearing before Kenley. The son was released in an hour, but the father was sent to Fort McHenry, then to Fort Lafayette, N.Y., and still later to Boston's Fort Warren. Several times Dr. MacGill was offered his release if he would take the oath to the Union, which he refused. He was eventually released in 1862 and returned home to continue his practice. In 1863, when Lee invaded Maryland, MacGill established a hospital at Hagerstown for the sick and wounded returning from Gettysburg, and those who were wounded in the fighting in Washington County. As Lee retreated across the Potomac, MacGill

went with him and was later appointed surgeon
of the Confederate Army by President Jefferson
Davis. He held this position until the end of
the war when he took up residence in Richmond,
where he established a private practice. He
retired in 1880 due to a paralysis of the
limbs. MacGill died at the home of his son-in-
law, Dr. S. D. Dewey, in Richmond, 5 May, 1881.
MacGill is credited with performing the very
first ligation of both carotid arteries in the
same person. While living in Hagerstown he and
his family associated with St. John's Episcopal
Church. He married Miss Mary Ragan, daughter of
a prominent Hagerstown merchant, and they
produced eleven children including four that
served in the Confederacy; William D., James
and Davidge, privates in Co. C, 1st Maryland
Cavalry; and Charles G. W., regimental surgeon
with the Stonewall Brigade. A daughter, Alice,
married Dr. Samuel Davies Dewey, of Richmond, a
surgeon in the Confederate Navy; and James, who
married Miss Belle Pierce, a niece of the
famous Confederate cavalry commander General J.
E. B. Stuart. Mollie R. MacGill was born at
Hagerstown before the start of the war. At its
start she was visiting friends in Texas and
upon being informed of the circumstances
returned home at once. Throughout the war
Mollie remained with her mother and became
famous throughout the region for her Southern
feelings and hospitality extended to Rebel
soldiers. After the Battle of Antietam she
brought two seriously wounded Rebels into their
home for treatment until they were able to
return to service. After the war she returned
to Texas where she died in 1917.

MACGILL, Charles G. W.   2rd Virginia Infantry
(CSA) Hagerstown.   The son of Dr. Charles
MacGill was raised in Hagerstown, and earned
his medical degree at the University of
Maryland in 1856.   He practiced in Hagerstown
until 1863 when he entered the Confederate army
as a surgeon in the 2nd Virginia Infantry in
the famous "Stonewall Brigade." Dr. Macgill
served until the end of the conflict and then

settled in Catonsville, Md., to continue his practice. His Hagerstown office was on the west side of South Potomac Street, next to Dr. Scott. After the war Dr. MacGill became one of only two instructors at the Maryland Military Institute, in Catonsville. (9)

MACGILL, Davidge.(Pvt.) Co. C, 1st Regiment Maryland Cavalry. (CSA) Hagerstown.

MACGILL, James. (Pvt.) Co. C, 1st Regiment Maryland Cavalry. (CSA) Hagerstown. (Huntsberry, 85)

MACGILL, William D. (Pvt.) Co. C, 1st Regiment Maryland Cavalry.(CSA) Hagerstown.(Huntsberry, 85)

(NOTE: Charles G. W., Davidge, James and William Macgill were the sons of Hagerstown physician Dr. Charles Macgill.)

MADDOX, Dr. Thomas Clay. (CSA) Surgeon. Born at Hagerstown, he enlisted in the Confederate service before serious fighting began, and was present near Fort Sumter as a surgeon. Later, served as surgeon at Barnsville, Ga., Hospital. Before the war he was instrumental in luring the first rail service to Washington County, in 1851. He served on the county Board of Health from District 2. In 1854 he was an organizer of the first Great Hagerstown Fair that is still held each summer, in Hagerstown. Dr. Maddox was a charter member of the Ringgold Manor Agricultural Society, and was twice elected a delegate to the Protestant Episcopal Church conventions. After the war he practiced in Richmond, Baltimore, and Hagerstown, where he retired. (Hartzler, 216; H.R.M.V., Vol. 1, 114; W.C.H.S., VF 926, 1,W; Scharf, Vol. 1, 1008-09, 1192, 1194, 1288)

MAIN, Joseph D. Hospital steward. (Pvt.) Co. A, 1st Regiment Potomac Home Brigade "Cole's" Cavalry. (US) Knoxville. Served from 10

August, 1861 to 19 August, 1864. Enlisted as
private and promoted to hospital steward.
(H.R.M.V., Vol. 1, 665, 669) (1890-C)

MAINE, William. (Cpl.) Co. F, 1st Regiment
Potomac Home Brigade Infantry. (US) Knoxville.
Served from 4 September, 1861 to 29 May, 1865.
(H.R.M.V., Vol. 1, 513) (1890-C)

MALONE, Benjamin L. (Pvt.) Co. H,   Co. H, 13th
Regiment Maryland Infantry, and 2nd Maryland
Volunteers. Served from 9 June, 1861 to 27
Feb., 1864. (H.R.M.V., Vol. 1, 453) (1890-C)

MANGAN (or Mangin) Martin A. (Cpl.) Co. A, 7th
Regiment Maryland Infantry. (US) Washington
County. Age 24. Served from 18 August, 1862 to
31 May, 1865. (Sharf, 226) (H.R.M.V., Vol. 1,
279 and MSA-S-936-17)

MANIUS, John. (Pvt.) Co. I, 1st Regiment
"Russell's" Maryland Cavalry, and Co. A, of the
same unit. (US) Hagerstown. Veteran. Served
from 1, September, 1861 to 8 August, 1865.
(H.R.M.V., Vol. 1, 734) (1890-C)

MANN,   Charles W. (2nd Lt.) Captain Firey's Co.
B, 1st Regiment Potomac Home Brigade "Cole's"
Cavalry. (US) Age 23. Carpenter. Clear
Spring. Entered service as a private, 4
September, 1861. Promoted quartermaster
sergeant, first sergeant, then second
lieutenant. Veteran volunteer. Wounded in
action, mustered out 28 June, 1865. (Scharf,
328) (H.R.M.V., Vol. 1, 670) (MSA-S-936-30)

MANN, Job.   (Sgt.) Co. A, 3rd Regiment Maryland
Infantry. (US) Age 24. Enlisted 15 June, 1861
at Williamsport. Discharged 15 June, 1864,
near Petersburg, Va. (H.R.M.V., Vol. 1, 119)
(MSA-AGR, Vol. 1, 236)

MANNING, Thomas. (Pvt.) Co. F, 1st Regiment
Potomac Home Brigade Infantry. (US) Millstone.
Served from 27 February, 1864 to 29 May, 1865.
Transferred to Co. F, 13th Maryland Infantry.

Gunshot wound in shoulder. (H.R.M.V., Vol. 1, 513) (1890-C)

MARKER, Benjamin. (Pvt.) Co. B, 3rd Regiment Potomac Home Brigade Infantry. (US) Age 29. Hagerstown. Enlisted at Hagerstown, 6 November, 1861. Transferred to Co. F. Discharged 6 November, 1864. (H.R.M.V., Vol. 1, 578) (Captain Maxwell's roster) (MSA-S-936-23)

MARKER, Samuel. (Pvt.) Co. B, 3rd Regiment Potomac Home Brigade Infantry. (US)   Age 35. Hagerstown. Enlisted at Hagerstown, 25 October, 1861. Transferred to Co. F. Discharged 25 May, 1865. (H.R.M.V., Vol. 1, 578) (Captain Maxwell's roster) (MSA-S-936-23)

MARKS, Benjamin. (Pvt.) Co. E, 1st Regiment Potomac Home Brigade Infantry. (US) Hagerstown. Age 21. Laborer. Enlisted at Hagerstown, 23 August, 1861. Wounded in action at Gettysburg on the third day (3 July, 1863). Sustained wound to right hand with partial loss of motion to the three last fingers. Hospitalized in Philadelphia. Transferred to 59th Co., 2nd Battalion V.R.C., 12 September, 1863. Discharged at Harrisburg, Pa., 4 October, 1864. Received a life pension. Family relocated to Sullivan, Missouri in 1879. (H.R.M.V., Vol. 1, 508) (additional information provided by Mr. Larry Kramer, of Cortland, NY, his great-grandson)

MARROW, John. (Pvt.) Co. H, 1st Regiment Potomac Home Brigade Infantry. (US)   Sharpsburg. Entered service 14 September, 1861, died three days later for reasons unknown.   Buried at Old Reformed graveyard, Sharpsburg.   (H.R.M.V., Vol. 1, 526) (WCCR 1, 86)

MARROW, James. (Pvt.) Co. A, 1st Regiment Potomac Home Brigade Infantry. (US) Sharpsburg.   Served from 14 September, 1861 to 25 October, 1864. Buried in Old Reformed graveyard, Sharpsburg. (H.R.M.V., Vol. 1, 526) (WCCR 1, 86)

MARROW, Andrew W. (Pvt.) Co. H, 1st Regiment
Potomac Home Brigade Infantry. (US) Sharpsburg.
Served from 14 September, 1861 to 1 December,
1864. Buried in Mountain View Cemetery,
Sharpsburg. (H.R.M.V., Vol. 1, 526) (WCCR Vol.
1, 9) (1890-C)

MARSH, John H. (Cpl.) Co. F, 3rd Regiment Potomac
Home Brigade Infantry. (US) Age 20. Beaver
Creek. Farmer. Enlisted at Hagerstown 10
December, 1861. Veteran. Discharged 29 May,
1865. (H.R.M.V., Vol. 1, 592. (Captain
Maxwell's roster) (MSA-S-936-23)

MARSHALL, M. (?) (Pvt.) Co. F, 2nd Regiment
Maryland Infantry. (US) Hagerstown. Served
from 9 September, 1863 to 5 January, 1866.
(1890-C)

MARSHALL, Robert. (Pvt.) Co. I, 7th Regiment
Maryland Infantry. (US) Age 27. Enlisted at
Hagerstown, 21 September, 1862. Discharged 31
May, 1865. (H.R.M.V., Vol. 1, 298) (MSA-AGR,
Vol. 1, 253)

MARTIN, Adam B. (Capt.) Co. H, 6th Regiment
Maryland Infantry. (US) Smithsburg. Entered
service 5 September, 1862. Wounded 27
November, 1863, Mine Run, Va., died 6 May,
1864, of wounds received at Wilderness, Va.
(Scharf, 328) (H.R.M.V., Vol. 1, 240) (1890-C)
(MSA-AGR-S-936-2)

MALONE, Benjamin. (Sgt.) Co. G, 2nd Regiment
(U.S.C.T.) (US) Eakle's Mill. Served from 9
September, 1863 to 16 January, 1866. Buried in
the Red Hill Cemetery, near Keedysville.
(WCCR, Vol. 5, 179) (1890-C)

MARTIN, Charles A. (Cpl.) Co. B, 1st Regiment
Potomac Home Brigade Infantry. (US) Age 18.
Boatman. Williamsport. Enlisted 4 September,
1861. Used his own horse and equipment.
Veteran. Reenlisted 14 February, 1864 at
Boliver, Va. Discharged 28 June, 1865.
(H.R.M.V., Vol. 1, 672) (MSA-S-936-30)

MARTIN, Daniel D. (1st Lt.) Battery A, 1st
Pennsylvania Artillery. (US) Hagerstown. Served
from 28 April, 1861 to 28 July, 1865. (1890-C)

MARTIN, James E. (Capt.) Co. I, 2nd Mississippi
Infantry, (CSA) Hagerstown. (Hartzler, 219)

MARTIN, John. (2nd Lt.) Co. E, 1st Regiment
Potomac Home Brigade Infantry. (US) Hagerstown.
Enlisted 23 August, 1861, resigned 29 April,
1862. (Scharf, 328) (H.R.M.V., Vol. 1, 505)

MARTIN, John M. (Pvt.) Co. H, 6th Regiment
Maryland Infantry. (US) Age 31. Enlisted at
Hagerstown, 21 August, 1862. Arrived several
days late for muster; deserted at Berryville,
Va., 20 June, 1865. (H.R.M.V., Vol. 1, 242)
(MSA-AGR, Vol. 1, 249 and 936-2)

MARTIN, Josiah. (Pvt.) Co. F, 13th Regiment
Maryland Infantry. (US) Weverton. Served from
27 February, 1865 to 29 May, 1865. (H.R.M.V.,
Vol. 1, 447) (1890-C)

MARTIN, Stephen G. (Sgt.) Co. H, 6th Regiment
Maryland Infantry. (US) Age 37. Edgewood.
Enlisted at Hagerstown 21 August, 1862.
Discharged at Washington, D.C., 30 June, 1865.
(H.R.M.V., Vol. 1, 242) (1890-C) (MSA-AGR, Vol.
1, 249 and S-936-2))

MASON, Dr. Augustine. Medical Director,
Department of Richmond. (CSA) A native of
Virginia, Mason moved to Hagerstown after the
war and practiced until 1911. His office was
located on South Jonathan Street. He and his
family were active in the community with St.
John's Church, Washington County Board of
Health and he was a charter member of the Penn
Mar Council No. 440, the Royal Arcanum. He
volunteered his services to the South and
served with distinction as surgeon and medical
director, Department of Richmond. (Hartzler,
216) (Scharf, Vol. 2, 1102, 1133, 1198)
(Tercentenary History of Maryland, Vol. 3,

801) (M.F.D., 735)

MASON, Daniel. (Pvt.) Co. F, 1st Regiment Potomac
Home Brigade Infantry. (US) Age 24. Laborer.
Washington County. Enlisted at Baltimore, 17
September, 1864. Transferred to Co. F, 13th
Regiment Maryland Infantry. Discharged 28 May,
1865. (H.R.M.V., Vol. 1, 513) (MSA-S-936-23)

MASON, Daniel. (2nd Lt.) Co. F, 1st Regiment
Potomac Home Brigade Infantry. (US) Clear
Spring. Entered service 21 August, 1861 as
sergeant; promoted to second lieutenant 13
February, 1863. (Scharf, 328) (H.R.M.V., Vol.
1, 510) (1890-C)

MASTERS, George. (Pvt.) Co. H, 6th Regiment
Maryland Infantry. (US) Age 21. Smithsburg.
Enlisted at Hagerstown, 21 August, 1862.
Discharged near Washington, D.C., 20 June,
1865. (H.R.M.V., Vol. 1, 242) (1890-C) (MSA-
AGR, Vol. 1, 249 and 936-2)

MASTERS, William. (Pvt.) Co. H, 6th Regiment
Maryland Infantry. (US) Age 18. Enlisted at
Hagerstown, 21 August, 1862. Taken prisoner 7
May, 1864, at Wilderness, Va. Paroled at
Wilmington, Del. Discharged 8 June, 1865, at
Annapolis, Md. (H.R.M.V., Vol. 1, 242) (MSA-
AGR, Vol. 1, 249 and 936-2)

MATHIAS, Jacob. (Pvt.) Co. F, 3rd Regiment
Potomac Home Brigade Infantry. (US) Boonsboro.
Enlisted 16 April, 1862. Discharged 16 April,
1864. (H.R.M.V., Vol. 1, 593) (MSA-S-936-24)

MATTHEWS, John D. (Pvt.) Co. F, 1st Regiment
Potomac Home Brigade Infantry. (US) Age 18.
Laborer. Washington County. Enlisted 27 Feb.,
1864. Transferred to Co. F, 13th Regiment
Maryland Infantry. Discharged 29 May, 1865.
(H.R.M.V., Vol. 1, 447, 513) (MSA-S-936-23)

MAUGANS, Levi. (or Lewis) (Pvt.) Co. I, 1st
Regiment Maryland Infantry. (US) Age 18.
Enlisted Hagerstown, 3 March, 1863. Mustered

in at Petersburg, Va., three days later.
Transferred to 7th Maryland 1 June, 1865. (MSA-
AGR, Vol. 1, 228) (H.R.M.V., Vol. 1, 64)

MAUGANS, Martin A. (Cpl.) Co. A, 7th Regiment
Maryland Infantry. (US) Age 26. Enlisted at
Hagerstown 18 August, 1862. Appointed corporal
1 November, 1862. Discharged at Arlington
Heights, Va., 31 May, 1865. (MSA-AGR, Vol. 1,
250) (H.R.M.V., Vol. 1, 279, shown as Mangan)

MAXWELL, Robert. (Capt.) Co. F, 3rd Regiment
Potomac Home Brigade Infantry. (US) Age 29.
Hagerstown. Second lieutenant of Co. A, 4th P.
H. B., and Co. B, 3rd Regiment. Promoted to
captain of Co. F, 3rd Regiment, 23 September,
1862. Maxwell was active in Hagerstown affairs
and on 26 January, 1861, was elected president
of the Independent Junior Fire Company.
(Scharf, 328) (H.R.M.V., Vol. 1, 592) (Captain
Maxwell's roster) (MSA-S-936-24) (Minutes of
The Independent Junior Fire Company for 26
January, 1861. The Western Maryland Room of the
Washington County Free Library)

MAY, Henry. (Cpl.) Co. A, 7th Regiment Maryland
Infantry. (US) Hagerstown. Age 24. Member
Independent Junior Fire Company of Hagerstown.
Enlisted for three years at Hagerstown, 16
August, 1862. Paid $25 bounty. Served to 26
July, 1865. Transferred to V.R.C. 12 February,
1864. (H.R.M.V., Vol. 1, 279) (1890-C) (MSA-
AGR, Muster-In Rolls, 936-17) (I.J.F.C.roster)
(Scharf, 226)

MAYBERRY, Peter J. (1st Lt.) Co. A, 4th Regiment
and Co. B, 3rd Regiment Potomac Home Brigade
Infantry. (US) Age 28. Hagerstown. Entered
service 11 October, 1861, mustered out 31
December, 1864. (Scharf, 328) (H.R.M.V., Vol.
1, 575) (1890-C) (Captain Maxwell's roster)
(MSA-S-936-24)

MAYHEW, Harvey. (Pvt.) Captain Firey's Co. B, 1st
Regiment Potomac Home Brigade "Cole's" Cavalry.
(US) Hancock. Served from 2 September, 1861

to 15 September, 1864. Taken prisoner.
(H.R.M.V., Vol. 1, 672) (1890-C)

MCALLISTER, Andrew J. (Pvt.) Co. F, 1st Regiment
Potomac Home Brigade Infantry. (US) Ernstville.
Teamster. Served from 4 September, 1861 to 1
September, 1862. Thrown from horse, suffering
broken ribs. (H.R.M.V., Vol. 1, 513) (1890-C)

MCATEE, Benjamin. (Pvt.) Co. B, 1st Potomac Home
Brigade "Cole's" Cavalry. (US) Washington
County. A school teacher. Enlisted at
Frederick, 24 August, 1861. Discharged with
physical disability, 23 November, 1861.
(H.R.M.V., Vol. 1, 672) (MSA-AGR-S-936-34)

MCATEE, Benjamin F. (2nd Lt.) Co. K, 1st Potomac
Home Brigade "Cole's Cavalry." (US) Washington
County. Served from 4 April, 1864 to 23 Nov.,
1864. (Scarf, 328) (H.R.M.V., Vol. 1, 693)

MCATEE, Thomas J. (2nd Lt.) Co. G, "Cole's
Cavalry." (US) Washington County. Served from 7
March, 1864 to 18 June, 1864. (Scharf, 328)
(H.R.M.V., Vol. 1, 686)

MCAWAY, John B. (Pvt.) Co. B, 3rd Regiment
Potomac Home Brigade Infantry. (US) Age 21.
Hagerstown. Enlisted at Hagerstown, 30 October,
1861. Transferred to Co. F. Discharged 30
October, 1864. (H.R.M.V., Vol. 1, 578) (Captain
Maxwell's roster) (MSA-S-936-23)

MCBRIDE, Edward. (2nd Lt.) Co. B, 3rd Regiment
Maryland Infantry. (US) Washington County.
Entered service as private, Co. C, 12 August,
1861. Promoted to second lieutenant 29
October, 1862. Resigned 26 June, 1863.
(Scharf, 328) (H.R.M.V., Vol. 1, 122)

MCBRIDE, John H. (Pvt.) Co. G, 1st Regiment
Potomac Home Brigade "Cole's" Cavalry. (US)
Hagerstown. Enlisted at Hagerstown, 4 August,
1864. Discharged 25 May, 1865. (H.R.M.V., Vol.
1, 688) (MSA-AGR-S-936-34)

MCCALLISTER, George. (Pvt.) 1st Regiment
Maryland Infantry. (US) Hagerstown. Served from
25 February, 1864 to 8 August, 1865. (1890-C)

MCCARDELL, Wilford C. (Pvt.) Co. I, 1st Regiment
"Russell's" Maryland Cavalry. (US)Williamsport.
Served from 3 September, 1861 to 26 September,
1863. (H.R.M.V., Vol. 1, 733) (1890-C)

MCCARTER, Albert W. (Pvt.) Co. I, 7th Regiment
Maryland Infantry. (US) Hagerstown. Age 27.
Entered service 27 August, 1862, at Hagerstown.
Missing in action 5 May, 1864. Died in
Andersonville, Ga., prison, 2 March, 1865.
(H.R.M.V., Vol. 1, 298.) (1890-C) (MSA-AGR,
Vol. 1, 253)

MCCARTER, George. (Pvt.) Co. M. 1st Regiment
Maryland Cavalry. (US) Age 21. Butcher.
Hagerstown. Enlisted at Hagerstown, 7 March,
1864. Discharged 8 August, 1865. (H.R.M.V.,
Vol. 1, 743) (MSA-AGR-S-936-36)

MCCARTER, Harrison. (Pvt.) Co. I, 7th Regiment
Maryland Infantry. (US) Washington Co. Age
24. Entered service 27 August, 1862, at
Hagerstown. Discharged 31 May, 1865. Buried in
Rose Hill Cemetery, Hagerstown. (H.R.M.V.,
Vol. 1, 298) (WCCR, Vol. 7, 239)

MCCARTY, Alexander. (Pvt.) Co. H, 1st Regiment
Maryland Cavalry. (US) Hancock. Service dates
not available. Reported to census that he
suffered a back injury in service. (1890-C)

MCCARTY, Barnabas. (Pvt.) Co. G., 1st Potomac
Home Brigade "Cole's" Cavalry. (US) Millstone
Point. Age 42. Enlisted at Frederick, Md.,
February 26, 1864. Reported missing in action
at Berryville, Va., September 4, 1864. Sent to
prison in Richmond, Va., then transferred to
prison in Salisbury, N. C., October 9, 1864,
where he died Nov. 22, 1864. Cause of death
unknown. (H.R.M.V., Vol. 1, 688) (Records held
by Mrs. Candy Gloyd, of Warfordsburg, Pa.)

MCCARTY, John. (Pvt.) Co. M, 1st Regiment Potomac
Home Brigade "Cole's" Cavalry. (US) Clear
Spring. Age 40. Laborer. Enlisted 17 October,
1864. A discharge date not available.
(H.R.M.V., Vol. 1, 700) U. S. National
Archives, Record Group No. 110, 4th Election
District)

MCCARTY, Robert. (Pvt.) Co. A, 13th Regiment
Maryland Infantry. (US) Downsville. Served
from 21 February, 1865 to 29 May, 1865.
(H.R.M.V., Vol. 1, 434) (1890-C)

MCCLAIN, Elias. (Pvt.) Co. D, 6th Regiment
Maryland Infantry. (US) Edgemont. Served from
20 August, 1862 to 30 June, 1865. Taken
prisoner and served time in Libby and Belle
Isle Prisons. Exchanged. Transferred to
V.R.C., 25 April, 1864. (H.R.M.V., Vol. 1, 234)
(1890-C)

MCCLAIN, John D. (Pvt.) Co. F, 1st Regiment
Potomac Home Brigade Infantry. (US) Age 26.
Taylor. Washington County. Enlisted 4
September, 1861. Veteran. Reenlisted 28
February, 1864, at Frederick, Md. Transferred
to Co. F, 13th Regiment Maryland Infantry.
Discharged 29 May, 1865. (H.R.M.V., Vol. 1,
513) (MSA-S-936-23)

MCCLANNAHAN, Matthew. (Pvt.) Co. I, 1st Regiment
"Russell's" Maryland Cavalry. (US)
Williamsport. Enlisted 3 September, 1861, at
Williamsport, for three year's service.
Mustered out 3 September, 1864. Moved from
Clear Spring to Williamsport when very young.
Educated in Williamsport schools and worked as
a clerk in a store, dealing in lumber and
building materials, owned by Samuel Culbertson,
at the corner of Potomac and Conococheague
Streets. Entered service as the war began.
Participated in battles at Brandy Station,
Gettysburg, and many others. After the war
returned to his clerking duties until 1873,
when he was named freight manager for the
Williamsport Station of the Western Maryland

Railroad. (Williams, Vol. 2, 698) (H.R.M.V., Vol. 1, 734) (1890-C) (McClannahan papers, 1) (M. F. D., 749)

MCCLELLAND, Thomas W. (Pvt.) Co. H, 1st Regiment Maryland Infantry. (US) Boonsboro. Entered service 29 February, 1864. Died in hospital after suffering gunshot wound to the head. (1890-C)

MCCLELLEN, John D.C. (Pvt.) Co. B, 3rd Regiment Potomac Home Brigade Infantry. (US) Age 31. Washington County. Enlisted 21 December, 1861. Veteran. Discharged 29 May, 1865. (H.R.M.V., Vol. 1, 578) (MSA-S-936-23)

MCCOLISTER, Franklin. (Pvt.) Co. D, 4th Regiment Maryland Volunteers. (U.S.C.T.) (US) Williamsport. Served from 28 August, 1863 to 26 June, 1865. (1890-C)

MCCOY, David W. (Pvt.) Co. B, 3rd Regiment Potomac Home Brigade Infantry. (US) Age 18. Washington County. Enlisted 30 December, 1861. Discharged 29 May, 1865. (H.R.M.V., Vol. 1, 578) (MSA-S-936-23)

MCCOY, Daniel. (Pvt.) Co. L, 1st Regiment Potomac Home Brigade "Cole's" Cavalry. (US) Hancock. Served from 4 October, 1864 to 28 June, 1865. (H.R.M.V., Vol. 1, page 607)

MCCOY, David W. (Pvt.) Co. D, 3rd Regiment Maryland Infantry. (US) Age 19. Hagerstown. Served from 5, June, 1864 to 29, May, 1865. Veteran. (1890-C) (H.R.M.V., Vol. 1, page 578) (MSA-S-936-24)

MCCOY, David W. (Pvt.) Co. F, 3rd Regiment Potomac Home Brigade Infantry. (US) Funkstown. Musician, (fife). Enlisted at Hagerstown, 30 December, 1861. Veteran. Discharged 29 May, 1865. (H.R.M.V., Vol. 1, 593) (Captain Maxwell's roster)

MCCOY, John H. (Capt.) Co. L, 1st Regiment

Potomac Home Brigade "Cole's Cavalry." (US)
Hancock. Served 23 April, 1864 to 28 June,
1865. (Scharf, 328) (H.R.M.V., Vol. 1, 695)

MCCOY, Joseph. (Pvt.) Co. H, 1st Regiment Potomac
Home Brigade Infantry. (US) Age 31. Laborer.
Washington County. Enlisted 19 December, 1861.
Discharged 19 December, 1864. (H.R.M.V., Vol.
1, 526) (MSA-S-936-23)

MCCOY, Robert. (Pvt.) Musician. Co. E, 1st
Regiment Potomac Home Brigade Infantry. (US)
Age 23. Wagonmaker. Rohrersville. Served from
14 September, 1861 to 1 October, 1864.
(H.R.M.V., Vol. 1, 508) (1890-C) (MSA-S-936-23)

MCCOY, Rigdon. (Pvt.) Co. I, 7th Regiment
Maryland Infantry. (US) Age 22. Enlisted at
Hagerstown, 31 August, 1862. Served to 31 May,
1865. (H.R.M.V., Vol. 1, 298) (MSA-AGR, Vol.
1, 253)

MCCOY, Timothy. (Pvt.) Co. H, 3rd Maryland
Cavalry Regiment. (US) Sharpsburg. Age 36.
Served from 28 September, 1863 to 7 September,
1865. (H.R.M.V., Vol. 1. 775) (1890-C) (MSA-
AGR, Vol. 1, 236)

MCCULLOUGH, George M. (Pvt.) Co. A, 3rd Regiment
Maryland Infantry. (US) Hancock. Served from
15 June, 1861 to 15 June, 1864. Buried in
Tonoloway Baptist Church Cemetert, north of
Hancock, in Pennsylvania, near the Mason and
Dixon line. (H.R.M.V., Vol. 1, 119) (WCCR Vol.
2, 170)

MCCLEARY, Robert. (Pvt.) Co. B, 103rd Regiment
Pennsylvania Infantry. (US) Chewsville.
Served from 8 August, 1861 to March, 1863.
Discharge lost. (1890-C)

MCCUSKER, Jacob. (Pvt.) Co. A, 3rd Regiment
Maryland Infantry. (US) Hancock. Age 21.
Enlisted at Hancock, 1 October, 1861.
Discharged 23 August, 1862. (H.R.M.V., Vol. 1,
119) (1890-C)

MCCUSKEY, Thomas. (Pvt.) Co. B, 3rd Regiment
Maryland Infantry. (US) Age 21. Entered
service at Hancock November 1, 1861. Wounded in
action 3 May, 1863 near Fredericksburg, Va.
Died at home, 10 February, 1864, while on
furlough, for disease contracted in service.
(H.R.M.V., Vol. 1, 124) (MSA-AGR, Vol. 1, 236)

MCCUSKER, John, Sr.(Pvt.) Co. B, 3rd Regiment
Maryland Infantry. (US) Hancock. Served from 21
August, 1863 to 3 October, 1865. (1890-C)

MCDONALD, James Edward. (Pvt.) Co. E, 2nd
Regiment Potomac Home Brigade Infantry. (US)
Hagerstown. Served from 11 August, 1862 to 23
May, 1865. (H.R.M.V., Vol. 1, 556) (1890-C)

MCFERRIN, Samuel. (Pvt.) 17th Regiment
Pennsylvania Cavalry. (US) Funkstown. Service
dates not available. Captured and confined to
Libby Prison, Richmond. (1890-C)

MCGRAW, Joseph. (Lt. Col.) Commissary of Supply,
and staff of Gen. John Pegram. (CSA) Age 20.
Sharpsburg. One of the most highly respected
officers in the Confederate Artillery Corps. A
teamster of Irish blood he rose quickly through
the ranks to lieutenant colonel of the Purcell
Battery. He was elected lieutenant 31 March,
1862; captain in May, 1863, and was in command
of the battery at the Confederate surrender.
Pegram, his commanding officer, described him
as a man with a powerful frame and possessing
the excellent ability to command.
   At Spottsylvania Court House, in May of 1864,
McGraw was struck by solid shot that tore away
his left arm at the shoulder, leaving only a
small stump in the socket. When aides rushed
to help, McGraw waved them off saying "Don't
mind me, I'm alright, giv'em hell!" Closing his
eyes he fell forward, out of his saddle to the
ground. He regained consciousness as he was
transported to a hospital area where he refused
an anesthetic suggested by a surgeon. When the
surgeon insisted, McGraw observed he was the

senior of the two officers and would have none. He then commanded removal of the bloody stump which was accomplished without a cry of pain as he puffed away on a pipe. Looking the surgeon in the eye he said dryly, "Reckin I'll be off duty for 30 days!"

He returned to active service at Petersburg where he commanded 24 cannon. As Richmond was consumed by flames in the death throws of the Confederacy, McGraw accompanied Gen. R. Lindsey Walker to Gen. Lee's headquarters to see what could be done. Lee, after some conversation, ordered the guns spiked and limber chests destroyed. His men were to "take to the woods" and join Gen. Joseph Johnston, in North Carolina to continue the struggle. When the order was passed on to McGraw's men, they obeyed, but many broke down and cried like young children.

The Hall of Delegates in Richmond was the scene of a reunion for survivors of Pegram's Battalion Association, on 21 May, 1886. The principal address was given by Maj. Thomas A. Brander, president of the association. He described the men who had served, including McGraw. He had extensive words of praise for him, his bravery, his ability to handle men in combat and his rapid advance through the ranks. He noted that McGraw was twice wounded, was a superb soldier who was marked for his bravery by an "empty sleeve." (Hartzler, 212) (CVM, Vol. XXXII, 59, 60) (S.H.S.P., Vol. XIV, page 14; XXVIII, pages 374-75, XLII, page 166)

MCKAIN, George. (Pvt.) Co. A. 7th Maryland Regiment. (US) Hagerstown. Age 24. Enlisted 11 August, 1862 at Hagerstown. Discharged 31 May, 1865. Hospitalized at Washington, D.C., suffering from chronic diarrhea. Discharged at Philadelphia, Pa., 23 May, 1865. Received pension of $6 per month. (Scharf, Vol. 1, 226) (H.R.M.V., Vol. 1, 279) (1890-C) (MSA-AGR, Vol. 1, 250 and MSA-S-936-17) (Pensions List, 157)

MCKAIN, Thomas. (Pvt.) Co. A, 7th Regiment Maryland Infantry. (US) Washington County.

Age 31. Served from 18 August, 1862 to 31 May, 1865. (Scharf, Vol. 1, 226) (H.R.M.V., Vol. 1, 279) (MSA-S-936-17)

MCKAIN, William. (Pvt.) Co. A, 7th Regiment Maryland Infantry. (US) Hagerstown. Age 22. Served from 16 August, 1862 to 24 June, 1865. Wounded in action, 19 June, 1864, at Petersburg, Va. Transferred to V.R.C. Buried in St. John's Episcopal Church Cemetery, Hagerstown. (H.R.M.V., Vol. 1, 279) (WCCR, Vol. 7, 457) (1890-C) (MSA-S-936-17)

DR. CHARLES E. S. McKEE (US)

MCKEE, Dr. Charles E.S. (Brevet Lt. Col.) Regimental surgeon. Co. B, 3rd Regiment, Potomac Home Brigade Infantry. (US) Born and raised in Hagerstown, he enlisted 15 February, 1863. Discharged 29 May, 1865. His office was located on North Potomac Street, in Hagerstown. Dr. KcKee obtained his M.D. degree from the University of Maryland in 1858. He began practice immediately and enjoyed much success. He entered the Union army in the spring of 1862 as a surgeon with the 3rd Regiment Potomac Home Brigade Infantry, and served until the close of the war. For faithful and efficient service he was made Brevet Lieutenant-Colonel, 13 March, 1865. Returning after the conflict he settled in Oakland, Allegany County, and practiced until 1870, when he returned to Hagerstown. In 1873 he retired and entered the hardware business at 28 North Potomac Street. In 1892 he sold it to his son, and retired. (5) It later became a Hagerstown landmark store known as R. D. McKee Hardware, named for his grandson, Richard D. McKee. Dr McKee served as mayor of Hagerstown from 1874-75. (6) (H.R.M.V., Vol. 1, page 571) (Captain Maxwell's roster) (M.F.D., 738)

MCKEE, James. (Pvt.) Co. C, 1st Regiment Maryland Cavalry. (CSA) Indian Springs. Served from 15 June, 1861 to August, 1865. Wounded in side and shoulder. (1890-C) (Huntsberry, 85)

MCKENNA, James P. (Pvt.) Co. H. 6th Regiment
Maryland Infantry. (US) Age 21. Washington
Co. Served from 14 August, 1862 to 20 June,
1865. Discharged at Washington, D.C. Buried
in St. Paul's Reformed Cemetery, Clear Spring.
(WCCR, Vol. 4, 271) (H.R.M.V., Vol. 1, 242)
(MSA-AGR-S-936-2)

MCKINLEY, Norval. (Capt.) Co. H, 2nd Regiment
Potomac Home Brigade Infantry. (US) Hancock.
Entered service as a second lieutenant of Co.
F, 9 December, 1862. Promoted to Captain of
Co. H, 1 February, 1864. Served to 30
September, 1864. Suffered gun shot wound to
right thigh. (Sharf, 328) (H.R.M.V., Vol. 1,
557, 562) (1890-C)

MCKINSEY, Jacob. Co.(Pvt.) E, 1st Regiment
Potomac Home Brigade Infantry. (US) Age 22.
Laborer. Enlisted at Hagerstown, 14 September,
1861. Reenlisted 23 February, 1864, at Sandy
Hook, Md. Dishonorably discharged 26 August,
1865. (H.R.M.V., Vol. 1, 508) (MSA-S-936-23)

MCKINSEY, William. (Pvt.) Co. B, 3rd Regiment
Potomac Home Brigade Infantry. (US) Age 21.
Beaver Creek. Enlisted at Hagerstown, 12
November, 1861. Veteran. Transferred to Co. F.
Discharged 29 May, 1865. (H.R.M.V., Vol. 1,
593) (Captain Maxwell's roster) (MSA-S-936-23)

MCLAUGHLIN, John I. (Pvt.) Co. G, 1st Regiment
Maryland Infantry. (US) Enlisted at
Williamsport, 6 May, 1861. Deserted at
Sharpsburg, Md., 23 October, 1861. (MSA-AGR,
Vol. 1, 228) (H.R.M.V., Vol. 1, 54)

MCMACHAN, Henry M. (Capt.) Co. I, 1st Regiment
Maryland Cavalry. (US) Age 23. Williamsport.
Enlisted at Williamsport, 3 September, 1861 as
a private. Served to 27 October, 1864.
Promoted first sergeant; second lieutenant 19
May, 1862; captain 28 August, 1863. (Scarf,
328) (H.R.M.V., Vol. 1, 731) (MSA-AGR-S-936-38)

MCMACHAN, Samuel. (Pvt.) Co. I, 1st Regiment
Maryland Cavalry. (US) Age 22. Enlisted at
Williamsport, 3 September, 1861. Drew $100
bounty. Transferred to V.R.C. Discharged 20
September, 1864 at Portland, Me. (H.R.M.V.,
Vol. 1, 734) (MSA-AGR-S-936-38)

MCMILLEN, James D. (Pvt.) Co. F, 1st Regiment
Potomac Home Brigade Infantry. (US) Age 23.
Farmer. Clear Spring. Enlisted 15 August,
1862. Died 8 February, 1865. (H.R.M.V., Vol. 1,
513) (MSA-S-936-23)

MCPHERSON, George W. (Pvt.) Co. I, 7th Regiment
Maryland Infantry. (US) Smoketown. Age 25.
Entered service 25 August, 1862. Deserted 15
November, 1862. (The census indicates
McPherson served until 18 May, 1865. The state
roster indicates his desertion as shown.)
(H.R.M.V., Vol. 1, 298) (1890-C)

MCPHERSON, John. (Pvt.) Co. D, 6th Regiment
Maryland Infantry. (US) Smithsburg. Served
from 4 September, 1862 to 20 June, 1865.
(H.R.M.V., part 1, 234) (1890-C)

MEAZELL, Lewis L. (Pvt.) Co. B, 7th Regiment
Maryland Infantry. (US) Age 21. Enlisted at
Hagerstown, 2 December, 1863. Deserted at
Hagerstown, 20 April, 1864. (H.R.M.V., Vol.
1, 282) (MSA-AGR, Vol. 1, 251)

MEISNER, James. (Pvt.) Co. B, 3rd Regiment
Potomac Home Brigade Infantry. (US) Age 19.
Farmer. Broadfording. Enlisted at Hagerstown,
30 December, 1831. Veteran. Transferred to Co.
F. Died 26 November, 1864. (H.R.M.V., Vol. 1,
593) (Captain Maxwell's roster) (MSA-S-936-23)

MEISNER. Solomon W. (Pvt.) Co. B, 3rd Regiment
Potomac Home Brigade Infantry. (US) Age 38.
Hagerstown. Enlisted at Hagerstown, 23
October, 1861. Veteran. Transferred to Co. F.
Discharged 29 May, 1865. (H.R.M.V., Vol. 1,
577) (Captain Maxwell's roster) (MSA-S-936-23)

MELLINGER, William. (Pvt.) Co. I, 7th Regiment
Maryland Infantry. (US) Age 20. Enlisted at
Hagerstown, 31 August, 1862. Discharged 31
May, 1865. (H.R.M.V., Vol. 1, 298) (MSA-AGR,
Vol. 1, 253)

MELLOTT, Stephenson. (Pvt.) Co. K, 12th Regiment
Pennsylvania Infantry. (US) Hancock. Served
from 20 August, 1861 to 15 July, 1865. (1890-C)

MENTZER, John M. (Capt.) Co. K, 2nd Kansas
Cavalry. His wife and two infant children are
buried with him in Rose Hill Cemetery,
Hagerstown. (WCCR, Vol. 7. 392)

MERRICK, Alfred D. (Pvt.) Age 31. Hagerstown.
Attorney. Rockbridge Va., Artillery. (CSA)
Member Hagerstown Bar and the Independent
Junior Fire Company of Hagerstown. (WCHS)
(Hartzler, 222) (I.J.F.C. roster)

METCALF, Thomas O. (Sgt.) (Quartermaster) Captain
Firey's Co. B, 1st Regiment Potomac Home
Brigade "Cole's" Cavalry. (US) Conococheague.
Served from 24 August, 1861 to 15 September,
1864. (H.R.M.V., Vol. 1, 672) (1890-C)

METZ, Jacob. (2nd Lt.) Captain Firey's Co. B, 1st
Regiment Potomac Home Brigade "Cole's Cavalry."
(US) Tilghmanton. Entered service 24 August,
1861, killed in action near Williamsport, Md.,
15 June, 1863. (Scharf, 328) (H.R.M.V., Vol.
1, 670) (1890-C)

MILLER, Benjamin. (Cpl.) Co. A, 3rd Regiment
Maryland Infantry. (US) Age 20. Enlisted at
Williamsport 15 June, 1861. Discharged 15 June,
1864. (MSA-AGR, Vol. 1, 236) (H.R.M.V., Vol.
1, 119)

MILLER, Charles. (Pvt.) Co. H, 6th Regiment
Maryland Infantry. (US) Age 23. Enlisted at
Hagerstown, 14 August, 1862. Wounded in action
6 May, 1864, at Wilderness, Va. Deserted at
Martinsburg, Va., 10 November, 1863.
(H.R.M.V., Vol. 1, 242) (MSA-AGR, Vol. 1, 249

and 936-2)

MILLER, George. (Pvt.) Co. A, 7th Regiment
Maryland Infantry. (US) Hagerstown. Age 28.
Entered service at Williamsport, 22 October,
1862. (A substitute for Walter Mobley) Miller
was on guard duty at company stables on
Maryland Heights, Friday, 9 February, 1863,
when he stole a horse belonging to Maj.
William Dallman, and rode quietly out of camp.
The army searched and telegraphed in all
directions without finding a trace of the
deserter-horse thief. (H.R.M.V., Vol. 1, 280)
Dorrance collection, letter 16 February, 1863.)
(MSA-AGR, Vol. 1, 251)

MILLER, George Washington. (Pvt.) Co. F, 1st
Regiment Potomac Home Brigade Infantry. (US)
Age 21. Laborer. Washington County. Enlisted
4 September, 1861. Died 16 May, 1864.
(H.R.M.V., Vol. 1, 513) (MSA-S-936-23)

MILLER, Jackson. (Pvt.) Co. G, 1st Regiment
Potomac Home Brigade "Cole's Cavalry." (US)
Age 23. A blacksmith. Leitersburg. Enlisted
21 February, 1864. Discharged 28 June, 1865.
(H.R.M.V., Vol. 1, 688) (MSA-AGR-S-936-38)

MILLER, John. (Pvt.) Co. B, 3rd Regiment Potomac
Home Brigade Infantry. (US) Age 20.
Hagerstown. Enlisted at Hagerstown, 6
November, 1861. Veteran. Transferred to Co. F.
Discharged 29 May, 1865. (H.R.M.V., Vol. 1,
593) (Captain Maxwell's roster) (MSA-S-936-23)

MILLER, Dr. John E. (Pvt.) Assistant Surgeon.
57th Regiment Pennsylvania Volunteers. (US)
Hagerstown. Served from 20 August, 1862 to 6
May, 1865. (1890-C)

MILLER, John P. (Pvt.) Co. D, 6th Regiment
Maryland Infantry. (US) Smithsburg. Served
from 4 September, 1862 to 20 June, 1865.
Member of the Washington County Medical
Society. (H.R.M.V., Vol. 1, 234) (1890-C)
(Scharf, Vol. 2, 1133)

MILLER, Joseph C. (Pvt.) 14th Regiment
Pennsylvania Cavalry. (US) Hagerstown. Served
from 26 August, 1865 to 30 November, 1865. A
veterinary surgeon. Injured when kicked by a
horse. (1890-C)

MILLER, Levi. (Cpl.) Co. H, 6th Regiment Maryland
Infantry. (US) Age 21. Edgemont. Served from 21
August, 1862 to 20 June, 1865. Contracted
typhoid fever. Discharged at Washington, D.C.
(H.R.M.V., Vol. 1, 242) (1890-C) (MSA-AGR, Vol.
1, 249 and 936-2)

MILLER, Michael. (Pvt.) Co. B, 3rd Regiment
Potomac Home Brigade Infantry. (US) Age 22.
Hagerstown. Served from 31 October, 1861 to 29
May, 1865. Veteran. Transferred to Co. F.
(H.R.M.V., Vol. 1, 593) (1890-C) (Captain
Maxwell's roster) (MSA-S-936-23)

MILLER, Samuel. (Pvt.) Co. A, 1st Regiment
Potomac Home Brigade Infantry. (US) Funkstown.
Age 21. Served from 15 August, 1861 to 27
August, 1864. (H.R.M.V., Vol. 1, 489) (1890-C)
(MSA-AGR, Vol. 1, 234)

MILLER, Samuel. (Pvt.) Co. I, 7th Regiment
Maryland Infantry. (US) Age 21. Enlisted at
Hagerstown, 14 August, 1862. Deserted at
Maryland Heights, 1 February, 1863. (H.R.M.V.,
Vol. 1, 298) (MSA-AGR, Vol. 1, 253)

MILLER, DR. Victor Davis. 78th Pennsylvania
Infantry Regiment. (US) Williamsport. Dr.
Miller was born near Williamsport in 1938. He
graduated from Jefferson College in 1861 and
began practice in Franklin County,
Pennsylvania. In 1862 he was appointed surgeon
of the 78th Regiment of Pennsylvania Volunteers
as a part of the Army of the Cumberland,
stationed at Nashville, Tennessee. During the
battle of Stone River he suffered a severe case
of exposure resulting in a physical disability
leading to his retirement from the service in
April, 1863. While the Stone River fight was

underway Dr. Miller attended an Indiana officer
in Gen. Thomas' Corps. As he closed a serious
leg wound two enemy bullets passed through the
doctor's coat without causing harm. Upon his
resignation he retired to Washington County and
practiced medicine in Antrim Township,
Pennsylvania.

MILLER, William H. (Pvt.) Co. I, 7th Regiment
Maryland Infantry. (US) Age 26. Enlisted at
Hagerstown, 29 August, 1862. Sick at
Washington, D.C. Mt. Pleasant Hospital until 31
May, 1865. Discharged 17 June, 1865. (H.R.M.V.,
Vol. 1, 298) (MSA-AGR, Vol. 1, 253)

MILLS, Amos A. (Pvt.) Co. D, 1st Regiment Potomac
Home Brigade "Cole's" Cavalry. (US) Four Locks.
Age 17. Laborer and foreman on the C & O Canal.
Saddled one of his father's team horses, went
to Hagerstown and enlisted 27 November, 1861.
Reenlisted at Boliver, Virginia, 26 February,
1864, in Co. I, "Cole's" Cavalry. Veteran
volunteer. Killed in action 15 May, 1864 at New
Market, Virginia. (H.R.M.V., Vol. 1, 680)
(Mildred Stoneman collected records and
National Archives)

MILLS, James Johnson (or John J.). (Sgt.)
Washington Co. Co. A, 3rd Maryland Infantry.
(US) Farmer. Age 18. Enlisted at Williamsport,
15 June, 1861, for three years. Reenlisted 5
Jan. 1864 at Cowans, Tenn. (Mildred Stoneman
collected records.

MILLS, Jeremiah. (Pvt.) Co. F, 13th Regiment
Maryland Infantry. (US) Millstone. Served from
21 February, 1865 to 29 May, 1865. (H.R.M.V.,
Vol. 1, 447) (1890-C)

MILLS, John. (Pvt.) Co. A, 12th Regiment Virginia
Cavalry. (CSA) Brownsville. Served from 17 May,
1861 to 1865. (1890-C)

MILLS, Robert Louis. (Pvt.) Co. G, 1st Regiment
Potomac Home Brigade "Cole's" Cavalry. (US)
Four Locks. Canal worker. Age 14. Enlisted 25

February, 1864. Discharged 10 June, 1865.
Suffered sabre wound in left side at fighting
at Keedysville, Maryland. His brother Amos, of
Co. D., sewed up his wound with a needle and
thread, then poured alcohol over it.
Hospitalized at Frederick, Maryland. Three
times his horse fell on him in battle. Was
docked a month's pay for losing his Enfield
rifle ($22.15) and a revolver ($4.00). Received
pension of $8 per month. Died 13 October, 1915
at 56 years, at Perryville, Ashland County,
Ohio, where he is buried. (H.R.M.V., Vol. 1,
688) (Mildred Stoneman collected records
National Archives)

MILLS, Samuel Luther, (Sgt.) (Quartermaster
sergeant) Captain Firey's Co. B, 1st Regiment
Potomac Home Brigade Cavalry. (US) Age 21.
Canal boatman. Indian Springs. Enlisted at
Hagerstown 4 September, 1861. Veteran.
Reenlisted at Boliver, Va., 14 February, 1864.
Discharged 28 June, 1865. Pensioned at age 50
at $8 per month. Died 3 July, 1905, at
Springfield, Clark County Ohio.
(MSA-S-936-30) (H.R.M.V., Vol. 1, 672) (Mildred
Stoneman collected records National Archives)

MITCHELL, Henry. (Pvt.) Co. A, 39th Regiment
Maryland Infantry. (U.S.C.T.) (US) Hagerstown.
Entered service April, 1864. Died in service.
The particulars are unknown. (1890-C)

MITCHELL, Henry F. (Pvt.) Co. G, 1st Potomac Home
Brigade Infantry. (US) Age 19. Knoxville.
Laborer. Enlisted at Point-of-Rocks, 24
October, 1861. Transferred to Co. D.
Discharged 29 May, 1865. (H.R.M.V., Vol. 1,
521) (MSA-S-936-23)

MOATZ, Jacob. (Cpl.) Co. A, 7th Regiment Maryland
Infantry. (US) Tilghmanton. Age 19. Enlisted
at Hagerstown 13 August, 1862. Appointed
corporal 1, November, 1862. Discharged at
Arlington Heights, Va., 31 May, 1865) (Sharf,
226) (H.R.M.V., Vol. 1, 279) (MSA-AGR, Vol. 1,
250 and MSA-S-936-17)

MOATS, Jonathan. (Pvt.) Co. A, 3rd Maryland
Infantry. (US) Washington Co. Enlisted at
Hagerstown, 28 July, 1861. Discharged with
surgeon's certificate as disabled, at Arlington
Heights, Va., 6 February, 1865. Buried in the
Bakersville Cemetery, near Eakle's Crossroads.
(WCCR, Vol. 5) (H.R.M.V., Vol. 1, 119)

MOATZ, William E. (Pvt.) Co. A, 7th Regiment
Maryland Infantry. (US) Tilghmanton. Age 24.
Began service 11 August, 1862. Deserted 18
March, 1864. (Scharf, Vol. 1 226) (H.R.M.V.,
Vol. 1, 279) (MSA-AGR, Vol. 1, 250 and MSA-S-
936-17)

MOBLEY, Carver E. (Pvt.) Co. A, 7th Regiment
Maryland Infantry. (US) Hagerstown. Age 17.
Entered service 18 August, 1862. A son of Col.
Edward Mobley of the same regiment. Patient at
Slough Barracks Hospital, Alexandria, Va.
Discharged 31 May, 1865, at Arlington Heights,
Va. (Scharf, Vol. 1, 226) (H.R.M.V., Vol. 1,
279) (MSA-AGR, Vol. 1, 250 and MSA-S-936-17)

MOBLEY, Edward M. "Ned" (Col.) Co. A, 7th
Regiment Maryland Infantry. (US) Hagerstown.
Age 37. Entered service as captain, 8 August,
1862, in Co. A, which he helped to raise;
promoted major 21 January, 1864; brevet
lieutenant-colonel 9 April, 1865 for gallant
and meritorious services during the campaign
terminating with the surrender of Lee's army;
brevet colonel 13 March, 1865 for faithful and
gallant services. Mobley was wounded in the
leg at Bethesda Church, Va., 27 May, 1864. He
bravely wrapped cloth around the bleeding leg,
refused to leave the battlefield, and continued
to direct his men. He was wounded again, this
time in the neck, 18 August, 1864 at Weldon
R.R., Va. When several regimental color
bearers fell to enemy fire, Mobley went to
their assistance, grabbing the staff as it was
about to touch the ground. Almost immediately
he was shot in the neck. His men rushed to his
assistance, raised him up, and the colors

continued to fly. During the war Col. Mobley
served as provost marshal at various times
including Williamsport and Harper's Ferry.
Before the war he engaged in the family
business of carriage manufacture and was
elected sheriff of Washington County on the
Union ticket in 1859, serving two years. The
1860 Census of Washington County lists Mobley
as the jailer with family members including
wife Ellen, 33, and children, Carver Edward 15,
Walter Albert 13, James, 10, William E., 8,
Henry, 5, Jesse M., 3 and Lewis 6/12. After the
war Mobley became a collector of taxes from
1866 to 1867 and later served sixteen years in
the assessor's office of the U. S. Internal
Revenue Service, at 4 Public Square. The
colonel died of paralysis, 4 April, 1906, at
his home, 525 North Locust Street. He was 81.
Burial services at Rose Hill Cemetery,
Hagerstown, were attended by many members of
the colonel's command, marching in a solemn
procession from his home to the site. Mobley's
recommendation for the brevet rank of Colonel
of Volunteers reads as follows;

        Washington, D.C., April 24, 1866.
To the Adjutant General.
        United States Army:

Sir: I respectfully beg leave to recommend for
brevet appointments a number of officers of the
volunteer service..(including) Major E. M.
Mobley, who, in much of the campaign of 1864,
commanded the Seventh Regiment Maryland
Volunteers, to be Colonel of Volunteers, by
brevet, for faithful and gallant service.

        Very respectfully
            Your obedient servant,
                G. K. Warren
    Former Major-General Vols., Comd,g Fifth
Army Corps.
(Scharf, 328) (H.R.M.V., Vol. 1, 277) (Dorrance
collection: letter 24 August, 1862.) (WCCR,
Vol. 7, 406) (1890-C) (Portrait and
Bibliographical Records of the Sixth

Congressional District, of Maryland, for 1898, pages 161-165) (Mobley Collection-various, including his obituary) (company roster, MSA-S-936-17) (M. F. D., 788) (Camper and Kirkley, 123, 223-24, 305) (The 1877-78 Sheriff's Hagerstown, Maryland Town Directory, page 111) (The Hagerstown Herald- Mail newspaper, 12 April, 1906)

MOBLEY, Walter A. (Cpl.) Co. A, 7th Regiment Maryland Infantry. (US) Hagerstown. Age 18. Served from 18 August, 1862 to 31 May, 1865. (Scharf, 226) (H.R.M.V., Vol. 1, 279) (MSA-AGR, Vol. 1, 250 and MSA-S-936-17)

MONATH, Jacob W. (Pvt.) Co. K, 107th Regiment of Pennsylvania Volunteers. (US) Hagerstown. Served in the first brigade, second division, 3rd Army Corps, Army of the Potomac. Fought at Cedar Mountain and Second Bull Run where he was severely injured in the right hip. Returned to Hagerstown after the war and became a barber. (Williams, Vol. 2, 1035)

MONG, William H. (Sgt.) Co. L, (sergeant of commissary) 1st Regiment Potomac Home Brigade "Cole's" Cavalry. (US) Huyetts. Served from 28 May, 1864 to 12 August, 1864. Deserted on latter date. Veteran. (H.R.M.V., Vol. 1, 697) (1890-C)

MONGAN, David F. (Pvt.) Co. H, 13th Regiment Maryland Infantry. (US) Hagerstown. Served from 31 January, 1865 to 29 May, 1865. (H.R.M.V., Vol. 1, 453) (1890-C)

MONGAN, Dennis. (Pvt.) Co. H, 1st Regiment Potomac Home Brigade Infantry. (US) Sharpsburg. Served 18 February, 1865 to 29 May, 1865. Also served in Co H, 13th Maryland Infantry. Buried at Mountain View Cemetery, Sharpsburg. (H.R.M.V., Vol. 1, 527) (WCCR Vol. 1, 14) (1890-C)

MONGAN, Henry W. (Pvt.) Co. A, 3rd Regiment Maryland Infantry. (US) Age 25. Enlisted 12

September, 1861. Served initially with Co. I,
Virginia Union Volunteers, later the 3rd
Maryland Infantry. Contracted chronic diarrhea
during the summer of 1862. Hospitalized at
Smoketown, near the Antietam Battlefield, after
battle of Antietam. In 1863, following the
battle of Gettysburg was hospitalized in
Virginia. Later transferred to V.R.C. 13
November, 1863. (H.R.M.V., Vol. 1, 119)
(Information provided by Justin Mayhew, of
Hagerstown, a descendent. Also from post-war
pension affidavits of Frederick Colbert, of
Hagerstown, Dr. John McPherson Scott, also of
Hagerstown and Martin L. Moats, of Fairplay.
Department of the Interior, Bureau of Pensions
file, dated 20 January, 1905)

MONGAN, Peter. (Pvt.) Co. A, 3rd Regiment
Maryland Infantry. (US) Age 38. Enlisted at
Williamsport, 12 August, 1861. Discharged 12
August, 1865. (H.R.M.V., Vol. 1, 119)
(MSA-AGR, Vol. 1, 236)

MONGAN, Samuel. (Pvt.) Co. A, 3rd Regiment
Maryland Infantry. (US) Age 38. Enlisted at
Williamsport, 15 June, 1861. Discharged 15
June, 1865. (H.R.M.V., Vol. 1, 119) (MSA-AGR,
Vol. 1, 236)

MONROE J. (or Munroe) G. (Pvt.) Co. A, 7th
Regiment Maryland Infantry. (US) Washington
County. Age 23. Entered service 12 August,
1862, at Hagerstown. Deserted 25 August, 1862,
at Baltimore. (H.R.M.V., Vol. 1, 279) (MSA-AGR,
Vol. 1, 251 and MSA-S-936-17)

MONTGOMERY, Joseph. (1st Sgt.) Co. K, 97th
Pennsylvania Volunteer Infantry. (US) Hancock.
Buried in Mt. Olivet Cemetery, west of
Hancock. (WCCR Vol. 2, 139)

MONTGOMERY, Solomon J. (Pvt.) Battery A, 1st
United States Artillery. (US) Trego. Served
from 14 November, 1862 to 14 November, 1865.
Census report indicates that in this period he
also served three months in the 2nd New York

Artillery and 18 months in the 91st New York
Artillery. (1890-C)

MOORE, John H. (Cpl.) Co. H, 6th Regiment
Maryland Infantry. (US) Hagerstown. Age 18.
Enlisted at Hagerstown 21 August, 1862.
Discharged at Washington, D.C., 20 June, 1865.
(H.R.M.V., Vol. 1, 242) (1890-C) (MSA-AGR, Vol.
1, 249 and S-936-2))

MOORE, John H. (Pvt.) Co. A, 1st Maryland Potomac
Home Brigade Infantry. (US) Hagerstown.
Served from 15 August, 1861 to 27 August, 1864.
Buried in Samples Manor Cemetery. (H.R.M.V.,
Vol. 1, 489) (WCCR, Vol. 4, 69-70)

MOORE, Mouter F. (Pvt.) (US) Indian Springs.
Teamster. Unit and dates of service not shown
on census report. (1890-C)

MOORE, Ridgley. (Pvt.) Co. A, 1st Maryland
Potomac Home Brigade. (US) Sharpsburg. Served
from 15 August, 1851 to 29 May, 1865.
Transferred to Co. A, 13th Maryland Infantry.
(H.R.M.V., Vol. 1, 489) (1890-C)

MOORE, William W. (Pvt.) Co. H, 6th Regiment
Maryland Infantry. (US) Age 24. Enlisted at
Hagerstown, 14 August, 1862. Died from the
premature discharge of his musket 13 November,
1862, at Williamsport, Md. (H.R.M.V., Vol. 1,
242) (MSA-AGR, Vol. 1, 289 and 936-2)

MORGAN, Jacob. (Pvt.) Co. G, 1st Regiment
Maryland Infantry. (US) Brownsville. Served
from 29 September, 1864 to 3 June, 1865.
(H.R.M.V., Vol. 1, 54) (1890-C)

MORGAN, Joseph. (Pvt.) Co. E, 3rd Regiment
Potomac Home Brigade Infantry. (US)
Brownsville. Served from 3 April, 1865 to 29
May, 1865. (H.R.M.V., Vol. 1, 590) (1890-C)

MORGAN, Lawson. (Pvt.) Co. D, 13th Regiment
Maryland Infantry. (US) Age 21. Boatman. Served
from 15 August, 1861 to 29 May, 1865. Veteran.

Transferred from Co. D, 1st Potomac Home
Brigade Infantry. (H.R.M.V., Vol. 1, 443, 504)
(MSA-AGR 936-22)

MORGAN, Levi. (Pvt.) Co. A, 7th Regiment Maryland
Infantry. (US) Age 23. Enlisted at Hagerstown,
3 March, 1863. No further information
available. (MSA-AGR, Vol. 1, 251)

MORGAN, William. (Pvt.) Co. I, 7th Regiment
Maryland Infantry. (US) Age 26. Enlisted at
Hagerstown, 19 August, 1862. Transferred to
brigade band 1 May, 1863. (H.R.M.V., Vol. 1,
298) (MSA-AGR, Vol. 1, 253)

MORRISON, Calvin B. (Pvt.) Co. M, 1st Regiment
Maryland Cavalry. (US) Age 29. Salesman.
Williamsport. Enlisted 22 February at
Williamsport. Discharged 8 August, 1865.
(H.R.M.V., Vol. 1, 743) (MSA-AGR-S-936-36)

MORRISON, George W. B. (1st Lt.) Co. A, 3rd
Regiment Maryland Infantry. (US) Hagerstown.
Began service as second lieutenant in 1st
Virginia Union Infantry 26 November, 1861,
later transferred to 3rd Maryland; first
lieutenant 1 May, 1862. Discharged 27 May,
1862. (Scharf, 328) (H.R.M.V., Vol. 1, 116)
(1890-C)

MORRISON, Josiah (Pvt.) Co. I, 1st Regiment
"Russell's" Maryland Cavalry. (US)
Williamsport. Boatman. Entered service at age
22, served from 3 September, 1861 to 3
September, 1864. (H.R.M.V., Vol. 1, 734)
(1890-C) (1860-C, 75)

MORT, William. (Pvt.) Co. G, 102nd Pennsylvania
Infantry Regiment. (US) Leitersburg. Served
from 20 May, 1864 to 28 June, 1865. (1890-C)

MONTGOMERY, Levi. (Pvt.) Co. E, 1st Regiment
Maryland Cavalry. (US) Williamsport. Served
from 22 February, 1864 to 8 August, 1865.
(H.R.M.V., Vol. 1, 721) (1890-C)

MOSE, Alfred. (Pvt.) Co. A, 1st Regiment Potomac
Home Brigade Infantry. (US) Sharpsburg. Served
from 15 August, 1861 to 27 August, 1864.
(H.R.M.V., Vol. 1, 489) (1890-C)

MOSE, Daniel. Co. A, 1st Regiment Potomac Home
Brigade Infantry. (US) Sharpsburg. Enlisted 15
August, 1861. Discharged 27 August, 1864.
(H.R.M.V., Vol. 1, page 489) (reference 824-
7506)

MOSE, Jacob. (Pvt.) Co. A, 1st Regiment Potomac
Home Brigade Infantry. (US) Sharpsburg. Served
15 August, 1861 to 27 August, 1864. Buried in
Mountain View Cemetery, Sharpsburg. (H.R.M.V.,
Vol. 1, 489) (WCCR Vol. 1, 51)

MOSE, Peter. (2nd Lt.) Co. H, 7th Maryland
Infantry. (US) Sharpsburg. Served from 10
September, 1861 to 25 Oct. 1866. (1890-C)

MOSE, Samuel. (Pvt.) Co. H., 1st Regiment Potomac
Home Brigade Infantry. (US) Sharpsburg. Served
from 8 February, 1865 to 29 May, 1865. Buried
in Mountain View Cemetery, Sharpsburg.
(H.R.M.V., Vol. 1, 527) (1890-C)

MOSE, William. (Pvt.) Co. A, 1st Regiment Potomac
Home Brigade Infantry. (US) Sharpsburg. Served
15 August, 1861 to 27 August, 1864. Buried in
Lutheran graveyard, Main Street, Sharpsburg.
(H.R.M.V., Vol. 1, 489) (WCCR Vol. 1, 74)

MOSIER, John. (US) (Pvt.) Indian Springs.
Teamster. Unit and dates of service not shown
on census report. (1890-C)

MOST, George. (Pvt.) (Unit unknown) Killed at
Gettysburg, 3 July, 1863. Age 18. Buried in
Rose Hill Cemetery, Hagerstown. (WCCR, Vol.
7, 230)

MOWEN, Adam R. (Pvt.) Co. K, 143 Pennsylvania
Volunteer Infantry. (US) Washington Co. (WCCR,
Vol. 7, 267)

MOWEN, John. (Pvt.) Co. D, 139th Regiment
Pennsylvania Infantry. (US) Broadfording.
Served from 21 October, 1862 to 21 August,
1863. (1890-C)

MOXLEY, Joseph. (Pvt.) Musician First Class,
Moxley's Number One Brigade Band. (U.S.C.T.)
(US) Born at Hancock, resided at Hagerstown. A
slave owned by Ranney Hunter. Before the war
was a member of brother "Robert Moxley's Band."
Worked as waiter and farmhand. Joined at
Hagerstown 8 September, 1863, mustered into
service 26 September, 1863, at Baltimore.
Mustered out 20 April, 1866, at Baltimore.
Died at Hagerstown 1 September 1884 of scurvy
contracted while at Brownsville, Texas. He
complained to his day of death of severe pain
in his side from forging the Rappahannock River
after the Battle of the Wilderness in 1864. He
applied for and received a pension for his
disabilities that included chronic rheumatism,
and impaired vision. Buried in Beautiful View
Cemetery, near State Line. (WCCR, Vol. 6, 60)

MOXLEY, Perry L. (Pvt.) Member Moxley's Number
One Brigade Band. (U.S.C.T.) (US) Age 23.
Hagerstown. Worked at Washington House and at
the Thomas Grove farm, near Hagerstown. Free
man at time of marriage 1 April, 1861.
Enlisted at Grove farm, 28 August, 1863.
Disabled due to chronic rheumatism, and kidney
disease. Discharged at Brownsville, Texas, 20
April, 1866. Died at Hagerstown 7 September,
1900. (Maryland State Archives summary sheet
of material from National Archives, not
numbered)

MOXLEY, Robert. (Pvt.) Leader "Moxley's Band," at
Hagerstown and Number One Brigade Band.
(U.S.C.T.) (US) Hagerstown. Laborer. Band was
mustered into service for recruiting at the
request of Gen. William Birney. Contracted
chronic rheumatism and disease of the eyes from
lying on wet ground while on duty in front of
Petersburg, Va., December, 1864. Discharged at
Brownsville, Texas, 20 April, 1866. (Bureau of

MOXLEY, William. (Pvt.) Co. B, 3rd Regiment
Potomac Home Brigade Infantry. (US) Age 32.
Hagerstown. Enlisted at Hagerstown, 30
October, 1861. Transferred to Co. F.
Discharged 31 October, 1864. (H.R.M.V., Vol. 1,
578) (Captain Maxwell's roster) (MSA-S-936-23)

MULL, George W. (Pvt.) Co. A, 13th Regiment
Maryland Infantry. (US) Downsville. Served from
15 February, 1865 to 29 May, 1865. (H.R.M.V.,
Vol. 1, 434) (1890-C)

MULLENDORE, Josiah E. (2nd Lt.) Co. E, 1st
Regiment Potomac Home Brigade Infantry. (US)
Rohrersville. (War Department records spell his
name Millendore) Began service as private, rose
to second lieutenant 20 December, 1863.
(Scharf, 328) (H.R.M.V., Vol. 1, 505.)

MUNSON, Calvin I. (Sgt.) Co. H, 3rd Maryland
Cavalry. (US) Washington Co. Served from 28
September, 1863 to 7 September, 1865. Buried
in Rose Hill Cemetery, Hagerstown. (H.R.M.V.,
Vol. 1, 775) (WCCR, Vol.6, 255)

MUNSON, Cyrus. (Pvt.) Co. H, 13th Regiment
Maryland Infantry. (US) Sharpsburg. Served from
18 February, 1865 to 29 May, 1865. (H.R.M.V.,
Vol. 1, 453) (1890-C)

MURPHY, William. (Pvt.) Co. B, 7th Regiment
Maryland Infantry. (US) Age 18. Enlisted at
Hagerstown, 3 November, 1862. Deserted at
Hagerstown, 22 December 1862. (H.R.M.V., Vol.
1, 282) (MSA-AGR, Vol. 1, 251)

MURRAY, Martin V. B. (Pvt.) Co. G, 1st Regiment
Potomac Home Brigade "Cole's" Cavalry. (US)
Green Spring Furnace. Served from 14 February,
1865 to 28 June, 1865. (H.R.M.V., Vol. 1, 688)
(1890-C)

MUSE, Alfred. (Pvt.) Co. A, 1st Regiment Potomac
Home Brigade Infantry. (US) Sharpsburg.

Served from 15 August, 1862 to 27 August, 1864. (H.R.M.V., Vol. 1, 489) (WCCR Vol. 1, 26)

MUST, Christian. (Pvt.) Co. I, 7th Regiment Maryland Infantry. (US) Age 25. Enlisted at Hagerstown, 29 August, 1862. Wounded in action, hospitalized at Baltimore. Transferred to V.R.C. 21 January, 1865. Discharged 7 July, 1865. (H.R.M.V., Vol. 1, 298) (MSA-AGR, Vol. 1, 253)

MYERS, Edwin H. (Pvt.) Co. M, 17th Pennsylvania Volunteer Cavalry. (US) Washington Co. Buried in Rose Hill Cemetery, Hagerstown. (WCCR, Vol. 7, 232)

MYERS, Emanuel. (Sgt.) Co. G, 1st Regiment Potomac Home Brigade "Cole's" Cavalry. (US) Green Spring Furnace. Served from 26 February, 1864 to 26 June, 1865. (H.R.M.V., Vol. 1, 687) (1890-C)

MYERS, Henry J. (Pvt.) (US) Unit unknown. (1890-C) (Scharf, Vol. 1, 226)

MYERS, John W. (Pvt.) Co. G, 1st Regiment Potomac Home Brigade "Cole's" Cavalry. (US) Hagerstown. Enlisted at Hagerstown, 4 August, 1864. Discharged 25 May, 1865. (H.R.M.V., Vol. 1, 688) (MSA-AGR-S-936-38)

MYERS, Josiah. (Pvt.) Co. A, 7th Regiment Maryland Infantry. (US) Washington County. Age 21. Entered service 14 August, 1862, at Hagerstown. Transferred to Co. C, 1st Maryland Infantry. Deserted 9 February, 1863. Returned 15 January, 1864 to complete obligation. (Scharf, Vol. 1 226) (H.R.M.V., Vol. 1, 279) (MSA-S-936-17)

MYERS, John. (Pvt.) Co. H., 1st Maryland Volunteer Infantry. (US) Washington Co. Served from 2 February, 1865 until 2 July, 1865. Wounded in action at Five Forks, Va., 1 April, 1865. Buried in the Sandy Hook Cemetery. (H.R.M.V., Vol. 1, 59) (WCCR, Vol. 4, 78.)

MYERS, Levi. (Pvt.) Co. F, 1st Regiment Potomac Home Brigade Infantry. (US) Millstone. Served from 15 August, 1862 to 29 May, 1865. Transferred to Co. F, 13th Maryland Infantry. (H.R.M.V., Vol. 1, 514) (1890-C)

MYERS, Reuben. (Pvt.) Co. B, 3rd Regiment Potomac Home Brigade Infantry. (US) Age 24. Farmer. Boonsboro. Enlisted at Hagerstown, 23 October, 1861. Veteran. Transferred to Co. F. Died 12 January, 1865. (H.R.M.V., Vol. 1, 593) (Captain Maxwell's roster) (MSA-S-936-23)

MYERS, Samuel. (Pvt.) Co. H., 1st Maryland Volunteer Infantry. (US) Washington Co. Buried in the Sandy Hook Cemetery. (WCCR, Vol. 4, 79)

MYERS, Soloman. (Pvt.) Co. G, 1st Regiment Potomac Home Brigade "Cole's" Cavalry. (US) Age 37. A laborer. Ringgold. Served from 20 February, 1864 to 28 June, 1865. Discharged with disease of the eyes. (H.R.M.V., Vol. 1, 688) (1890-C) (MSA-AGR-S-936-38)

MYERS, Walter S. (Pvt.) Co. B, 1st Potomac Home Brigade (Cole's) Cavalry. (US) Clear Spring. Served 24 August, 1861 to 15 September, 1864. Taken prisoner 10 January, 1864. Sent to Andersonville, Ga., prison where he died. (H.R.M.V., Vol. 1, 678) (National Archives)

MYERS, William. (Pvt.) Co. B, 3rd Regiment Potomac Home Brigade Infantry. (US) Millstone. Served from 6 November, 1861 to 6 November, 1864.(H.R.M.V., Vol. 1, 578) (1890-C)

MYERS, William H. (Pvt.) Co. E, 3rd Regiment Potomac Home Brigade Infantry. (US) Four Locks. Served from 12 November, 1861 to 29 May, 1865. Veteran. (H.R.M.V., Vol. 1, 590) (1890-C)

-- N --

NAIL, John. (Pvt.) Co. I, 7th Regiment Maryland Infantry. (US) Age 36. Enlisted at Hagerstown,

22 September, 1862. Discharged 31 May, 1865.
(H.R.M.V., Vol. 1, 255) (MSA-AGR, Vol. 1, 255)

NAPE, John. (2nd Lt.) Co. B, 3rd Regiment
Maryland Infantry. (US) Washington County.
Began service 16 December, 1861 as private in
Co. D, later sergeant-major. Veteran volunteer.
Second lieutenant 2 March, 1865. Died 15 April,
1865 of wounds received in action 25 March,
1865. (Scharf, 328) (H.R.M.V., Vol. 1, 122)

NEGLEY, Robert P. (Pvt.) 5th Regiment Virginia
Infantry. (CSA) Hagerstown. Service dates not
available. Shot in left hand. (1890-C)

NELSON, William. (Pvt.) Co. D, 13th Regiment
Maryland Infantry. (US) Washington County.
Served from 12 August, 1862 to 29 May, 1865.
Buried in graveyard on the Charles Virts farm
near Sandy Hook. (H.R.M.V., Vol. 1, 443) (WCCR,
Vol. 4, page 80)

NESBITT, Alexander A. (Capt.) Co. I, 1st
Regiment Maryland Cavalry. (US) Clear Spring.
Entered service as first lieutenant of 1st
Virginia Union Cavalry 20 August, 1861;
promoted captain 9 September, 1862. Died 9
March, 1863, at age 29. Buried in St. John's
Episcopal Church Cemetery, Hagerstown.
(Scharf, Vol. 1, 328; Vol. 2, 1087) (H.R.M.V.,
Vol. 1, 731) (WCCR, Vol. 7, 454)

NESBITT, Henry C. (Pvt.) Co. A, 7th Regiment
Maryland Infantry. (US) Washington County. Age
19. Served from 12 August, 1862 to 31 May,
1865. (Scharf, Vol. 1, 226) (H.R.M.V., Vol. 1,
279) (MSA-S-936-17)

NESBITT, Thomas S. (1st Lt.) 7th Regiment
Maryland Infantry. (US) Age 24. Clear Spring.
Began service as private in Co. A, later
sergeant-major, then first lieutenant and on 8
September, 1862, regimental quartermaster.
(Scharf, 328) (H.R.M.V., Vol. 1, 277) (Camper
and Kirkley, 123) (MSA-AGR, Vol. 1, page 255
and MSA-S-936-17)

NEWBRY, John W. (Pvt.) Co. H, 17th North Carolina
Infantry. (CSA) Smithsburg. (Hartzler, 233)

NEWCOMER, Jacob F. (Pvt.) Co. H, 6th Regiment
Maryland Infantry, (US) Age 18. Hagerstown.
Entered service at Hagerstown, 2 Aug., 1862.
Wounded in action 27 Nov., 1863, at Mine Run,
Va. (H.R.M.V., Vol. 1, 242) (MSA-AGR, Vol. 1,
255 and 936-2)

NEWMAN, Joseph. (Pvt.) Co. E, 1st Regiment
Potomac Home Brigade Infantry. (US) Age 20.
Laborer. Washington County. Enlisted 1 August,
1862. Transferred to Co.E, 13th Regiment
Maryland Infantry. Discharged 29 May, 1865.
(H.R.M.V., Vol. 1, 509. (MSA-S-936-23)

NICKOLS, William Augustas. (Cpl.) Co. A, 7th
Regiment Maryland Infantry. (US) Age 24.
Hagerstown. Enlisted at Hagerstown 9 Aug.1862.
Appointed corporal 1 March, 1865. Wounded in
action 1 April, 1865, at Five Forks, Va.
Hospitalized in Douglas U. S. General Hospital,
Washington, D.C. Discharged at Washington D.C.,
June, 1865. (Sharf, 226) (H.R.M.V., Vol. 1,
280) (MSA-AGR, Vol. 1, 255) and MSA-S-936-17)

NICODEMUS, Ezra H. (Pvt.) Co. B, 11th Regiment
Maryland Infantry.(US) Sharpsburg. Served from
26 May, to 29 Sept. 1864. (H.R.M.V., Vol. 1,
379) (1890-C) (Scharf, Vol. 1, 226)

NIGH, John W. (Pvt.) Co. C, 1st Regiment Potomac
Home Brigade "Cole's" Cavalry. (US)
Leitersburg. Served from 17 Sept. 1862, to 25
May, 1865. Discharged with disease. (H.R.M.V.,
Vol. 1, 676) (1890-C)

NIGH, Samuel T. (Cpl.) Co. A, 7th Regiment
Maryland Infantry. (US) Age 25. Enlisted at
Hagerstown 15 Aug. 1862. Transferred to brigade
band, 1 May, 1863. No record of discharge.
(Scharf, 226) (H.R.M.V., Vol. 1, 280) (MSA-AGR,
Vol. 1, 255 and MSA-S-936-17)

NITZELL, William L. (Pvt.) Co. I, 1st Regiment

"Russell's" Maryland Cavalry. (US)
Williamsport. Enlisted at Williamsport, 17
Dec. 1862. Discharged 8 August, 1865.
(H.R.M.V., Vol. 1, 732) (MSA-AGR-S-936-28)

NOEL, Gilbert. (Pvt.) Co. I, 1st Regiment Potomac
Home Brigade "Cole's" Cavalry. (US) Age 22.
Laborer. Williamsport. Enlisted Williamsport,
16 February, 1864. No further record available.
(MSA-AGR-S-936-36)

NOILE, John T. (2nd Lt.) Co. G, 1st Regiment
Potomac Home Brigade "Cole's" Cavalry. (US)
Hancock. Served from 26 Feb. 1864 to 28 June,
1865. Entered service as private in Co. G;
promoted first sergeant; second lieutenant, 20
August, 1864. Mustered out 20 June, 1865.
(Scharf, 328) (H.R.M.V., Vol. 1, 686) (1890-C)

NORFORD, Joseph G. (Pvt.) Co. H, 6th Regiment
Maryland Infantry.(US) Age 32. Smithsburg.
Entered service 21 Aug. 1862. Sick, left camp
at Williamsport, Md., 23 Oct. 1862, Returned to
service. Captured at Winchester, Va. 15 June,
1863. Confined at Richmond, Va. Paroled at City
Point, Va., 23 July, 1863. Reported to Camp
Parole, Md, 24 July, 1863. Returned to regiment
12 October, 1863. Missing in action after
Wilderness campaign, 5 May, 1864. Paroled at
Charleston, SC, 11 Dec. 1864. Captured later in
Dec. 1864, and died while a prisoner of war.
Pension No. 119649. (H.R.M.V., Vol. 1, 242)
(1890-C) (MSA-AGR-S-936-2) (Additional
information provided by Mr. Ronald G. Norford,
of Hagerstown)

NORRIS, John Williams. (Pvt.) Co. H, 1st
Regiment Potomac Home Brigade Infantry. (US)
Rohrersville. Enlisted 1 Oct. 1861. Drowned
while crossing the Potomac River with two
companions 21 May, 1862. Son of George and
Katherine Kefauver Norris. (Williams, 875)
(H.R.M.V., Vol. 1, 509) Pensions on the Roll as
of Jan. 1, 1883. Vol. 5. U. S. Government
Printing Office, Wash. D.C.

NORRIS, Nathan. (Pvt.) Co. F, 1st Regiment
Potomac Home Brigade Infantry. (US) Age 44.
Farmer. Hancock. Enlisted at Hancock, 28
February, 1864. Died 26 September, 1864.
(H.R.M.V., Vol. 1, 514) (MSA-S-936-23)

NORRIS, Otha. (Pvt.) Co. G, 1st Regiment Potomac
Home Brigade Cavalry. (US) Williamsport.
Saddler. Served from 26 February, 1864 to 28
June, 1865. He is buried in a Cumberland, Md.,
cemetery. (H.R.M.V., Vol. 1, 688)

NORRIS, Silas H. (Pvt.) Co. E, 13th Regiment
Maryland Infantry. (US) Age 19. Farmer.
Brownsville. Enlisted at Sandy Hook, 26 Jan.
1865. Discharged 29 May, 1865. (H.R.M.V., Vol.
1, 445) (1890-C) (MSA-AGR-S-936-22)

NORRIS, William H. (Pvt.) Co. D, 1st Regiment
Potomac Home Brigade Infantry. (US) Age 18.
Laborer. Enlisted at Sandy Hook, 12 Oct.1864.
Transferred to Co. D, 13th Regiment Maryland
Infantry. Discharged 29 May, 1865. (H.R.M.V.,
Vol. 1, 443) (MSA-AGR-S-936-22)

NOWEL, William. (Pvt.) Co. I, 1st Regiment
"Russell's" Maryland Cavalry. (US)Williamsport.
Served from 3 Sept. 1861 to 3 September, 1864.
(H.R.M.V., Vol. 1, 734) (1890-C)

NULL, James A. (Pvt.) Co. F, 1st Regiment Potomac
Home Brigade Infantry. (US) Age 19. Laborer.
Washington County. Enlisted 4 Sept. 1861.
Transferred to Co. F, 13th Regiment Maryland
Infantry. In confinement at time of scheduled
discharge. No further record. (H.R.M.V., Vol.
1, 514. (MSA-S-936-23)

NUSE, Daniel. (Pvt.) Co. D, 1st Regiment Potomac
Home Brigade Infantry. (US) Age 19. Laborer.
Sharpsburg. Enlisted Sharpsburg, 15 Aug. 1861.
Veteran. Transferred to Co. D, 13th Regiment
Maryland Infantry. Discharged 29 May,
1865.(H.R.M.V., Vol. 1, 504)(MSA-AGR-S-936-22)

NUSE, Hezikiah. (Pvt.) Co. D, 1st Regiment

Potomac Home Brigade Infantry. (US) Age 21.
Laborer. Sharpsburg. Enlisted at Sharpsburg, 15
Aug. 1861. Veteran. Transferred to Co. D, 13th
Regiment Maryland Infantry. Discharged 29 May,
1865.(H.R.M.V., Vol. 1, 504) (MSA-AGR-S-936-22)

-- O --

OAKER, Charles. (Cpl.) Co. B, 3rd Regiment
Potomac Home Brigade Infantry. (US)   Age 22.
Hagerstown.   Enlisted at Hagerstown 14 October,
1861.   Transferred to Co. F.   Discharged 14
October, 1864.   (H.R.M.V., Vol. 1, 578)
(Captain Maxwell's roster) (MSA-S-936-23)

O'BRIST (?), John. (Sgt.) 8th Regiment Maryland
Infantry. (US) Brownsville. Served from 1861 to
1866. (1890-C)

ODEN, (or Owden) Nathaniel A. (Pvt.) Co. F, 1st
Regiment Potomac Home Brigade Infantry.   (US)
Chewsville.   Served from 2, April, 1864 to 29
May, 1864.   Transferred to Co. F, 13th Maryland
Infantry. (H.R.M.V., Vol. 1, 514) (1890-C)

O'HIRK (?) Jacob R. (Pvt.) Co. B, 3rd Regiment
Maryland Infantry. (US) Hagerstown. Entered
service 2 October, 1861. Other dates not
available. (1890-C)

O'NEAL, Thomas. (Pvt.) Co. I, 1st Regiment
"Russell's" Maryland Cavalry. (US)   Age 25.
Laborer.   Williamsport.   Enlisted at
Williamsport, 17 December, 1862. Discharged 8
August, 1865.   (H.R.M.V., Vol. 1, 734) (1890-C)
(1860-C, 91) (MSA-AGR-S-936-38)

OSTER, John. (Pvt.) Co. D, 12th Regiment Maryland
Infantry. (US)   Chewsville.   Served from 26
July, 1864 to 6 November, 1864. Discharge lost.
(H.R.M.V., Vol. 1, 428) (1890-C)

-- P --

PACUTT (?), Ephram W. (Pvt.) Co. H, 7th Regiment
Maryland Infantry.   (US)   Hagerstown.   Served

from February, 1862 to 19 November, 1865.
Chronic dysentery. (1890-C)

PAMPELL, Jerome E. (Sgt.) Co. B, 3rd Regiment
Maryland Infantry. (US) Age 24. Williamsport.
Enlisted at Williamsport 3 June, 1861. Wounded
in action 9 November, 1863, in Tennessee. Loss
of left arm and portion of right hand.
Discharged for disability 1 June, 1864.
(H.R.M.V., Vol. 1, 125) (MSA-AGR, Vol. 1, 291)

PARKER, William G. (Pvt.) Co. I, 1st Regiment
"Russell's" Maryland Cavalry. (US)
Williamsport. Painter. Age 19. Served from 21
October, 1861 to 1 October, 1864. Wounded at
Deep Bottom, Va., 16 August, 1864. (H.R.M.V.,
Vol. 1, 734)(McClannahan papers, 4)(1860-C, 90)

PARKS, George. (Pvt.) Co. I, 7th Regiment
Maryland Infantry. (US) Age 37. Enlisted at
Hagerstown, 21 August, 1863. Died 9 December,
1863 of disease contracted in service.
(H.R.M.V., Vol. 1, 298) (MSA-AGR, Vol. 1, 296)

PEACHER, Oliver. (Pvt.) Co. A, 1st Regiment
Potomac Home Brigade Infantry. (US) Hagerstown
and Harpers Ferry. Signed up at age 21. A farm
laborer. Served from 15 August, 1861 to 27
August, 1864. Buried in Samples Manor
Cemetery. (H.R.M.V., Vol. 1, 490) (WCCR, Vol.
4, 68) (1860-C, 68)

PEAR, James. (Pvt.) Co. A, 7th Regiment Maryland
Infantry. (US) Age 47. Enlisted at Hagerstown,
26 February, 1864. Wounded in action 24 May
1864, at North Anna River, Va. Transferred to
V.R.C. 8 March, 1865. Discharged with
surgeon's certificate 5 May, 1865. (H.R.M.V.,
Vol. 1, 280) (MSA-AGR, Vol. 1, 296)

PELTON, Emery W. (2nd Lt.) Co. G, 2nd Regiment
Potomac Home Brigade Infantry. (US) Hancock.
Served from 16 August, 1861 to 12 March, 1865.
Entered service as sergeant. Promoted second
lieutenant 1 April, 1862. (H.R.M.V., Vol. 1,
560) (1890-C)

PELTZ, James. (Sgt.) Co. A, 7th Regiment Maryland
Infantry. (US) Age 21. Washington County.
Enlisted at Hagerstown 12 August, 1862. Taken
prisoner 18 August, 1864 at Weldon Railroad,
Va. Hospitalized at Camp Parole, Md.
Discharged at Annapolis, Md., 9 June, 1865.
(Scharf, 226) (H.R.M.V., Vol. 1, 280) (MSA-AGR,
Vol. 1, 296 and MSA-S-936-17)

PENNELL, David. (2nd Lt.) Co. A, 1st Regiment
Potomac Home Brigade Infantry. (US) Hagerstown.
Served 15 August, 1861 to 27 August, 1864.
Entered service as first sergeant; promoted
second lieutenant 9 February, 1863. (Scharf,
328) (H.R.M.V., Vol. 1, 486)

PENNELL, George M. (Pvt.) Co. A, 1st Regiment
Potomac Home Brigade. (US) Age 20. Laborer.
Sharpsburg. Enlisted at Sharpsburg, 15 August,
1861. Veteran. Discharged 29 May, 1865. Buried
in Lutheran graveyard, Sharpsburg. (WCCR Vol.
1, 69) (1890-C) (Scharf, Vol. 1, 226)
(H.R.M.V., Vol. 1, 443, 504) (MSA-AGR-S-936-22)

PENNELL, Hezekiah C. (1st Lt.) Co. K, 1st
Regiment Potomac Home Brigade Infantry. (US)
Age 30. School teacher. Sharpsburg. Served from
15 Aug. 1861 to 29 May, 1865. Promoted to first
lieutenant 2 March, 1865. Veteran volunteer.
Later assigned to Co. K, 13th Maryland
Infantry. Discharged 29 May, 1865. (Scharf,
328) (H.R.M.V., Vol. 1, 534) (MSA-AGR-S-936-22)

PENNELL, Isaac. (Pvt.) Co. D, 1st Regiment
Potomac Home Brigade Infantry. (US) Age 19.
Boatman. Enlisted Sharpsburg, 15 August, 1861.
Veteran. Transferred to Co. D, 13th Regiment
Maryland Infantry. Discharged 29 May, 1865.
(H.R.M.V., Vol. 1, 504) (MSA-AGR-S-936-22)

PENNER, Jacob. (Pvt.) (US) Indian Springs.
Teamster. Age 21. Unit and dates of service not
shown on census report. (1890-C)

PENNER, John. (Pvt.) Co. H, 6th Regiment Maryland

Infantry. (US) Age 23. Enlisted at Hagerstown,
21 August, 1862. Deserted at Franklintown, Md.,
7 September, 1862. (H.R.M.V., Vol. 1, 242)
(MSA-AGR, Vol. 1, 295 and S-936-2))

PENNER, John. (Pvt.) Co. F, 2nd Regiment
Pennsylvania Cavalry. (US) Cavetown. Served
from 8 March, 1864 to 16 July, 1865. (1890-C)

PENNER, Samuel. (Pvt.) Captain Firey's Co. B, 1st
Regiment Potomac Home Brigade "Cole's" Cavalry.
(US) Indian Spring. Served from 30 December,
1864 to 28 June, 1865.(H.R.M.V., Vol. 1, 678)
(1890-C)

PERKINS, Dr. William Henry. (Sgt.) "Alexander's"
Baltimore Light Artillery. (US) Born at
Lewistown, in Frederick County, in 1841, he
became a teacher, educating himself in local
schools. After the war he studied medicine at
the University of Maryland and the Long Island
College Hospital of Medicine, in New York. He
graduated in 1866. Moving to Hancock he
established a very successful practice.
Perkins enlisted in the Baltimore Light
Artillery Association, Maryland Volunteers, 14
August, 1862, and was appointed corporal of the
day. After Antietam his battery was assigned to
the Maryland Brigade, commanded by Brig. Gen.
John R. Kenly, U.S. Volunteers, attached to the
Eighth Army Corps, defending the upper Potomac.
His conduct in various engagements, including
Winchester, and Martinsburg, in 1862, and after
Gettysburg, earned a promotion to sergeant. In
1864 he fought at Cedar Creek and the Monocacy.
(Williams, Vol. 2, 917) (H.R.M.V., Part 1, 822)

PERROT, Alexander. (Pvt.) Co. K, 100th Regiment
Pennsylvania Infantry. (US) Four Locks. Served
22 February, 1865 to 24 July, 1865.(1890-C)

PETERKIN, Rev. George William. (Cpl.) (CSA) Clear
Spring. Aide de Camp to Lt. Gen. W. N.
Pendleton. Peterkin was the first rector of
St. Andrews Episcopal Church, at Clear Spring,
Md. (Hartzler, 242) (Local)

PETERS, Louis. (Pvt.) Co. B, 3rd Regiment Potomac
Home Brigade Infantry. (US) Age 40.
Hagerstown. Enlisted at Hagerstown, 19
November, 1861. Transferred to Co. F. Died of
wounds received at Buchanan, W.Va., 24
February, 1865. (H.R.M.V., Vol. 1, 579, 594)
(Captain Maxwell's roster) (MSA-S-936-23)

PICKETT, George P. (Pvt.) Co. H., 6th Regiment
Maryland Cavalry. (US) Age 18. Enlisted at
Hagerstown, 16 August, 1862. Wounded in action
21 September, 1864, at Fisher's Hill, Va.
Discharged near Washington, D. C., 20 June,
1865. (H.R.M.V., Vol. 1, 242) (MSA-AGR, Vol. 1,
291 and 936-2)

PILE, Michael. (Pvt.) Co. H, 3rd Regiment
Maryland Cavalry. (US) Hancock. Served from 28
September, 1863 to 7 September, 1865.
(H.R.M.V., Vol. 1, 776) (1890-C)

PINKNEY, James W. (Pvt.) Co. B, 19th Regiment
Infantry. (U.S.C.T.) (US) Born and raised in
Washington County. Credited to state of
Massachusetts. Laborer. Enlisted Norfolk, Va.,
1 Sept. 1864. Discharged 25 May, 1865.
Disability. Also carried on rolls as John W.
Pinckney.(H.R.M.V., Vol. 2, 212) (MSA-S-936-49)

PITTMAN, Sylvester. (Pvt.) Co. B, 3rd Regiment
Potomac Home Brigade Infantry. (US) Hancock.
Served from 16 November, 1861 to 29 May, 1865.
Veteran. (H.R.M.V., Vol. 1, 578) (1890-C)

PLATT, George A. (Sgt.) Co. I, 1st Regiment
Maryland Cavalry. (US) Washington County.
Entered service 2 December, 1861. (The History
and Roster of Maryland Volunteers lists Platt
as a private and a deserter on 1 September,
1863, page 734. The McClannahan papers list
him as a sergeant and being killed at Brandy
Station on 9 June, 1863, page 4)

POFFENBERGER, Charles. (Pvt.) Co. A, 7th Regiment
Maryland Infantry. (US) Age 17. Hagerstown.

Served from 13 Aug. 1862 to 31 May, 1865. Taken prisoner 16 Sept. 1864. Sent Richmond's Libby Prison where his health deteriorated. (Scharf, Vol. 1, 226) (H.R.M.V., Vol. 1, 280) (1890-C) (MSA-S 936-36 and MSA-S-936-17)

POFFENBERGER, Henry J. (Pvt.) Co. L, 1st Regiment Potomac Home Brigade "Cole's" Cavalry. (US) Chewsville. Served from 29 March, 1864 to 28 June, 1865. (H.R.M.V., Vol. 1, 697) (1890-C)

PORTER, George. (2nd Sgt.) Co. A, 1st Regiment Maryland Infantry. (US) Hagerstown. Served from 12 August, 1861 to 20 September, 1864. (1890-C)

PORTER, Levi. (Sgt.) Co. D, 13th Regiment Maryland Infantry. (US) Sharpsburg. Served from 15 August, 1861 to 29 May, 1865. Veteran soldier. Buried in Mountain View Cemetery, Sharpsburg. (H. R. M. V., Vol. 1, 443) (WCCR, Vol. 1, 8) (1890-C)

POTTER, Noah. (Pvt.) Co. B, 3rd Regiment Maryland Infantry. (US) Age 25. Enlisted at Hancock, 1 October, 1861. Discharged with disability from Baltimore hospital, 1 October, 1864. (H.R.M.V., Vol. 1, 125) (MSA-AGR, Vol. 1, 291)

POTTER, John B. (Pvt.) Co. F, 1st Regiment Potomac Home Brigade Infantry. (US) Age 21. Farmer. Washington County. Enlisted at Sandy Hook, Md., 20 January, 1865. Transferred to Co. F, 13th Regiment Maryland Infantry. Discharged 29 May, 1865. (H.R.M.V., Vol. 1, 514) (MSA-S-936-23)

POTTERFIELD, Jacob A. (Pvt.) Co. F, 13th Regiment Maryland Infantry. (US) Hagerstown. Served from 30 January, 1865 to 29 May, 1865. (H.R.M.V., Vol. 1, 448) (1890-C)

POTTS, Daniel. (Pvt.) Co. E, 1st Regiment Maryland Cavalry. (US) Age 27. Farmer. Hagerstown. Enlisted at Hagerstown, 7 March, 1864. Discharged 8 August, 1865. (H.R.M.V., Vol. 1, 721) (MSA-AGR-S-936-36)

POWELL, Abraham. (Pvt.) Co. C, 3rd Regiment
Potomac Home Brigade Infantry. (US) Chewsville.
Served from 16 October, 1861 to 29 May, 1865.
Veteran. Reenlisted after discharge. Wounded
in action 9 July, 1864. Died 22 July, 1864.
(H.R.M.V., Vol. 1, 582) (1890-C)

POWELL, Basil M. (Pvt.) Co. C, 3rd Regiment
Potomac Home Brigade Infantry. (US) Chewsville.
Served from 21 December, 1861 to 29 May, 1865.
Veteran. (H.R.M.V., Vol. 1, 582) (1890-C)

PRATHER, Samuel G. (Capt.) Co. F, 1st Regiment
Potomac Home Brigade Infantry. (US) Clear
Spring. Prather helped organize his company in
August, 1861. His untimely death, at Frederick,
Md., two months later, at age 29, saddened his
men and his home town. He is buried at Rose
Hill Cemetery, near Clear Spring. His grave is
marked by a tall monument, inscribed in part as
follows; "He was a true man to his country, his
family and posterity...this shaft is erected by
the officers and men of Co. F, 1st Maryland
Regiment, P.H.B." (H.R.M.V., Vol. 1, 510)
(Clear Spring Alumni Association publication
"Windmills of Time," 20 May, 1989)

PRATHER, Thompson Isaac. (Pvt.) Co. F, 1st
Regiment Potomac Home Brigade Infantry. (US)
Clear Spring. Age 26. Laborer. Served from 4
September, 1861 to 5 February, 1863. Died at
home, August, 1863. Buried in the Prather
family cemetery, west of Clear Spring. A
relative of Captain Samuel G. Prather of the
same company and regiment. (U.S National
Archives, Record Group No. 110, 4th Election
District) (H.R.M.V., Vol. 1, 514) (Prather
family history)

PRETZMAN, David C. (Pvt.) Co. A, 1st Maryland
Cavalry, (CSA) Hagerstown. (Hartzler, 248)
(Huntsberry, 83) (Goldsborough, 230)

PRICE, Adrian D. (Cpl.) Co. B, 21st Virginia
Infantry, (CSA) Hagerstown. (Hartzler, 248)

PRICE, Kennedy. (Pvt.) Co. A, 1st Regiment
Maryland Infantry. (CSA) Hagerstown. Service
dates unknown. (1890-C) (Huntsberry, 83)

PRICE, Michael. (Pvt.) Co. A, 184th Regiment
Pennsylvania Infantry. (US) Hancock. Served
from 28 February, 1864 to 16 July, 1865.
Suffered gunshot wound. (1890-C)

PRICE, Samuel R. (Pvt.) (unit unknown) (CSA)
Smithsburg. (Hartzler, 249)

PRICE, Thomas. (Pvt.) Co. D, 1st Regiment Potomac
Home Brigade Infantry. (US) Age 21. Boatman.
Sharpsburg. Enlisted Sharpsburg, 15 Aug. 1861.
Veteran. Transferred to Co. D, 13th Regiment
Maryland Infantry. Discharged 29 May, 1865.
(H.R.M.V., Vol. 1, 504) (MSA-AGR-S-936-22)

PROCTOR, Nelson. (Pvt.) Co. B, 4th Regiment
Infantry. (U.S.C.T.) Maryland Volunteers.
(US) Hancock. Served from 26 August, 1863 to 4
May, 1866. (H.R.M.V., Vol. 2, 135) (1890-C)

PROVIDANCE, James. (Pvt.) Co. G., 3rd Maryland
Infantry. (US) Washington Co. Buried in
Harbaugh's German Reformed Church Cemetery,
near Ringgold. (WCCR, Vol. 4, 123)

PRYOR, James. (Pvt.) Co. I, 1st Regiment
"Russell's" Maryland Cavalry. (US) Hagerstown.
Served from 1 January, 1864 to 23 July, 1865.
(1890-C)

PRYOR, James E. S. (Pvt.) Co. I, 1st Wisconsin
Cavalry. (US) Born near Hagerstown in 1841.
Teacher in Election District 13, at Cearfoss,
until 1863. Relocated to Ogle County, Ill., the
same year and enlisted. Served until 23 July,
1865, under Gen. Sherman. Participated in the
battles of Atlanta and other conflicts. At the
close of the war he returned to Washington
County and taught school again. Later was
admitted to the bar and continued his studies
with Judge A. K. Syester, of Hagerstown. He

also served as surveyor and city engineer for
Hagerstown. (Portrait and Biographical Record
of Sixth Congressional District ofMaryland,
1898, pages 516-17) (Scharf, Vol. 2, 795)

PURNELL, Frederick. (Pvt.) Co. F, 1st Regiment
Potomac Home Brigade Infantry. (US) Hancock.
Served from 4 September, 1861 to 5 February,
1863. (H.R.M.V., Vol. 1, 554) (1890-C)

-- Q --

QUINN, William H. (Pvt.) Co. A, 5th United States
Cavalry. (US) Chewsville. Enlisted in the
general mounted service in 1859 and was sent to
Ft. Smith, Arkansas. Arrived in December of
that year after passing through several Indian
nations. Initially assigned to the 2nd U.S.
Cavalry (later the 5th) and remained at Ft.
Smith until the following summer. Then took up
the trail of the dangerous Comanche Indians who
had committing atrocities among the settlers.
In one engagement the Indians inflicted
numerous wounds on the Federal soldiers,
including Lt. Fitzhugh Lee, a nephew of Gen.
Robert E. Lee. An arrow pierced his right arm,
near the shoulder. Quinn's company remained in
tact as the war began and was designated Co. A,
5th U.S. Cavalry, attached to Brig. Gen.
Wesley Merritt's Reserve Brigade, Gen. John
Buford's 1st Cavalry Division. These men
fought at Martinsburg, Bunker Hill, Cedar Hill,
Yorktown, South Mountain, and Antietam. During
Lee's retreat from Gettysburg, in 1863, in
Washington County, they fought Williamsport,
Funkstown, Boonsboro and along the Falling
Waters Road. (Williams, Vol. 1, 1282)

-- R --

RAMSEY, Sylvester. (Pvt.) 1st United States
Volunteers. (US) Benevola. Served from 1
January, 1864 to 29 June, 1863. General order
discharge. (1890-C)

RATCLIFF, William D. (Capt.) Co. I, 7th Regiment

Maryland Infantry. (US) Hagerstown. Entered
service 5 September, 1862 as first lieutenant;
promoted captain 23 December, 1864. Discharged
31 May, 1865. (Scharf, 328) (H.R.M.V., Vol. 1,
297) (Camper and Kirkley, 123, 305)

RAY, Samuel. (Pvt.) Co. D, 1st Regiment Potomac
Home Brigade Infantry. (US) Hagerstown. Served
from 12 August, 1862 to 29 May, 1865. Wounded
in leg at Gettysburg, July 1863. Transferred
to Co. F, 13th Regiment Maryland Infantry.
(H.R.M.V., Vol. 1, 504) (1890-C)

REAGAN, John. (Pvt.) Captain Firey's Co. B, 1st
Regiment Potomac Home Brigade "Cole's" Cavalry.
(US) Age 23. Hancock. Enlisted 27 August,
1864. Transferred to Co F. Discharged 28 June,
1865. (H.R.M.V., Vol. 1, 669) (MSA-S-936-30)

REAPSOMER, John M. (Pvt.) Co. A, 13th Regiment
Maryland Infantry. (US) Boonsboro. Served from
10 February, 1865 to 29 May, 1865. (H.R.M.V.,
Vol. 1, 434) (1890-C)

RECKER, Frederick M. (Pvt.) Co. E, 12th Regiment
Maryland Infantry. (US) Hagerstown. Served
from 27 July, 1864 to 6 November, 1864.
(H.R.M.V., Vol. 1, 429) (1890-C)

REED, Francis. (Pvt.) Co. I, 7th Regiment
Maryland Infantry.(US) Age 35. Enlisted at
Hagerstown, 22 Aug. 1862. Discharged 31 May,
1865. (H.R.M.V., Vol. 1, 298) (MSA-AGR, Vol.
1, 370)

REED, Jeremiah E. S. (Pvt.) "Alexander's"
Baltimore Battery, Light Artillery. (US)
Hancock. Entered service 14 August, 1862.
Died in service 17 May, 1864. (H.R.M.V., Vol.
1, 822) (1890-C)

REED, Thomas W. (Pvt.) Co. K, 2nd Regiment
Maryland Infantry. (US) Age 24. Enlisted at
Maryland Heights, 9 February, 1864. Veteran.
Discharged near Alexandria, Va., 17 July, 1864.
(H.R.M.V., Vol. 1, 107) (MSA-AGR, Vol. 1, 313)

REEDER, Andrew J. (Pvt.) Co. E, 3rd Regiment
Potomac Home Brigade Infantry. (US)
Brownsville. Served from 31 March, 1864 to 29
May, 1865. (H.R.M.V., Vol. 1, 591) (1890-C)

REESE, Ezra. (Pvt.) Co. F, 3rd Regiment Maryland
Infantry. (US) Funkstown. Served from 29
February, 1862 to 20 June, 1863. Wounded in
right hand. (1890-C)

REICHARD, J. T. (Pvt.) Co. A, 7th Regiment
Maryland Infantry. (US) Age 19. Washington
County. Served from 15 August, 1862 to 31 May,
1865. Discharged at Arlington Heights, Va.
(Scharf, Vol. 1, 226) (H.R.M.V., Vol. 1, 280)
(MSA-AGR, Vol. 1, 370 and MSA-S-936-17)

REITZ, Samuel D. (Pvt.) Co. A, 3rd Regiment
Maryland Infantry. (US) Age 40. Enlisted at
Williamsport, 15 June, 1861. Veteran.
Discharged 15 June, 1864. (H.R.M.V., Vol. 1,
120) (MSA-AGR, Vol. 1, 314)

RENNER, Adolphus. (Pvt.) Co. H, 1st Regiment
Potomac Home Brigade Infantry. (US) Age 19.
Boatman. Sharpsburg. Enlisted 16 May, 1862.
Transferred to Co. H, 13th Maryland Infantry 19
January, 1864. Discharged 29 May, 1865.
(H.R.M.V., Vol. 1, 527) (MSA-S-936-23)

REPP, David. (Pvt.) Co. F, 13th Regiment Maryland
Infantry. (US) Served from 21 February, 1865
to 29 May, 1865. (H.R.M.V., Vol. 1, 448) (1890-
C)

REPP, John. (Pvt.) Co. F, 13th Regiment Maryland
Infantry. (US) Age 27. Farmer. Clear Spring.
Served from 27 February, 1864 to 29 May, 1865.
(H.R.M.V., Vol. 1, 448) (1890-C) (MSA-S-936-23)

RESLEY, James. (1st Lt.) Also Quartermaster, 4th
Potomac Home Brigade Infantry. (US) Hancock.
Served from 4 March, 1862 to 11 September,
1862. Contracted Typhoid Fever. (Scharf, 328)
(1890-C)

REYNOLD, George C. (Pvt.) Co. H, 6th Regiment
  Maryland Infantry. (US) Age 20. Enlisted at
  Hagerstown, 21 August, 1862. Discharged 20
  June, 1865. (H.R.M.V., Vol. 1, page 242) (MSA-
  AGR, Vol. 1, page 322 and 936-2)

REYNOLD, William F. (Pvt.) Co. B, 7th Regiment
  Maryland Infantry. (US) Age 18. Enlisted at
  Hagerstown, 11 April, 1863. Deserted 18
  August, 1863 at Maryland Heights. (H.R.M.V.,
  Vol. 1, page 282) (MSA-AGR, Vol. 1, page 370)

RHODES, Elisha R. (Pvt.) Co. E, 1st Regiment
  Potomac Home Brigade Infantry. (US) Age 35.
  Laborer. Washington County. Enlisted at Sandy
  Hook, Md., 30 January, 1865. Transferred to Co.
  F, 13th Regiment Maryland Infantry. Discharged
  29 May, 1865. (H.R.M.V., Vol. 1, page 514)
  (MSA-S-936-23)

RICHARDS, Henry. (Pvt.) Co. H, 1st Regiment
  Maryland Cavalry. (US) Age 24. Enlisted at
  Hancock, 3 December, 1861. Discharged 26
  October, 1864. (H.R.M.V., Vol. 1, page 730)
  (MSA-AGR-S-936-38)

RICHARDS, Isaac. (Cpl.) Co. F, Co. F, 2nd
  Regiment Potomac Home Brigade Infantry. (US)
  Hancock. (Listed on 1890 census as corporal
  and in the H.R.M.V., Vol. 1, 559 as a private.)

RICHARDSON, John. (Pvt.) Co. B, 3rd Regiment
  Potomac Home Brigade Infantry. (US) Sharpsburg.
  Enlisted at Hagerstown, 26 May, 1862.
  Discharged 26 May, 1865. (H.R.M.V., Vol. 1,
  page 578) (Captain Maxwell's roster)

RICHARDSON, John W. (Pvt.) Co. F, 4th Regiment
  Maryland Infantry. (US) Chewsville. Served from
  12 August, 1862 to 31 May, 1865. (H.R.M.V.,
  Vol. 1, 169) (1890-C)

RICHARDSON, William S. (Pvt.) Co. B, 7th Regiment

Maryland Infantry. (US) Age 24. Enlisted at
Hagerstown, 18 August, 1862. Discharged 31 May,
1865. (H.R.M.V., Vol. 1, page 282) (MSA-AGR,
Vol. 1, page 370)

RIDENOUR, Cyrus. (Cpl.) Co. I, 7th Regiment
Maryland Infantry. (US) Hagerstown. Entered
service 29 August, 1862. (H.R.M.V., Vol. 1,
298) (WCCR, Vol.7, 465) (1890-C)

RIDENOUR, Cyrus. (Cpl.) Co. I, 7th Regiment
Maryland Infantry. (US) Hagerstown. Enlisted 28
August, 1862. Saw heavy action at the
Wilderness, in May, 1864. When a ball tore
through his right leg about three inches above
the ankle, he was removed to a hospital in
Fredericksburg, where an amputation was
performed. Discharged 13 November, 1864, due to
wounds. Buried in Shiloh United Brethren Church
Cemetery near Fiddlersburg. Ridenour was
educated in Washington County schools and
worked at farming until he entered the service.
After discharge he made his home in Washington,
D. C. and worked at the Commissary Department
until the assassination of President Lincoln.
Then, returned to Washington County, working at
various jobs until he settled into shoe making.
(Williams, Vol. 1, 634) (H.R.M.V., Vol. 1, 298)

RIDENOUR, Daniel C. (Pvt.) Co. L, 1st Regiment
Potomac Home Brigade "Cole's" Cavalry. (US)
Edgemont. Served from 29 March, 1864 to 28
June, 1865. (H.R.M.V., Vol. 1, 697) (1890-C)

RIDENOUR, Isaac M. (Pvt.) Co. G, 7th Regiment
Maryland Infantry. (US) Hagerstown. Served from
20 August, 1862 to 31 May, 1865. (H.R.M.V.,
Vol. 1, 294) (1890-C)

RIDENOUR, Martin F. (Pvt.) Co. B, 3rd Regiment
Maryland Infantry. (US) Age 20. Enlisted at
Williamsport, 26 June, 1861. Discharged 15
June, 1865. (H.R.M.V., Vol. 1, page 125) (MSA-
AGR, Vol. 1, page 314)

RIDENOUR, Thomas J. (Pvt.) Co. A, 9th Regiment
Indiana Cavalry. (US) Smithsburg. Served from 2
October, 1863 to 31 May, 1865. (1890-C)

RIDENOUR, William F. (Pvt.) Co. D, 5th Regiment
Maryland Infantry. (US) Ringgold. Served from
21 September, 1864 to 14 June, 1865. (H.R.M.V.,
Vol. 1, 196) (1890-C)

RIFE, David. (Pvt.) Co. H, 6th Regiment Maryland
Infantry. (US) Age 21. Enlisted at Hagerstown,
21 August, 1862. Discharged for physical
disability from U.S. general hospital, Harpers
Ferry, 3 July, 1863. (H.R.M.V., Vol. 1, page
242) (MSA-AGR, Vol. 1, page 322 and 936-2)

RIGGS, James. (Pvt.) Co. B, 7th Regiment Maryland
Infantry. (US) Age 22. Enlisted at Hagerstown,
18 August, 1862. Discharged 31 May, 1865.
(H.R.M.V., Vol. 1, page 282) (MSA-AGR, Vol.
1, page 370)

RILEY, George M. (Pvt.) Co. A, 1st Regiment
Maryland Infantry. (US) Keedysville. Served
from 26 September, 1864 to 3 June, 1865.
Discharged with general disability. (H.R.M.V.,
Vol. 1, 23) (1890-C)

RILEY, Thomas. (Pvt.) Co. G, 1st Regiment
Maryland Infantry. (US) Hagerstown. Entered
service 17 November, 1864. Deserted 20 August,
1865. (H.R.M.V., Vol. 1, 208) (1890-C)

RINEHART, John T. (Pvt.) Co. A, 7th Regiment
Maryland Infantry. (US) Washington County.
Age 21. Served from 15 August, 1862 to 31 May,
1865. (H.R.M.V., Vol. 1, 280) (Scharf, Vol. 1,
226) (MSA-S-936-17)

RINEHART, Moses S. (Pvt.) Co. A, 7th Regiment
Maryland Infantry. (US) Age 22. Washington
County. Served from 18 April, 1862 to 31 May,
1865. (H.R.M.V., Vol. 1, 280) (Scharf, Vol. 1,
226) (MSA-AGR, Vol. 1, page 370)

RINGER, Samuel Jr. (Pvt.) Co. A, 13th Regiment
Maryland Infantry. (US) Boonsboro. Served from
13 February, 1865 to 29 May, 1865. (H.R.M.V.,
Vol. 1, 434) (1890-C)

RINGGOLD, Cadwalader. (Rear Admiral) (USN) The
son of General Samuel Ringgold (*), and a
distinguished officer in the United States
Navy. He was born at Fountain Rock, in
Washington County, in 1802. Appointed
midshipman on 4 March, 1819 and then lieutenant
17 May, 1828; lieutenant commander, 16 July,
1849; Reserved List, 13 September, 1855;
captain on Active List 2 April, 1856; commodore
16 July, 1862 and rear-admiral retired list in
March, 1866. He commanded the schooner Weazel
in action against West Indies pirates during
the late 1820's and later served in the Pacific
and the Mediterranean, assisting with surveying
and explorations of the North Pacific and China
Seas. He became inactive in the later 1850's,
but returned at the outbreak of the Civil War.
As it began he was transferred to command of
the frigate Sabine. On Thursday, 2 January,
1862 while on blockading duty off the coast of
South Carolina, Sabine encountered a terrifying
storm with excessively high winds. A nearby
steamer, Governor, with a battalion of Marines
on board, was found to be severely storm-
battered. Captain Ringgold went to its rescue
and in extreme conditions saved the marines and
the crew just moments before the Governor went
under. Captain Ringgold's personal account of
the incident was reported from New York, on 6
January, to Hon. Gideon Wells, Secretary of the
Navy. In general, it stated the following.
"The squadron under the command of Flag Officer
S. F. DuPont encountered the memorable gale on
the evening of 2 January 1862. On the following
day at 1 p.m., Georgetown S. C. light-house
bearing N. W., 35 miles, the wind veered to W.
S. W., but blowing very strong, with heavy
seas. As Sabine returned to her former station,
two vessels in close company were encountered.
Determined them to be two steamers in tow, one
appearing to be crippled. A flag was observed

with its Union upside down, meaning it was in
distress. A side-wheel steamer rolled heavily,
rudder gone, smokestack overboard and her deck
crowded with humans. A small screw steamer was
standing by scarcely able to take care of
herself. Serious doubt existed about rescue
efforts in the relentless weather.
Notwithstanding the hazard, two officers were
dispatched to the scene and determined it was
impossible to board. The ship was the storm-
battered Governor, of Flag Officer DuPont's
squadron, and she was leaking badly. A
battalion of U.S. Marines was on board
commanded by Major Reynolds. Rank and file
totalled 400, and all hands were engaged in
bailing and pumping, but the water was gaining
rapidly on them. The propeller in company was
the Isaac Smith and a smaller bark was the
gunboat Young Rover. There was little time for
deliberation. First impulse was to take the
Governor in tow to Georgetown. That, however,
would have destroyed the last hope of rescue.
There was also the apprehension of a collision
of our boats in the storm's fury. We came to
anchor in 13 fathoms (78 feet) of water.
Governor was ordered to drop anchor and a
rescue was planned from the stern of the
Sabine, using the spanker boom for a derrick to
hoist them aboard. The vessels were secured in
due time and the job of perilous rescue began
with every effort to protect the crew of the
Sabine as well. As the operation began, two
small rescue boats were swept overboard and
blown into the sea by the storm's continuing
fury. They were smashed to atoms against the
Sabine's hull. At 10 p.m. work began in
earnest. Progress was slow at first and just
as the routine began to flow smoothly the sea
renewed it savage turbulence. Both ships
strained at anchor. The Governor pitched in a
furious manner lurching first to port and then
to starboard, burying her sharp bow deep into
the pounding waters. Each time seemed to be
her last, but she would emerge again,
protecting her priceless crew. Then, a hawser
connecting the two ships, gave way, and then

another. The situation was now acute in the extreme, but the anchor of the Governor held steady. Volunteers were called to secure the fasts again and in moments, under exhausting conditions, they succeeded and the rescue continued. Then another misfortune. The main, heavy chain cable holding the two ships together broke and the Governor fell astern and began to go under. By this time only 30 men had been rescued from her decks. Just one hawser was holding the two heaving ships together, a thin line at most. The Governor was pulled slowly to the starboard side of the Sabine and the remaining Marines and crew members ordered to "leap for their lives," to the deck of the Sabine." Ringgold watched as another 30 or more men jumped to safety just seconds before the two vessels collided with a violent impact. Twenty feet of the Governor's deck rail was torn violently away, and she was found to be in immediate danger of breaking in two and sinking. Here, the Governor's anchor and chain held, by some miracle, which proved her eventual salvation. As the two ships slammed together a second time, two Marines fell overboard and one was crushed to death. Six others jumped overboard in an attempt to gain the Sabine, and were drowned. The scene was one of total horror. The screams of men about to drown, the violence of the storm, confusion on board both boats, the unnatural glare of the sea and sky caused by the rockets and the red and blue lights signaling for assistance to the Isaac Smith and the Young Rover. Then a miracle! The fierceness of the sea began to abate and the Governor began to settle down, and further rescue attempts were postponed until dawn. At daylight the work continued with the remaining Marines and crew members jumping overboard and climbing into a small boat to be brought to the Sabine and safety. The Young Rover and Isaac Smith sustained substantial damage and were unable to assist in the rescue which was concluded by 11:30 a.m. The Sabine also suffered serious damage, but limped successfully to port with

900 men safely on board. After news of the heroic work of Captain Ringgold and his crew was reported to the public, various honors came their way. On 20 January the city of New York's mayor and council presented a special resolution to Ringgold and the crew of the Sabine, citing their "heroic, humane and successful effort." Another accolade, including a gold metal, was awarded by the Life Saving Benevolent Association of the City of New York. on 28 February. Ringgold's home state recognized his dauntless effort as the general assembly adopted a resolution tendering their thanks, signed by Governor A. W. Bradford. Then on 7 March, 1864, Ringgold and the crew of the Sabine received a Congressional Citation which read: *"To Commodore Ringgold, the officers, petty officers and men of the United States Ship SABINE, for the daring and skill displayed in rescuing the crew of the steam transport Governor wrecked in a gale on the first day of November, eighteen hundred and sixty one, having on board a battalion of United States marines under the command of Major John G. Reynolds, and in the search for, and rescue of, the United States line-of-battle ship VERMONT, disabled in a gale upon the twenty-sixth day of February last, with her crew and freight.*

March 7, 1864

During the Civil War Ringgold contributed much to the successful blockading of Southern ports, especially in operations against Port Royal. After the war, in 1866, Ringgold was named General Superintendent of Ironclads, and President of the Board of Claims. Its duties required reviewing all claims of extra work by contractors and extra charges submitted to the Navy. The claims were examined and either approved and passed on to the Bureau of Construction and Repair for payment, or rejected and not paid. Eventually two boards were merged for contract consideration and became known as The Ringgold Board. He died in New York City, 29 April, 1867.

FUTURE HONORS

In later years two ships were named in his
honor. The first Ringgold, a twin-screw
destroyer, was launched 14 April, 1918. After
a variety of operations it was decommissioned
17 June, 1922. Two decades later it was
recommissioned 23 August, 1940, and
transferred, along with 40 other older ships,
to Great Britain, to fight the German submarine
menace. It was manned by a British crew and
renamed Newark. She suffered minor bomb damage
in a night air attack at Belfast, 4-5 May,
1941. In another attack it was damaged by a
German torpedo. Newark was scrapped 18
February, 1947. The second Ringgold, also a
destroyer, was commissioned 11 November, 1942,
and christened by Mrs. Arunah Sheperdson,
grandniece of Rear Adm. Ringgold. After
training it reported to the Pacific fleet at
Pearl Harbor, and joined a task force that
included the Yorktown and Essex. Ringgold
participated in operations around the Gilbert
Islands and Tarawa. At the latter, destroyers
Ringgold and Santa Fe lead the assault that
carried battle-hardened Marines, veterans of
the terrible fighting on Guadalcanal, into a
small lagoon, blasting away at the beaches.
They exited only when the major naval
bombardment commenced. The lagoon proved too
small for large ships to enter so the frontal
fire on the beaches was provided by Ringgold,
Pursuit, Requisite and Dashiell. Ringgold took
two hits, both duds, but one knocked out her
port engine. Her chief engineer literally
plugged himself in the hole while the repairs
were made. Ringgold also participated in the
capture of Kwajalein, and Eniwetok Atolls,
Hollandia, Dutch New Guinea, the Guam invasion
and operations near the Marianas Islands.
Early in 1945 Ringgold took part in the first
carrier strikes on the Island of Japan. After
repairs it returned to take part in more
strikes against the Japanese mainland,
bombarding the town of Shimizu. During Pacific
operation at the close of the war Ringgold
acted as escort for Antietam to Guam for
repairs. Ringgold was decommissioned 23 March,

1946 and placed in the Atlantic Reserve Fleet
at Charleston, S. C., where she remained until
1959. Then she was modernized and transferred
to the German Naval Fleet, 14 July, 1959, and
renamed Z-2. (Scharf, Vol. 2, 1026) (Lord, 352)
(Information on history and sale of the U. S.
S. Ringgold provided by the office of Maryland
U. S. Sixth District Congresswoman Beverly
Byron) (Dictionary of American Naval Fighting
Ships, Vol. 6, 111-13) (H.R.M.V., Vol. 2, 12)
(Official Records of the Union and Confederate
Navies, Series 1, Vol. 14, pages 131, 149, 239-
43, 250-52) (The Union, 481) (*) General Samuel
Ringgold, an officer in the regular army of the
United States, was born near Hagerstown in
1796. A graduate of West Point Military
Academy in 1818, he was commissioned a second
lieutenant of artillery when only 18 years old.
He served as an aide-de-camp to Gen. Winfield
Scott and earned a brevet major promotion for
his outstanding service in the Florida War
against the Seminole Indians. Major Ringgold
organized a corp of flying artillery that
attracted much attention.
He was killed at Point Isabel, Texas, on 11
May, 1846, during the Mexican War. The mansion
that was his home is located next to St. James
College. (Schoch, W.C.H.S., 929.2 S) (H.R.M.V.,
Vol. 2, 12) (The History of Maryland, page
143-44) (Scharf, Vol. 2, 1024)

RINGGOLD, George Hay. (Col.) (US) Also the son of
Gen. Samuel Ringgold, was born at Hagerstown
in 1814 and educated at West Point Military
Academy. He was appointed second lieutenant of
the 6th Infantry Regiment, 1 July, 1833 and
served on the American frontier. Ringgold
resigned in 1837 to engage in the manufacture
of flour. Later, from 1842 to 1846 he served
in the U. S. Ordnance Bureau in Washington and
was reassigned to the army in August, 1846 with
the rank of paymaster. During the Civil War he
served as deputy Paymaster General with the
rank of lieutenant-colonel. He died 4 April,
1864, at San Francisco. Ringgold was a gifted
scholar, accomplished draughtsman and an

amateur poet. In 1860 he published a volume of
poetry titled "Fountain Rock, Amy Weir and
Other Metrical Pastimes." (Schoch, 42)

RISER, William. (Pvt.) Captain Firey's Co. B, 1st
Regiment Potomac Home Brigade "Cole's" Cavalry.
(US) Indian Spring. Served from 24 August, 1861
to 15 September, 1864. (H.R.M.V., Vol. 1, 678)
(1890-C)

REICHARD, Benjamin F. (Capt.) Co. B, 12th
Regiment Maryland Infantry. (US) Hagerstown.
Served from 8 July, 1864 to 6 November, 1864.
(H.R.M.V., Vol. 1, 423) (1890-C)

REYNOLD, Amos. (Cpl.) Co. H, 6th Regiment
Maryland Infantry. (US) Age 22. Enlisted at
Hagerstown 21 August, 1862. Promoted corporal
2 April, 1865. Discharged 20 June, 1865.
(H.R.M.V., Vol. 1, 242) (MSA-AGR, Vol. 1, 322
and 936-2)

REYNOLD, Daniel B. (Cpl.) Co. H, 6th Regiment
Maryland Infantry. (US) Age 27. Smithsburg.
Enlisted at Hagerstown 21 August, 1862.
Severely wounded in action 1 June 1864, at Cold
Harbor, Va. Taken prisoner. Died 29 January,
1865, at post hospital, Hagerstown, Md., of
disease contracted at Andersonville, Ga.,
prison. (H.R.M.V., Vol. 1, 242) (1890-C) (MSA-
AGR-S-936-2)

RIVERS, Jonathan L. (Capt.) Co. B, 1st Regiment
Potomac Home Brigade "Cole's Cavalry." (US)
Washington County. Entered service 30 August,
1861, as private; promoted quartermaster
sergeant; second lieutenant 9 September, 1863;
captain 23 November, 1864; wounded in action 10
January, 1864. (Scharf, 328) (H.R.M.V., Vol.
1, 670)

ROBERTS, Alexander M. (Sgt.) Co. I, 7th Regiment
Maryland Infantry. (US) Hagerstown. Served from
18 August, 1862 to 30 June, 1865. Discharged at
Annapolis, Md. (H.R.M.V., Vol. 1, 298) (1890-C)
(MSA-AGR, Vol. 1, 370)

ROBEY, James A. (Pvt.) Co. H, 3rd Regiment
Maryland Cavalry. (US) Hancock. Served from
28 September, 1863 to 7 September, 1865.
(H.R.M.V., Vol. 1, 776) (1890-C)

ROBINSON, Cyrus D. (Pvt.) Co. C., 13th Regiment
Maryland Infantry. (US) Washington Co. Buried
in the Mt. Carmel Evangelical Church Cemetery,
at Big Pool, Md., near Fort Frederick. (WCCR,
Vol. 4, 125).

ROBINSON, James A. (2nd Lt.) Co. H, 6th Regiment
Maryland Infantry.(US) Age 21. Washington
County. Entered service 21 August, 1862 as
first sergeant; promoted second lieutenant 11
February, 1863. Resigned 17 March, 1864.
(Scharf, 328) (H.R.M.V., Vol. 1, 240) (MSA-AGR-
S-936-2)

ROBINSON, James B. (Pvt.) Co. G, 7th Virginia
Cavalry, (CSA) Sharpsburg. (Hartzler, 258)

ROBINSON, Peter. (Pvt.) Co. E, 1st Regiment
Potomac Home Brigade Infantry. (US) Smithsburg.
Served from 14 September, 1861 to 1 October,
1864. (H.R.M.V., Vol. 1, 509) (1890-C)

ROBISON, Samuel. (Pvt.) Co. B, 22nd Pennsylvania
Cavalry. (US) Clear Spring. Served from 20
January, 1863 to 17 January, 1864. (1890-C)

ROCK, John L. (Pvt.) Co. F, 3rd Regiment Potomac
Home Brigade Infantry. (US) Age 21.
Hagerstown. Enlisted 28 March, 1861.
Discharged 28 March, 1864. (H.R.M.V., Vol. 1,
594) (MSA-S-936-23)

ROCKWELL, Thomas. (Pvt.) (Co.?) 1st Maryland
Cavalry. (US) Ernstville. Served from January,
1862 to June, 1863. Suffered broken hip when
kicked by horse. (1890-C)

ROHRER, Daniel W. (Pvt.) Co. E, 13th Regiment
Maryland Infantry. (US) Age 23. Laborer.
Beaver Creek. Served from 1 October, 1861 to 29

May, 1865. Reenlisted 23 February, 1864 at
Sandy Hook, Md. Veteran. Transferred to Co. E,
13th Maryland Infantry. (H.R.M.V., Vol. 1, 445)
(1890-C) (MSA-S-936-23)

ROHRER, Joshua W. (Capt.) Co. D, 2nd Maryland
Cavalry. (US) Keedysville. Served from 3
August, 1861 to 19 September, 1865. His
education at Mt. Morris, Ill., was interposed
by the start of the war when he enlisted at St.
Louis, in 1861, and spent his first year
chasing bridge burners. He participated in the
fighting at Little Rock, Ark., and Camden and
Soline River, Mo. In 1864 he was assigned to
the command of Gen. George Thomas, at
Nashville, and near Atlanta, Ga., his regiment
captured more than 3,000 Confederate soldiers.
He also participated in the chase to catch
Confederate President Jefferson Davis at the
end of the war, but his men arrived too late to
share in the honors. He was promoted to
captain near the end of the war and returned
home to settle in Keedysville. (1890-C)
(Williams, Vol. 2, 965)

ROHRER, Henry C. (Pvt.) Co. A, 1st Regiment
Potomac Home Brigade Infantry. (US)
Sharpsburg. Served from 15 August, 1861 to 27
August, 1864. (H.R.M.V., Vol. 1, 490) (1890-C)
(Scharf, Vol. 1, 226)

ROHRER, Solomon. (Cpl.) Co. I, 7th Regiment
Maryland Infantry. (US) Smithsburg. Enlisted 31
August, 1861. Wounded in the Battle of the
Wilderness, 8 May, 1864 and died 6 June, 1864
from the wounds. Buried in Trinity Church
Graveyard, Smithsburg. (H.R.M.V., Vol. 1, 298)
(Scharf, Vol. 2, 1274)

ROOP, James P. (Pvt.) Co. B, 11th Regiment
Maryland Infantry. (100 days.) (US) Hagerstown.
Served from 27 May, 1864 to 29 September, 1864.
(H.R.M.V., Vol. 1, 379) (1890-C)

RONEY, James H. (Pvt.) Co. I, 1st Regiment
"Russell's" Maryland Cavalry. (US)

Conococheague. Served from 3 September, 1861 to
3 September, 1864. (H.R.M.V., Vol. 1, 734.)
(1890-C)

ROSS, David. (Pvt.) Co. B, 3rd Regiment Potomac
Home Brigade Infantry. (US) Age 18.
Washington County. Enlisted 27 December, 1861.
Transferred to Co. F. Discharged 29 May, 1865.
Veteran. (H.R.M.V., Vol. 1, 578) (MSA-S-936-23)

ROSS, David H. (Pvt.) Co. K, 2nd Regiment
Maryland Infantry. (US) Age 24. Enlisted at
Maryland Heights, 9 February, 1864. Veteran.
Discharged 17 July, 1865 near Alexandria, Va.
(H.R.M.V., Vol. 1, page 107) (MSA-AGR, Vol. 1,
313 and S-936-23)

ROSS, Henry H. (Sgt.) Co. K, 1st Regiment
Maryland Cavalry. (US) Ringgold. Served from 24
November, 1861 to 8 August, 1865. (H.R.M.V.,
Vol. 1, 737) (1890-C)

ROSS, James. (Pvt.) Co. B, 3rd Regiment Potomac
Home Brigade Infantry. (US) Hagerstown.
Enlisted at Hagerstown, 19 November, 1861.
Discharged 19 November, 1864. (H.R.M.V., Vol.
1, page 578) (Captain Maxwell's roster)

ROTROFF, David P. (Pvt.) Captain Firey's Co. B,
1st Regiment Potomac Home Brigade "Cole's"
Cavalry. (US) Age 23. Miller. Hagerstown.
Enlisted 4 September, 1861. Veteran.
Reenlisted 14 February, 1864, at Boliver, Va.
(H.R.M.V., Vol. 1, page 673) (MSA-S-936-30)

ROWE, Thomas J. (Pvt.) Co. B, 12 Regiment
Maryland Infantry. (US) Downsville. Served from
18 July, 1864 to 6 November, 1864. Died 6
November, 1864 in military hospital.
(H.R.M.V., Vol. 1, 424) (1890-C)

ROWAN, James. (Pvt.) Co. A, 2nd Regiment Maryland
Infantry. (US) Age 19. Enlisted at Maryland
Heights, 10 February, 1864. Taken prisoner 25
July, 1864, at Petersburg, Va. Veteran.
Discharged near Salem, Va., 17 July, 1865.

(H.R.M.V., Vol. 1, page 77) (MSA-AGR, Vol. 1, page 312)

ROWLAND, John. (Pvt.) Co. I, 7th Regiment Maryland Infantry. (US) Age 43. Hagerstown. Served from 28 August, 1862 to 31 May, 1865. (H.R.M.V., Vol. 1, 298) (1890-C) (MSA-AGR, Vol. 1, page 371)

RUDISILL, John (Pvt.) Co. L, 1st Regiment Potomac Home Brigade "Cole's" Cavalry. (US) Smithsburg. Served from 29 March, 1864 to 28 June, 1865. (H.R.M.V., Vol. 1, 697) (1890-C)

RUNYON, Joseph. (Pvt.) Co. H, 158th Regiment Pennsylvania Infantry. (US) Hancock. (WCCR 1, 170)

RUSHMORE, John. (Pvt.) Co. I, 7th Regiment Maryland Infantry. (US) Age 41. Enlisted at Hagerstown, 28 August, 1862. Transferred to V. R. C. 11 March, 1865. Discharged with surgeon's certificate of disability, 23 June, 1865. (H.R.M.V., Vol. 1, page 298) (MSA-AGR, Vol. 1, page 371)

RUSSELL, Charles H. (Major) Co. I, 1st Regiment Maryland Cavalry. (US) Williamsport. Entered service 5 August, 1861, as captain, 1st Virginia Union Cavalry. Transferred to Co. I, 1st Maryland Cavalry, 28 Jan. 1862; promoted major 9 Oct., 1862; discharged 31 Dec. 1863. (Scharf, 328) (H.R.M.V., Vol. 1, 704, 731)

RUSSELL, David. (Pvt.) Co. B, 7th Regiment Maryland Infantry. (US) Age 24. Enlisted at Hagerstown, 11 August, 1862. Deserted 10 October, 1862, at Williamsport, Md. (H.R.M.V., Vol. 1, page 282) (MSA-AGR, Vol. 1, page 370)

RUTHERFORD, George W. (Pvt.) Co. I, 1st Regiment "Russell's" Maryland Cavalry. Enlisted at Williamsport, 17 December, 1862. Discharged 8 August, 1865. (H.R.M.V., Vol. 1, page 732) (MSA-AGR-S-936-38)

RYAN, Reverend Abram Joseph. (Pvt.) Chaplain, 8th Tennessee Infantry, (CSA) Hagerstown. Known as the "Poet-Priest of the Southland," He was baptized in old St. Mary's Church, Hagerstown. (Hartzler, 261) (Confederate Veteran Magazine, Vol. XXXVI, page 118 and Vol. XXXVII, page 262)

RYAN, Amos. (Pvt.) Co. E, 1st Regiment Potomac Home Brigade Infantry. (US) Hagerstown. Served from 1 October, 1861 to 1 October, 1864. (H.R.M.V., Vol. 1, 509) (1890-C)

RYAN, Michael H. (Pvt.) Co. F, 1st Regiment Potomac Home Brigade Infantry. (US) Age 25. Saddler. Hagerstown. Served from 4 September, 1861 to 29 May, 1865. Transferred to Co. F, 13th Maryland Infantry. (H.R.M.V., Vol. 1, 514) (1890-C) (MSA-S-936-23)

RYAN, Patrick. (Pvt.) Co. K, 2nd Regiment Virginia Infantry. (CSA) Hagerstown. Served from 6 June, 1861 to 6 December, 1862. (1890-C)

-- S --

SAGER, John. (Cpl.) Co. A, 7th Regiment Maryland Infantry. (US) Age 36. Washington County. Enlisted at Hagerstown 9 August, 1862. Appointed corporal 1 January, 1864. Wounded in action 1 April, 1865, at Five Forks, Va. Confined to Lincoln Hospital, Washington, D.C. Discharged 24 June, 1865. (H.R.M.V., Vol. 1, 280) (MSA-AGR, Vol. 1, 350 and MSA-S-936-17)

SANDERS, William H. (Pvt.) Co. E, 1st Regiment Potomac Home Brigade Infantry. (US) Age 19. Laborer. Rohrersville. Enlisted 1 August, 1861. Transferred to Co. E, 13th Maryland Infantry. Discharged 29 May, 1865. (H.R.M.V., Part 1, page 509) (MSA-S-936-23)

SANDMAN, Benjamin F. (Cpl.) Co. A. 1st Regiment Potomac Home Brigade. (US) Sharpsburg. Served from 15 August, 1861 to 27 August, 1864.

Transferred to Co. A 13th Maryland Infantry. (H.R.M.V., Vol. 1, 490) (1890-C)

SANDS, George W. (Pvt.) Co. I, 77th Regiment Pennsylvania Infantry. (US) Hagerstown. Served from 6 March, 1865 to 8 July, 1865. (1890-C)

SANDS, Robert M. (Pvt.) Co. I, 1st Regiment "Russell's" Maryland Cavalry. (US) Hagerstown. Served from 3 Sept. 1861 to 26 Sept. 1864. Wounded at Brandy Station, Va., 9 June, 1863. Suffered gunshot wound of neck. Received pension of $4 per month. (Pensions List, 157) (H.R.M.V., Vol. 1, 734) (McClannahan papers, 4) (1890-C)

SANDSBURG, John O. (Pvt.) Co. I, 2nd Regiment Infantry. (US) (U.S.C.T.) Hagerstown. (MSA-S-936-45)

SANTMAN, James. (Pvt.) Co. H, 1st Regiment Potomac Home Brigade Infantry. (US) Age 20. Laborer. Washington County. Enlisted 3 December, 1861. Discharged 3 December, 1864. (H.R.M.V., Vol. 1, 527) (MSA-S-936-23)

SAWYER, Henry. (Pvt.) Co. F, 1st Regiment Potomac Hone Brigade Infantry. (US) Age 36. Laborer. Washington County. Wnlisted 29 February, 1864, at Hagerstown. Transferred to Co. F, 13th Regiment Maryland Infantry. Discharged 29 May, 1865. (H.R.M.V., Vol 1, 514) (MSA-S-936-23)

SAYLOR, Daniel. (Pvt.) Co. B, 3rd Regiment Potomac Home Brigade Infantry. (US) Hagerstown. Enlisted at Hagerstown, 27 October, 1861. Discharged 27 October, 1864. (H.R.M.V., Vol. 1, 578) (Captain Maxwell's roster)

SAYLOR, Harry. (Pvt.) Co. A, 1st Potomac Home Brigade Infantry. (US) Sharpsburg. Served 15 August, 1851 until 27 August, 1864. Buried in Lutheran graveyard, Sharpsburg. (1890-C) (H.R.M.V., Vol. 1, 490) (WCCR, Vol. 1, 71)

SAYLOR, Samuel W. (Pvt.) Co. B, 3rd Regiment

Potomac Home Brigade Infantry. (US) Age 22.
Washington County. Enlisted 26 November, 1861.
Discharged 29 May, 1865. Veteran. (H.R.M.V.,
Vol. 1, 579) (MSA-S-936-23)

SAYLOR, William H. H. (Pvt.) Co. B, 7th Regiment
Maryland Infantry. (US) Age 21. Enlisted at
Hagerstown, 18 August, 1862. Discharged 31
May, 1865. (H.R.M.V., Vol. 1, 282) (MSA-AGR,
Vol. 1, 351)

SCHINDEL, S. Milford. (Pvt.) Confederate Cavalry,
unit unknown. (CSA) Hagerstown. Born on All
Saints' Day in 1847, he met and talked with
abolitionist John Brown when Brown sold Bibles
to farmers of Washington County in 1859. In
1863 he served briefly as a courier in the Army
of Northern Virginia. Transferred to the
cavalry in 1864, participating in the
Shenandoah Valley campaign. Schindel was with
Gen. John McCausland when he extracted $20,000
from his hometown, Hagerstown, in July, 1864,
and when Chambersburg was burned in the same
month. At the end of the war Schindel moved to
Texas and participated in the Mexican War.
Afterwards, he managed a large cattle ranch and
returned to Hagerstown on the death of his
sister, Ada. After marriage to Anna Brendel,
he became manager of Huyett and Schindel's
Commercial Fertilizer Mill. In 1886 he
developed several new hybrids of wheat that
earned a commendation from the U. S.
Government. He also invented the first
practical corn husking machine and in 1888
organized the first company to weave silk
fabrics, south of the Mason Dixon Line, and
also established, in Hagerstown, the first
company in the south to build bicycles.
Schindel held 17 patents including the
punctureless double-tube pneumatic and self-
healing, single-tube tires. (Williams, Vol. 2,
1143) (Hartzler, 263) (1860-C, 43)

SCHLEIGH, Charles A. (Pvt.) Bugler. Captain
Firey's Co. B, 1st Regiment Potomac Home

Brigade "Cole's" Cavalry. (US) Age 24. Saddler.
Clear Spring. Enlisted 4 September, 1861.
Veteran. Reenlisted 14 February, 1864.
(H.R.M.V., Vol. 1, 673) (MSA-S-936-30)

SCHNEBLEY, (?) (Pvt.) Co. I, 7th Regiment
Maryland Infantry. (US) Age 21. Enlisted at
Hagerstown, 25 August, 1862. Deserted at
Williamsport, Md., 6 September 1862.
(H.R.M.V., Vol. 1, 298) (MSA-AGR, Vol. 1, 354)

SCHUFF, William L. (Pvt.) Co. A, 7th Regiment
Maryland Infantry. (US) Washington County.
Served from 9 August, 1862 to 6 June, 1865.
Wounded in action 25 May, 1864 at North Anna
River, Va. Taken prisoner 31 March, 1865.
(H.R.M.V., Vol. 1, 280) (1890-C)

SCOTT, Daniel W. (Pvt.) Co. B, 3rd Regiment
Potomac Home Brigade Infantry. (US) Age 31.
Enlisted at Hagerstown, 23 October, 1861.
Transferred to Co. F. Discharged 2 October,
1864. Veteran. (H.R.M.V., Vol. 1, 578, 594)
(MSA-S-936-23)

SCOTT, Perry W. (Pvt.) Co. K, 4th Regiment
Maryland Infantry. (US) (U.S.C.T.) Hagerstown.
Served from 1 September, 1863 to 4 May, 1866.
(H.R.M.V., Vol. 2, 154) (1890-C)

SCUFFIN, Charles H. (Pvt.) Co. I, 7th Regiment
Maryland Infantry. (US) Age 35. Boonsboro.
Served from 29 August, 1862 to 31 May, 1865.
Wounded in hips and knees, and left thigh.
Received pension of $6.00 per month. (Pensions
List, 156) (H.R.M.V., Vol. 1, 298) (1890-C)
(MSA-AGR, Vol. 1, 354)

SEALER, John H. (Pvt.) Co. F, 1st Regiment
Potomac Home Brigade Infantry. (US) Age 23.
Farmer. Washington County. Enlisted at Sandy
Hook, Md., 30 Jan. 1865. Transferred to Co. F,
13th Regiment Maryland Infantry. Discharged 29
May, 1865.(H.R.M.V., Vol. 1, 514)(MSA-S-936-23)

SEALER, Robert J.V. (Pvt.) Co. F, 1st Regiment

Potomac Home Brigade Infantry. (US) Age 18.
Farmer. Enlisted at Sandy Hook, Md., 30
January, 1865. Transferred to Co. F, 13th
Regiment Maryland Infantry. Discharged 29 May,
1865. (H.R.M.V., Vol. 1, 514) (MSA-S-936-23)

SEAMAN, James, (Pvt.) Co. A, 1st Regiment Potomac
Home Brigade Infantry. (US) Sharpsburg. Served
15 August, 1861 to 27 August, 1864. Buried in
Mountain View Cemetery, Sharpsburg. (H.R.M.V.,
Vol. 1, 490) (WCCR, Vol. 1, 6)

SECORE, George W. (Pvt.) Co. H, 6th Regiment
Maryland Infantry (US) Age 37. Enlisted at
Hagerstown, 15 August, 1862. Deserted 23
August, 1864, at Camp Parole, near Annapolis,
Md. (H.R.M.V., Vol. 1, 242) (MSA-AGR, part 1,
350 and S-936-2)

SEELER, Robert M. (Pvt.) Co. B, 11th Regiment
Maryland Infantry. (US) Trego. Served from 10
June, 1864 to 29 Sept. 1865. Disease contracted
during service resulted in shaking palsy, in
1865.(H.R.M.V., Vol. 1, 379) (1890-C)

SEIDENSTRICKER, William H. (Capt.) Co. E, 1st
Regiment Potomac Home Brigade Infantry. (US)
Age 23. Baker. Hagerstown. Entered service 1
October, 1861 as private; promoted to sergeant.
Reenlisted at Sandy Hook, Md., 2 February,
1864. Promoted captain 1 March, 1865; veteran
volunteer; later transferred to Co. E, 13th
Maryland Infantry. Discharged 29 May, 1865.
Buried in Rose Hill Cemetery, Hagerstown.
(Scharf, 328) (H.R.M.V., Vol. 1, 443, 505)
(WCCR, Vol. 7, 242) (1890-C) (MSA-S-936-23)

SEIGLER, Abraham. (Pvt.) Co. B, 3rd Regiment
Potomac Home Brigade Infantry. (US) Age 22.
Boonsboro. Enlisted at Hagerstown, 3 December,
1861. Transferred to Co. F. Discharged 3
December, 1864. (H.R.M.V., Vol. 1, 578)
(Captain Maxwell's roster) (MSA-S-936-23)

SEIGLER, William. (Pvt.) Co. B, 3rd Regiment
Potomac Home Brigade Infantry. (US) Washington

County. Enlisted 30 December, 1861.
Discharged 30 December, 1864. Veteran.
(H.R.M.V., Vol. 1, 578) (MSA-S-936-23)

SHAFFER, Jacob T. (Pvt.) Co. G, 3rd Regiment
Maryland Infantry. (US) Hagerstown. Served
from 9 May, 1865 to 10 June, 1865. (1890-C)

SHAEFFER, Jeremiah. (Pvt.) Co. A, 7th Regiment
Maryland Infantry. (US) Enlisted at Hagerstown,
25 February, 1864. Died of wounds received in
action at Gravel Run, Va., 1 April, 1865.
(H.R.M.V., Vol. 1, 280) (MSA-AGR, Vol. 1, 351)

SHANK, Adam. (Sgt.) Co. H, 6th Regiment Maryland
Infantry. (US) Age 38. Enlisted at Hagerstown
21 August, 1862. Wounded in action 5 May, 1864
at Wilderness, Va. Patient at Lincoln Hospital,
Washington, D.C., and Frederick, Md., General
Hospital. Discharged at Frederick with
disability 26 May, 1865. (H.R.M.V., Vol. 1,
242) (MSA-AGR, Vol. 1, 350 and 936-2)

SHANK, Henry. (Sgt.) Co. G, 1st Regiment Potomac
Home Brigade "Cole's" Cavalry. Four Locks.
Served from 26 February, 1864 to 28 June, 1865.
(H.R.M.V., Vol. 1, 688) (1890-C)

SHANK, Jonathan. (Sgt.) Co. G, 1st Regiment
Potomac Home Brigade "Cole's" Cavalry. (US)
Ernstville. Served from 26 February, 1864 to
28 June, 1865. (H.R.M.V., Vol. 1. 688) (1890-C)

SHAW, Henry Clay. (Sgt.) Co. A, 3rd Regiment
Potomac Home Brigade Infantry. (US) Washington
Co. Served from 1 May, 1862 to 1 May, 1865.
Buried in Rose Hill Cemetery, Hagerstown.
(H.R.M.V., Vol. 1, 574) (WCCR, Vol.7, 330)

SHELBY, Isaac. (Pvt.) Co. M, 22nd Pennsylvania
Cavalry. (US) Clear Spring. Served from 22
February, 1864 to 31 October, 1865. (1890-C)

SHEPHERD, William. (Pvt.) Co. F, 2nd Regiment
Potomac Home Brigade Infantry. (US) Hancock.
Served from 31 Aug. 1861 to 30 Sept. 1864.

Back injury. (H.R.M.V., Vol. 1, 559) (1890-C)

SHERLEY, C. S. (Pvt.) Co. G, 1st Maryland Potomac Home Brigade. "Cole's Cavalry." (US) Clear Spring. Buried in Union Bethel Cemetery, Blair's Valley. (WCCR, Vol. 2, 69)

SHIELDS, John H. (Pvt.) Co. H, 6th Regiment Maryland Infantry. (US) Age 38. Enlisted at Hagerstown, 21 August, 1862. Wounded by a sharpshooter at Spotsylvania, Va., 9 May, 1864, lost an arm. Discharged for disability 3 February, 1865. (H.R.M.V., Vol. 1, 242) (MSA-AGR-Vol. 1, 350 and S-936-2)

SHILHOWER, (?) Abraham, W. (Pvt.) Co. B, 2nd Regiment U. S. Cavalry. (US) Boonsboro. Served 24 November, 1862 to 4 April, 1865. (1890-C)

SHILLING, Joseph. (Pvt.) Co. A, 7th Regiment Maryland Infantry. (US) Cavetown. Age 19. A laborer. Enlisted at Hagerstown, 29 February, 1864. Transferred to Co. 1st Maryland Infantry. Mustered out 3 June, 1865. (H.R.M.V., Vol. 1, 280) (MSA-S, 936-17) (MSA-AGR, Vol. 1, 325, 351)

SHIPLEY, William. (Pvt.) Co. B, 3rd Regiment Potomac Home Brigade Infantry. (US) Age 23. Hagerstown. Enlisted at Hagerstown, 7 February, 1863. Veteran. Discharged 29 May, 1865. (H.R.M.V., Vol. 1, 579) (MSA-S-936-23)

SHIPWAY, John C. (Pvt.) Co. B, 3rd Regiment Potomac Home Brigade Infantry. (US) Hancock. Served from 16 November, 1861 to 16 November, 1864. (H.R.M.V., Vol. 1, 579) (1890-C)

SHIVES, Dayton O. (Pvt.) Co. B, 3rd Regiment Potomac Home Brigade Infantry. (US) Age 22. Hancock. Enlisted 9 March, 1864. Discharged 29 May, 1865.(H.R.M.V., Vol. 1, 578)(MSA-S-936-24)

SHIVES, Francis.(Pvt.) Co. H, 13th Regiment Maryland Infantry. (US) Hancock. Served from 24 February, 1865 to 29 May, 1865. Reported eye

injury. (H.R.M.V., Vol. 1, 454) (1890-C)
(H.R.M.V., Vol. 1, 454)

SHOEMAKER, David B. (Pvt.) Co. F, 79th
Pennsylvania Infantry Regiment. (US)
Leitersburg. Served from 22 February 1865 to
12 July, 1865. (1890-C)

SHOVER, John D. (Pvt.) Co. E, 1st Regiment
Potomac Home Brigade Infantry. (US) Age 20.
Shoemaker. Enlisted at Hagerstown, 1 October,
1861. Reenlisted 23 February, 1864, at Sandy
Hook, Md. Transferred to Co. E, 13th Maryland
Infantry. Discharged 29 May, 1865. (H.R.M.V.,
Vol. 1, 509) and MSA-S-936-23)

SHOW, Robert L. (Pvt.) Co. A, 1st Regiment
Maryland Infantry. (US) Williamsport. Served
from 7 Jan. 1864 to 3 Dec. 1864. (1890-C)

SHRADER, John. (Pvt.) Co. K, 102nd Regiment
Pennsylvania Infantry. (US) Downsville.
Service dates not known. (1890-C)

SHUFF, William. (Pvt.) Co. A, 7th Regiment
Maryland Infantry. (US) Age 27. Enlisted at
Hagerstown, 9 August, 1862. Wounded in action
25 May, 1864, at North Anna River, Va. Taken
prisoner 31 March, 1865, near Appomattox Court
House, Va. Discharged 6 June, 1865, at
Annapolis, Md. Charged $4.35 for loss of two
tents and one knapsack. (H.R.M.V., Vol. 1,
280) (MSA-AGR, Vol. 1, 351 and MSA-S-936-17)

SIDENSTRICKER, Abraham. (Cpl.) Co. H, 6th
Regiment Maryland Infantry. (US) Age 20.
Enlisted at Hagerstown 21 August, 1862.
Discharged with physical disability 29 April,
1864. (H.R.M.V., Vol. 1, 242) (MSA-AGR, Vol.
1, 350 and S-936-2)

SIGLER, Samuel B. (2nd Lt.) Co. D, 1st Regiment
Maryland "Cole's Cavalry." (US) Washington
County. Entered service as private; promoted
to commissary sergeant; 1st sergeant; second
lieutenant 25 August, 1863; taken prisoner 18

Aug. 1863 and mustered out 2 Dec. 1864.(Scharf, 328) (H.R.M.V., Vol. 1, 678) (MSA-AGR-S-936-2)

SIGLER, William. (Pvt.) Co. B, 3rd Regiment Potomac Home Brigade Infantry. (US)   Age 33. Boonsboro. Enlisted at Hagerstown, 30 Dec. 1861. Transferred to Co. F. Discharged 30 Dec. 1864. (H.R.M.V., Vol. 1, 594) (Captain Maxwell's roster) (MSA-S-936-23)

SIMMONS, David. (Pvt.) Co. B, 3rd Regiment Potomac Home Brigade Infantry. (US) Age 22. .Hancock. Enlisted 29 March, 1864. Discharged 29 May, 1865.(H.R.M.V., Vol. 1, 578)(MSA-S-936-24)

SIMMONS, John A. (Sgt.) Co. B, 3rd Regiment Potomac Home Brigade Infantry. (US) Age 23. Hagerstown. Enlisted 24 October, 1861. Discharged 24 October, 1864. (H.R.M.V., Vol. 1, 578) (MSA-S-936-24)

SIMMS, Jackson. (Pvt.) Co. H, 55th Massachusetts Regiment. (U.S.C.T.) (US) Hagerstown. Served from 1 July, 1863 to 1 November, 1865. (1890-C)

SIMPSON, John. (Pvt.) Co. D, 6th Regiment Pennsylvania Infantry. (U.S.C.T.) (US) Hagerstown. Served from fall of 1864 to fall of 1865. (1890-C)

SIMS, Richard. (Pvt.) Co. A, 30th Infantry Regiment. (U.S.C.T.) (US) Maryland Volunteers. Knoxville. Served from May, 1864 to 1865. (1890-C)

SINN, John L. (Pvt.) Co. B, 7th Regiment Maryland Infantry (US) Age 19. Enlisted at Hagerstown, 14 August, 1862. Reported sick in Alexandria, Va., hospital. Mustered out near Washington, D. C., 13 June, 1865. (H.R.M.V., Vol. 1, 282) (MSA-AGR, Vol. 1, 351)

SITES, Andrew J. (Pvt.) Co. H, 6th Regiment Maryland Infantry. (US)   Age 24.   Enlisted at Hagerstown, 7 August, 1862. Wounded in action 27 November, 1863 at Mine Run, Va. Transferred

to the V. R. C. Discharged 27 September, 1864.
(H.R.M.V., Vol. 1, 242) (MSA-AGR, Vol. 1, 350
and S-936-2)

SLICK, James F. (Pvt.) Co. G, 1st Regiment
Potomac Home Brigade "Cole's" Cavalry. (US)
Hagerstown. Served from 20 March, 1865 to 28
June, 1865. (H.R.M.V., Vol. 1, 688) (1890-C)

SLICK, Robert H. (Pvt.) Co. G, 1st Regiment
Potomac Home Brigade "Cole's" Cavalry. (US) Age
32. A laborer. Leitersburg. Served from 29
February, 1864 to 28 June, 1865. (H.R.M.V.,
Vol. 1,688) (1890-C) (MSA-AGR-S-936-38)

SLIFER, Joshua. (Pvt.) Co. E, 3rd Regiment
Potomac Home Brigade Infantry. (US)
Brownsville. Served from 28 March, 1864 to 29
May, 1865. (H.R.M.V., Vol. 1, 591) (1890-C)

SLIFER, Randolph. (Pvt.) Co. I, 7th Regiment
Maryland Infantry. (US) Age 30. Enlisted at
Hagerstown, 29 August, 1862. Discharged 31
May, 1865. (H.R.M.V., Vol. 1, 298) (MSA-AGR,
Vol. 1, 353)

SMALL, Leander. (Pvt.) Co. F, 1st Regiment
Potomac Home Brigade Infantry. (US) Age 21.
Shoemaker. Washington County. Enlisted 4
September, 1861. Transferred to Co. F, 13th
Regiment Maryland Infantry, at Frederick, Md.,
28 February, 1864. Discharged 29 May, 1865.
(H.R.M.V., Vol. 1, 514) (MSA-S-936-23)

SMALL, Melvin R. (1st Lt.) Also Adjutant, 6th
Regiment Maryland Infantry. (US) Age 18.
Hagerstown. Began service as first lieutenant
of Co. H, promoted adjutant 11 February, 1863;
died 19 October, 1864 from wounds received at
Cedar Creek. Buried in Rose Hill Cemetery,
Hagerstown. (Scharf, Vol. 1, 328; Vol. 2, 1099)
(H.R.M.V., Vol. 1, 224, 240) (WCCR, Vol. 6,
193)

SMALL, R. H. (Pvt.)Potomac Home Brigade, unit
unknown. (US) Clear Spring. Age 29. Shoemaker.

(U.S. National Archives, Record Group No. 10, 4th Election District)

SMITH, Adolphus W. (Cpl.) Captain Firey's Co. B, 1st Regiment Potomac Home Brigade "Cole's" Cavalry. (US) Age 21. Farmer. Clear Spring. Enlisted 4 September, 1861. Veteran. Reenlisted 14 February, 1864, at Boliver, Va. (H.R.M.V., Vol. 1, 678) (MSA-S-936-30)

SMITH, Albert. (Pvt.) Co. B, 9th Virginia Infantry, (CSA) Sharpsburg. (Hartzler, 272)

SMITH, Albert H. (Cpl.) Co. I, 13th Regiment Maryland Cavalry. (US) Brownsville. Served from 5 September, 1863 to 29 May, 1865. Deserted. (The census records Smith as a private while the roster lists him as a corporal) (H.R.M.V., Vol. 1, 456) (1890-C)

SMITH, Alexander. (Sgt.) Co. C, 1st Regiment Potomac Home Brigade Infantry. (US) Hagerstown. Served from 12 September, 1861 to 1 October, 1864. (1890-C)

SMITH, Alfred. (Pvt.) Co. I, 1st Regiment "Russell's" Maryland Cavalry. (US) Age 20. Apprentice shoemaker. Williamsport. Entered service 17 December, 1862. Killed in action at Deep Bottom, Va, 16 August, 1864. (H.R.M.V., Vol. 1, 734) (McClannahan papers, 4) (1860-C, 90) (MSA-AGR-S-936-38)

SMITH, Amos.(Pvt.) Co. A, 7th Regiment Maryland Infantry. (US) Washington Co. 33. Joined 16 August 1862, at Hagerstown. Died 20 April, 1865, from wounds received in action at Five Forks, Va., 5 April, 18965. (Scharf, Vol. 1, 226) (H.R.M.V., Vol. 1, 280) (MSA-AGR, Vol. 1, 351 and MSA-S-936-17)

SMITH, Andrew J. (Pvt.) Co. E, 3rd Regiment Potomac Home Brigade Infantry. (US) Trego. Served from 31 May, 1864 to 29 May, 1865. Buried in Lutheran Church Cemetery at Locust Grove. (H.R.M.V., Vol. 1, 591) (WCCR, Vol. 3,

165) (1890-C)

SMITH, Charles. (Cpl.) Co. H, 6th Regiment
Maryland Infantry. (US) Age 25. Enlisted at
Hagerstown 21 August, 1862. Reduced from rank
of sergeant 2 April, 1865. Discharged near
Washington, D.C., 20 June, 1865. (H.R.M.V.,
Vol. 1, 242) (MSA-AGR, Vol. 1, 350 and S-936-2)

SMITH, Charles F. (Pvt.) Co. H, 7th Regiment
Maryland Infantry. (US) Hagerstown. Served from
June, 1862 to May, 1865. (1890-C)

SMITH, Charles R. (Pvt.) Co. I, 7th Regiment
Maryland Infantry. (US) Age 17. Hagerstown.
The son of attorney George W. Smith, he served
from 18 August, 1862 to 31 May, 1865. Lost his
health in Richmond Libby Prison. (H.R.M.V.,
Vol. 1, 298) (1890-C) (1860-C, 29) (MSA-AGR,
Vol. 1, 353)

SMITH, Dallas E. (Pvt.) Co. H, 3rd Regiment
Maryland Cavalry. (US) Boonsboro. Served from
28 September, 1863 to 7 September, 1865.
(H.R.M.V., Vol. 1, 776) (1890-C)

SMITH, Daniel. (Pvt.) Co. A, 1st Maryland
Cavalry, (CSA) Downsville. (Hartzler, 272)
(Huntsberry, 83)

SMITH, David Hilary. (Pvt.) Co. B, 11th Regiment
Potomac Home Brigade Infantry. (100 days) (US)
From near Rohrsville/Boonsboro area. Age 21.
Enrolled at Sharpsburg, 5 June, 1864.
Discharged 29 September, 1864, at Baltimore.
Moved to Saline, Kansas after the war with
wife, Isabella Kuhn Smith, and a two year old
son. Applied for and received land in
accordance with the Homestead Act, and engaged
in farming. Later he and his wife owned and
operated a retirement home in Culver, Kansas,
where they spent their senior years. David
Smith died 8 May, 1925, and is buried in the
Walnut Grove (Wolff) Cemetery, in Pleasant
Valley Township, Saline, Kansas. (H.R.M.V.,
Vol. 1, 379 (Major portion furnished by Mrs.

Helen C. Dingler, of Enterprise, Kansas,
through Mr. and Mrs. Richard Smith, of
Hagerstown)

SMITH, David L. (Sgt.) Co. A, 7th Regiment
Maryland Infantry. (US) Age 27. Washington Co
Enlisted at Hagerstown 16 August, 1862.
Reported sick in Philadelphia hospital.
Discharged 2 June, 1865. Buried in Rose Hill
Cemetery, Hagerstown. (Scharf, 226) (H.R.M.V.
Vol. 1, 280) (WCCR, Vol. 7, 277) (MSA-AGR, Vol
1, 350 and MSA-S-936-17)

SMITH, Edward E. (Pvt.) Co. I, 1st Regiment
"Russell's" Maryland Cavalry. (US) Hagerstown.
Served from 15 August, 1861 to September, 1864
(1890-C)

SMITH, Eugene E. (Pvt.) Co. I, 1st Regiment
Maryland Cavalry. (US) Hagerstown. Enlisted a
Hagerstown 3 September, 1862. Sustained
gunshot wound to right foot. Discharged 23
September, 1864. Transferred to V.R.C.

SMITH, George P. (Pvt.) Co. I, 7th Regiment
Maryland Infantry. (US) Age 35. Hagerstown.
Enlisted at Hagerstown, 29 August, 1862.
Discharged 31 May, 1865. Fought in 26 battles.
(H.R.M.V., Vol. 1, 298) (1890-C) (MSA-AGR, Vol
1, 353)

SMITH, George S. (Pvt.) Co. A, 1st Regiment
Potomac Home Brigade "Cole's" Cavalry. (US)
Hancock. Enlisted 1 February, 1862.
Discharged 1 February, 1865. (H.R.M.V., Vol. 1
670) (MSA-S-936-30)

SMITH, George W. (Pvt.) Co. H, 3rd Regiment
Maryland Cavalry. (US) Hagerstown. Served
beginning 28 September, 1863. Died 30 August,
1865. (H.R.M.V., Vol. 1, 776) (1890-C)

SMITH, John. (Pvt.) Co. I, 1st Regiment
"Russell's" Maryland Cavalry. (US) Hagerstown.
Served from 2 December, 1861 to 8 August, 1865
Lost sight in left eye. Received pension of $4

per month. (Pensions List, 157) (H.R.M.V.,
Vol. 1, 734) (1890-C)

SMITH, John H. (Pvt.) Co. G, 5th Regiment
Maryland Infantry. (US) Smoketown. Served from
22 October, 1864 to 1 September, 1865. (1890-C)

SMITH, John K. (1st Lt.) Co. G, 7th Regiment
Maryland Infantry. (US) Washington County.
Began service 12 September, 1862 and resigned
11 January, 1863. (Scharf, 328) (H.R.M.V., Vol.
1, 292)

SMITH, Jonathan. (Pvt.) Co. F, 13th Regiment
Maryland Infantry. (US) Smithsburg. Served from
13 February, 1865 to 29 May, 1865. (H.R.M.V.,
Vol. 1, 448) (1890-C)

SMITH, Joseph E. (Pvt.) Co. H, 1st Regiment
Potomac Home Brigade Infantry. (US) Sharpsburg.
Served from 14 September, 1861 to 25 October,
1864. Buried in Mountain View Cemetery,
Sharpsburg. (H.R.M.V., Vol. 1, 528) (WCCR, Vol.
1, 8)

SMITH, M. H. (Cpl.) Co. B, 11th Regiment
Pennsylvania Infantry. (US) Trego. Served from
15 June, 1864 to 29 September, 1864. (1890-C)

SMITH, Marvin T. (Pvt.) Co. E, 1st Potomac Home
Brigade Infantry. (US) Sharpsburg. Served from
31 March, 1864 to 29 May, 1865. (1890-C)

SMITH, Samuel. (Pvt.) Co. E, 3rd Regiment Potomac
Home Brigade Infantry. (US) Brownsville.
Served from 31 March, 1864 to 29 May, 1865.
(H.R.M.V., Vol. 1, 591) (1890-C)

SLEIGH, Charles A. (Sgt.) Captain Firey's Co. B,
1st Regiment Potomac Home Brigade "Cole's"
Cavalry. (US) Clear Spring. (also spelled
Schleigh. Listed in the 1890 census as a
sergeant and in the H.R.M.V., as a bugler.)
Served from 4 September, 1861 to 28 June, 1865.
(H.R.M.V., Vol. 1, 678) (1890-C)

SNELL, George. (Pvt.) Co. I, 7th Regiment
Maryland Infantry. (US) Age 45. Enlisted at
Hagerstown, 29 August, 1862. Transferred to
V.R.C. March, 1865. Discharged near Washington,
D.C., 26 June, 1865. (H.R.M.V., Vol. 1, 298)
(MSA-AGR, Vol. 1, 354)

SNIVELY, George W. (1st Lt.) Co. I, 3rd Regiment
Maryland Cavalry. (US) Clear Spring. Began
service 3 November, 1863 as second lieutenant;
promoted first lieutenant 31 May, 1865.
Discharged 7 September, 1865. (Scharf, 328)
(H.R.M.V., Vol. 1, 776.)

SNIVELY, Isaac. (Pvt.) Co. I, 1st Regiment
"Russell's" Maryland Cavalry. (US) Hagerstown.
Entered service 3 September, 1861. Killed in
action at Front Royal, Va, 19 August, 1862.
(H.R.M.V., Vol. 1, 734) (McClannahan, 4)

SNIVLEY, Jacob. (Pvt.) Co. I, 179th Regiment
Pennsylvania Infantry. (US) Hagerstown. Served
1 February, 1865 to 1 August, 1865. (1890-C)

SNIVLEY, Samuel K. (Pvt.) Co. B, 2nd Maryland
Cavalry. (US) Williamsport. Served from 19
April, 1861 to 1 November, 1865. (1890-C)

SNOW, John M. (Pvt.) Co. A, 1st South Carolina
Infantry. (CSA) Keedysville. Served from
August, 1861 to February, 1863. (1890-C)

SNOWDEN, William. (Pvt.) Co. K, 39th Regiment
Infantry. (U.S.C.T.) (US) Washington County.
Owned by Samuel Piper. Enlisted at Baltimore,
31 March, 1864. Absent from wounds received 30
July, 1864, at The Crater, near Petersburg, Va.
(H.R.M.V., Vol. 2, 284) (MSA-S-936-51)

SNYDER, Andrew. (Pvt.) Co. I, 1st Regiment
"Russell's" Maryland Cavalry. (US) Enlisted at
Williamsport, 17 December, 1862. Discharged 8
August, 1865. (H.R.M.V., Vol. 1, 734) (MSA-AGR-
S-936-38)

SNYDER, Charles T. (Pvt.) Co. I, 7th Regiment

Maryland Infantry. (US) Age 22. Enlisted at Hagerstown, 22 August, 1862. Discharged at Williamsport, Md., 20 December, 1862, due to disability. (H.R.M.V., Vol. 1, 298) (MSA-AGR, Vol. 1, 359)

SNYDER, Christian P. (Cpl.) Co. B, 12th Regiment Maryland Infantry. (US) Downsville. Served from 18 June, 1864 to 6 November, 1864. (H.R.M.V., Vol. 1, 425) (1890-C)

SNYDER, Daniel. (Pvt.) Co. I, 1st Regiment "Russell's" Maryland Cavalry. (US) Enlisted at Williamsport, 17 December, 1862. Discharged 8 August, 1865. (H.R.M.V., Vol. 1, 734) (MSA-AGR-S-936-38)

SNYDER (or SNIDER) Peter. (Pvt.) Co. M, 1st Regiment Maryland Cavalry. (US) Age 26. Boatman. Hagerstown. Enlisted at Hagerstown, 7 March, 1864. Discharged 8 August, 1865. (H.R.M.V., Vol. 1, 744) (MSA-AGR-S-936-3

SNYDER, Samuel. (Pvt.) Co. B, 3rd Regiment Maryland Infantry. (US) Age 27. Clear Spring. Enlisted at Williamsport, 2 September, 1861. Discharged 2 September 1864. H.R.M.V., Vol. 1, 125) (1890-C) (MSA-AGR, Vol. 1, 324)

SNYDER, Thomas H. (Pvt.) Co. G., 1st Regiment Potomac Home Brigade "Cole's" Federal Cavalry. (US) Millstone. Served from 26 February, 1864 to 28 June, 1865. Buried in the Dunkard Church Cemetery, near Millstone. (H.R.M.V., Vol. 1, 688) (WCCR, Vol. 4, 187) (1890-C)

SOCEY, Abraham L. (Pvt.) Bugler, Captain Firey's Co. B, 1st Regiment Potomac Home Brigade "Cole's Cavalry". (US) Clear Spring. Enlisted 2, September, 1861. Killed in action 20 January, 1864 in action against Mosby's Guerillas near Romney, W.Va. Buried in St. Peter's Lutheran Cemetery, Clear Spring. (H.R.M.V., part 1, 678) (WCCR, Vol. 2, 342)

SOCKS, George P. (Pvt.) Co. F, 3rd Regiment

Potomac Home Brigade Infantry. (US) Age 34.
Hagerstown. Served from 29 February, 1864 to
29 May, 1865. (H.R.M.V., Vol. 1, 594) (1890-C)
(MSA-S-936-23)

SOWDERS, Michael. (Pvt.) Co. F, 2nd Regiment
Potomac Home Brigade Infantry. (US) Age 25.
Farmer. Washington County. Enlisted 16
September, 1861. Transferred to Co. C.
Veteran. Discharged 29 May, 1865. (H.R.M.V.,
Vol. 1, 559) (MSA-S-936-24)

SPARROW, Jacob. (Pvt.) Co. D, 1st Regiment
Potomac Home Brigade Infantry. (US) Blacksmith.
Antietam Furnace, Md. Died 23 November, 1911,
at Harrisburg, Pa. Enrolled at Harpers Ferry 13
August, 1862. Transferred 8 April, 1865 to
13th Maryland Infantry. Discharged 29 May,
1865, at Baltimore. Captured at Harpers Ferry,
15 September, 1862, by forces commanded by
Stonewall Jackson. Paroled on the same date.
Sent to Aldie, Va., November, 1862. Present
with company in September, 1863. (Information
from records of that period furnished by his
great-grand son Mr. George B. Sparrow, of Ann
Arbor, Michigan. Also (H.R.M.V., Vol. 1, 505,
734) (Pensions List, 157)

SPEAKER, Christopher. (Pvt.) Co. H, 1st Regiment
Maryland Cavalry. (US) Age 18. Farmer.
Downsville. Entered service 3 September, 1861.
Died 8 April, 1864. (H.R.M.V., Vol. 1, 734)
(1890-C) (MSA-S-936-23)

SPESSARD, John. (Pvt.) Co. B, 123 Illinois
Infantry. (US) Washington County. Died 2
January, 1863, of lung fever. (Spessard, 16)

SPIGLER, John N. (Pvt.) Co. I, 1st Regiment
"Russell's" Maryland Cavalry. (US) Age 37.
Williamsport. Served from 17 December, 1862 to
8 August, 1865. Wounded in left foot
Hospitalized. (H.R.M.V., Vol. 1, 734) (1890-C)
(MSA-AGR-S-936-38)

SPRINGER, George W. (Pvt.) Co. B, 3rd Regiment

Potomac Home Brigade Infantry. (US) Age 18.
Washington County. Enlisted 8 November, 1861.
Discharged 8 November, 1864. (H.R.M.V., Vol.
1, 578) (MSA-S-936-23)

SPRINGER, John M. (Pvt.) Co. A, 5th Regiment
Maryland Infantry. (US) Keedysville. Served
from 29 October, 1864 to 1 September, 1865.
(H.R.M.V., Vol. 1, 186) (1890-C)

SPRINGER, John. (Pvt.) Co. A, 2nd Regiment
Maryland Infantry. (US) Trego. Served from 9
June, 1864 to 15 May, 1865. Wounded in action
25 May, 1865. (H.R.M.V., Vol. 1, 78) (1890-C)

SPIDDLE, Jacob B. (Pvt.) Co. A, 1st Regiment
Maryland Infantry. (US) Age 22. Enlisted at
Williamsport, 10 May, 1861. Deserted 25
September, 1861. (H.R.M.V., Vol. 1, 23) (MSA-
AGR, Vol. 1, 323)

SPIELMAN, Daniel. (Pvt.) Co. I, 7th Regiment
Maryland Infantry. (US) Age 18. Funkstown.
Enlisted at Hagerstown, 14 August, 1862. Died
30 August, 1864, in Philadelphia military
hospital of disease contracted in service.
(H.R.M.V., Vol. 1, 298) (1890-C) (MSA-AGR, Vol.
1, 354 and MSA-S-936-17)

SPIELMAN, Frisby. (Pvt.) Co. A, 7th Regiment
Maryland Infantry. (US) Age 20. Washington Co.
Enlisted at Hagerstown, 15 August, 1862. Died
3 February, 1865 while a prisoner of war at
Florence, Ala. (Scharf, Vol. 1, 226)
(H.R.M.V., Vol. 1, 280) (MSA-AGR, Vol. 1, 351)

SPONG, John L. (Cpl.) Co. A, 1st Regiment Potomac
Home Brigade Infantry. (US) Age 18. Enlisted
at Sharpsburg 21 August, 1861. Taken prisoner
in Loudoun Co., Va., 6 May, 1862. (H.R.M.V.,
Vol. 1, 291) (MSA-AGR, Vol. 1, 323)

SPONG, Mathias. (Pvt.) Co. A, 1st Regiment
Potomac Home Brigade Infantry. (US) Sharpsburg.
Served from 15 August, 1851 to 27 August, 1864.
Buried at Mountain View Cemetery, Sharpsburg.

(H.R.M.V., Vol. 1, 491) (WCCR 1, 32) (1890-C)

SPRECHER, Clegget D. (Pvt.) Co. M, 1st Regiment
Potomac Home Brigade "Cole's" Cavalry. (US)
Huyetts. Served from 15 April, 1864 to 25
April, 1865. Wounded in action. Transferred
to V. R. C. (H.R.M.V., Vol. 1, 699) (1890-C)

STAFFORD, Simon P. (Pvt.) Co. B, 7th Regiment
Maryland Infantry. (US) Age 20. Enlisted at
Hagerstown, 27 November, 1862. Discharged 31
May, 1865. (H.R.M.V., Vol. 1, 282) (MSA-AGR,
Vol. 1, 351)

STALEY, Stephen G. (Pvt.) Co. A, 7th Regiment
Maryland Infantry. (US) Age 45. Enlisted at
Hagerstown, 5 March, 1864. Died at U. S.
Hospital, David's Island, N.Y., 26 June, 1864.
(H.R.M.V., Vol. 1, 280) (MSA-AGR, Vol. 1, 351)

STATTON, Thomas H. (Pvt.) Co. F, 39th Regiment
Infantry. (U.S.C.T.) (US) Cavetown. Served
from 30 March, 1864 to 17 April, 1864.
Transferred to the Navy. (H.R.M.V., Vol. 2,
276) (1890-C)

STAUBS, Josiah F. (Pvt.) Co. H, 1st Regiment
Potomac Home Brigade Infantry. (US) Sharpsburg.
Served from 25 October, 1861 to 25 October,
1864. Transferred to Co. H, 13th Maryland
Infantry. Buried at Mountain View Cemetery,
Sharpsburg. (H.R.M.V., Vol. 1, 528) (WCCR,
Vol. 1, 28)

STEEL, Daniel A. (Pvt.) Co. B, 7th Regiment
Maryland Infantry. (US) Age 42. Enlisted at
Hagerstown, 11 August, 1862. Discharged near
Washington, D.C., 31 May, 1865. (H.R.M.V.,
Vol. 1, 282) (MSA-AGR, Vol. 1, 351)

STINEMETZ, John. (Lt. Col.) Co. H, 13th Maryland
Volunteer Infantry. (US) Clear Spring. Entered
service as second lieutenant, 28 February,
1865, in Co. F, 1st Potomac Home Brigade
Infantry. Promoted 2nd lieutenant 1 March,
1865. Later assigned to Co. H, 13th Regiment.

(Washington County Cemetery Records records his
discharge rank as lieutenant colonel) Buried in
Rose Hill Cemetery, Clear Spring. (WCCR, Vol.)

STEPHENSON, William H. (Pvt.) Co. D, 5th Regiment
Maryland Infantry. (US) Ringgold. Served from
21 September, 1864 to 14 June, 1865. (H.R.M.V.,
Vol. 1, 197) (1890-C)

STEPHY, David. (Pvt.) Co. A, 7th Regiment
Maryland Infantry. (US) Washington Co. Age
16. Joined 15 August, 1862, at Hagerstown.
Killed in action 16 June, 1864, at Petersburg,
Va. (Scharf, Vol. 1, 226) (H.R.M.V., Vol. 1,
280) (MSA-AGR, Vol. 1, 351 and MSA-S-936-17)

STERLING, George M. (Pvt.) Co. I, 1st Regiment
"Russell's" Maryland Cavalry. (US) Indian
Springs. Enlisted at Williamsport, 17
December, 1862. Wounded at Deep Bottom, Va.,
16 August, 1864. Discharged 11 June, 1865.
(H.R.M.V., Vol. 1, 732) (McClannahan papers, 4)
(MSA-AGR-S-936-38)

STERLING, Samuel B. (Pvt.) Co. H, 6th Regiment
Maryland Infantry. (US) Age 20. Farmer.
Indian Springs. Enlisted at Hagerstown, 20
August, 1862. Wounded in action 27 November,
1865, at Mine Run., Va. Transferred to 1st
Maryland Volunteer Infantry. Discharged under
Presidential proclamation 4 May, 1865.
(H.R.M.V., Vol. 1, 242) (1890-C) (MSA-AGR-S-
936-2)

STERN, William H. (Pvt.) Co. E, 1st Regiment
Potomac Home Brigade Cavalry. (US) Boonsboro.
Served from 1 October, 1861 to 1 October, 1864.
Suffered physical defects from a gunshot wound
to the upper right chest. (H.R.M.V., Vol. 1,
509) (1890-C)

STEVENS, David. (Pvt.) Co. B, 3rd Regiment
Potomac Home Brigade Infantry. (US) Age 20.
Beaver Creek. Enlisted at Hagerstown, 1
August, 1862. Discharged 29 December, 1864.
(H.R.M.V., Vol. 1, 579) (Captain Maxwell's

roster) (MSA-S-936-23)

STEVENS, Isaiah. (Pvt.) Co. B, 3rd Regiment
Potomac Home Brigade Infantry. (US) Age 20.
Washington County. Enlisted 20 April, 1862.
Discharged 20 April, 1865. (H.R.M.V., Vol. 1,
579) (MSA-S-936-23)

STEWART, Asbury. (Pvt.) Co. K, 19th Regiment
Infantry. (U.S.C.T.) (US) Boonsboro. Entered
service 10 May, 1863. Discharged 10 May, 1866.
(1890-C) (H.R.M.V., Vol. 2, 232)

STILLWELL, James. (Pvt.) Co. I, 1st Regiment
"Russell's" Maryland Cavalry. (US) Enlisted at
Williamsport, 2 December, 1861. Died 2 March,
1863. (H.R.M.V., Vol. 1, 734) (MSA-AGR-S-936-
38)

STILLWELL, John W. (Pvt.) Co. B, 3rd Regiment
Potomac Home Brigade Infantry. (US) Age 19.
Hancock. Enlisted 30 May, 1864. Discharged 29
May, 1865. (H.R.M.V., Vol. 1, 578) (MSA-S-936-
24)

STINE, Henry. (Pvt.) Co. B, 5th Regiment Maryland
Infantry. (US) Hancock. Served from 21
September, 1864 to 14 June, 1865. (H.R.M.V.,
Vol. 1, 190) (1890-C)

STINE, Lawson. (Pvt.) Co. B, 11th Regiment
Maryland Infantry. (US) Brownsville. Served
from 26 May, 1864 to 29 September, 1865.
(H.R.M.V., Vol. 1, 379) (1890-C)

STINEMETZ, John. (2nd Lt.) Co. E, Twelfth
Regiment Maryland Infantry. (US) Age 28. Clear
Spring. Served 31 July, 1864 to 6 November,
1864. Transferred to Co. H, 13th Maryland
Infantry. (Scharf, 328) (H.R.M.V., Vol. 1,
428) (1890-C)

STIPP, Abraham V. (Pvt.) Co. B, 3rd Regiment
Potomac Home Brigade Infantry. (US) Age 23.
Washington County. Enlisted 1 August, 1862.
Discharged 29 May, 1865. (H.R.M.V., Vol. 1,

578) (MSA-S-936-23)

STOCKMAN, William. H. (Pvt.) Co. H, 1st Regiment
Potomac Home Brigade Infantry. (US)   Age 18.
Enlisted 13 February, 1863. Mustered out at
U.S. General Hospital Cumberland, Md., 20 June,
1865.(H.R.M.V., Vol. 1, 528) (MSA-S-936-23)

STONEBREAKER, Edward L. (Pvt.) 2nd Maryland
Cavalry. (CSA) Funkstown. (Hartzler, 281)

STONEBREAKER, Joseph R. (Pvt.) Co. C, 1st
Maryland Cavalry. (CSA) Funkstown. The son of
Henry and Angelic E. Rench Stonebreaker, he was
born in Mississippi, where the family kept a
hotel for several years. In 1847 they returned
to their native Maryland, and stayed with
grandfather Rench until a disastrous fire
destroyed the home. Henry moved his family to
Funkstown, where Joseph, his brothers and
sisters grew up on Green Street. Joseph's
Sunday school teacher tried, without success,
to make a preacher out of him. He admitted
enjoying the sermons of Rev. Robert Douglas, of
Sharpsburg, the father of Henry Kyd Douglas.
Children who could remember most of what Rev.
Douglas had to say in his sermon were often
rewarded with a penny, and Joseph collected
many of them. On a clear June night in 1859 a
tall man with a long beard stopped at Hammer's
Tavern in Funkstown, and asked for feed for his
horse. The stranger said his wagon was loaded
with fork handles, but that made everyone
suspicious. The stranger was John Brown, on
his way to a small farm south of Sharpsburg.
Later, he failed to take over the Federal
arsenal at Harper's Ferry. The tavern incident
prompted George Alfred Townsen to pen a poem
about Brown's visit.
"Legend of Funkstown."

Nick Hammer sat in Funkstown
Before his tavern door---
The same old blue stone tavern
The wagoners knew of yore,
When the Conestoga Schooners

Came staggering under their load
And the line of slow pack-horses
Stomped over the National Road.

One day in June two wagons
Came over Antietam bridge,
And a tall, old man behind them,
Strode up the Turnpike ridge,
His beard was long and grizzled
His face was gnarled and long,
His voice was keen and nasal,
And his mouth and eye were strong.

One wagon was full of boxes,
And the other full of poles,
As the weaver's wife discovered,
While the weaver took the tolls.

Two young men drove the horses,
And neither the people knew,
But young Nick asked a question,
And the old man looked him through.

In 1860, the Republicans nominated Abraham
Lincoln for president. The Democrats split,
with the northern wing selecting Stephen A.
Douglas, of Illinois, and the southern, John C.
Breckenridge, of Kentucky. The Union party
selected John Bell of Tennessee. Funkstown, a
Democratic stronghold for years, with most of
the eligible voters being for "States Rights,"
supported Breckenridge. The Whigs got what was
left and not a single vote was cast for
Lincoln. As the war began and Fort Sumter made
the newspaper headlines, some citizens
displayed their sentiments with flags and
banners. One individual, Hanson Beachley, a
eccentric clerk at the Davis General Store,
boasted loud and long that he was ready to go
fight, and defend Washington. But, when the
time came he was turned down. Hanson had no
teeth. In the early days of the war Henry
Stonebreaker was the postmaster, and Joseph
helped make up the bundles carried daily by a
four-horse stage coach between Hagerstown and
Frederick. On 9 August, 1862 the ascension of
a giant balloon was scheduled from the

Hagerstown public square, a spectacular event, attracting much attention. Joseph, anxious to see his first "big balloon," went to town. Before he could enter the public square he was arrested by a Federal soldier. He did not know Hagerstown was under martial law and governed by a provost marshall. Stonebreaker was taken before the "provo" who demanded that he take the oath to the Union. The youth said he was not yet out of his teens, had never committed an overt act against the government, and should not be held accountable for his southern feeling, since he was born there. The provo's reply was curt, "Take the oath, or go to jail!" Joseph went to jail. There he found Joseph Williams and Sol Keller, also from Funkstown. Both had been locked up several days before along with other local citizens. All were packed tightly into a small cell. On 18 August, along with five others, including Judge John T. Mason, they departed the Cumberland Valley Depot, under guard, for Harrisburg, Pa., then to confinement in Baltimore. They were released om 27 August. A few weeks after returning home the battle of Antietam was fought at Sharpsburg, and Funkstown witnessed the passing of the armies and hundreds of wounded soldiers. In July of the following year Gettysburg was contested and the retreating Confederates fell back upon Washington County. On the 8th, prior to the fighting at Boonsboro, Rebel cavalry commander Jeb Stuart visited Stonebreaker's home on Green Street, and before departing, signed his sister's notebook. The Battle of Funkstown was fought on the 10th, and Joseph witnessed much of it from the garret window of Sol Keller's home. He watched army surgeons treat the wounded, amputate arms and legs, and cover over those who could not be saved, at the Chaney house, across the street. As he observed, a sniper's bullet smashed into the window frame, barely missing his peering eyes. The dark memories of that day remained etched in his mind for many years afterwards. Joseph followed the Rebel army south and eventually joined Co. C, of the 1st Maryland Cavalry, in

the Maryland Line, Army of Northern Virginia.
He was present for the battles of Third
Winchester, Fisher's Hill and Cedar Creek. He
returned home at the war's end.

The Maryland Line Confederate Soldiers' Home
was established at an abandoned Federal
arsenal, near Baltimore, in 1888. Selected
rooms honored various Confederate soldiers,
officers and fighting units, and one,
substantially furnished, was named by Joseph R.
Stonebreaker as a memorial to his brother,
Edward L. Stonebreaker, who fought with the
2nd Maryland Cavalry. (37) (Hartzler, 281)
(Goldsborough, 232)

STONER, Abraham. (Pvt.) Co. H, 6th Regiment
Maryland Infantry. (US) Age 19. Enlisted at
Hagerstown, 21 August, 1862. Deserted 18
January, 1863, at Harper's Ferry, Va.
(H.R.M.V., Vol. 1, 242) (MSA-AGR, Vol. 1, 350
and S-936-2)

STOOPS, James.(Cpl.) Co. D, 4th Regiment
Infantry. (U.S.C.T.) (US) Hagerstown. Served
from 28 August, 1863 to 4 May, 1866. (H.R.M.V.,
Vol. 2, 140) (1890-C)

STOOPS, William. (Pvt.) Co. H, 13th Regiment
Maryland Infantry. (US) Knoxville. Served
from 21 January, 1865 to 29 May, 1865.
(H.R.M.V., Vol. 1, 454) (1890-C)

STOTTLEMEYER, Andrew J. (Pvt.) Co. A, 1st
Regiment Potomac Home Brigade, "Cole's
Cavalry." (US) Hancock. Served from 10 August,
1861 to 28 June, 1865. Suffered a sabre wound
to the shoulder 2 September, 1862, at Leesburg,
Va. Taken prisoner 18 June, 1863. Veteran.
(H.R.M.V., Vol. 1, 669) 1890-C)

STOUCH, Jerome. (Pvt.) Co. M, 1st Regiment
Potomac Home Brigade "Cole's" Cavalry. (US)
Huyetts. Served from 25 February, 1864 to 28
June, 1865. (H.R.M.V., Vol. 1, 699) (1890-C)

STOUFFER, Benjamin F. (Pvt.) Co. E, 1st Regiment
Potomac Home Brigade Infantry. (US) Age 18.
Laborer. Washington County. Enlisted 19
January, 1865. Transferred to Co. E, 13th
Regiment Maryland Infantry. Discharged 29 May,
1865. (H.R.M.V., Vol. 1, 509) (MSA-S-936-23)

STOUFFER, Henry M. (Pvt.) Co. L, 1st Regiment
Potomac Home Brigade "Cole's" Cavalry. (US)
Edgemont. Served from 29 November, 1864 to 28
June, 1865. Suffered from jaundice for 23
years after the war. (H.R.M.V., Vol. 1, 697)
(1890-C)

STOUFFER, John C. (Pvt.) Co. L, 1st Regiment
Potomac Home Brigade "Cole's" Cavalry. (US)
Edgemont. Served 31 March, 1864 to 28 June,
1865. Crippled back resulting from fall during
service. (H.R.M.V., Vol. 1, 697) (1890-C)

STOUFFER, Peter. (Pvt.) Co. D, 5th Regiment
Maryland Infantry. (US) Smoketown. Served
from 29 October, 1864 to 1 September, 1865.
(H.R.M.V., Vol. 1, 197) (1890-C)

STOUT, John. (Pvt.) Co. H, 1st Regiment Potomac
Home Brigade Infantry. (US) Age 18. Laborer.
Enlisted at Sandy Hook, 22 January, 1865.
Transferred to Co. H, 13th Maryland Infantry.
Discharged 29 May, 1865. (H.R.M.V., Vol. 1,
528)

STOUGH, Charles F. (Pvt.) Co. A, 7th Regiment
Maryland Infantry. (US) Age 35. Enlisted at
Hagerstown, 11 March, 1864. Transferred to Co.
C, 1st Maryland Infantry, 31 May, 1865.
(H.R.M.V., Vol. 1, 280) (MSA-AGR, Vol. 1, 324)

STOVER, Martin. (Pvt.) Co. B, 3rd Regiment
Potomac Home Brigade Infantry. (US) Age 28.
Washington County. Enlisted 3 December, 1861.
Discharged 3 December, 1864. (H.R.M.V., Vol.
1, 578) (MSA-S-936-23)

STRAUSE, Frisby G. D., (1st Sgt.) Co. I, 7th
Regiment Maryland Infantry. (US) Age 22.

Transferred to V.R.C. 8 October, 1864.
Mustered out near Washington, D.C., 3 June,
1865. (H.R.M.V., Vol. 1, 298) (MSA-AGR, Vol.
1, 354)

STRAUSE, George. (or Straus) (Pvt.) Co. I, 7th
Regiment Maryland Infantry. (US) Age 21.
Enlisted at Hagerstown, 28 August, 1862.
Discharged 31 May, 1865. (H.R.M.V., Vol. 1,
298) (MSA-AGR, Vol. 1, 353)

STRIDE, (or Strine) Rufus. (Pvt.) Co. A, 1st
Regiment Potomac Home Brigade Infantry. (US)
Sharpsburg. Served from 15 August, 1861 to 27
August, 1864. (H.R.M.V., Vol. 1, 491) (1890-C)

STRONG, Elias. (Pvt.) Co. A, 1st Regiment Potomac
Home Brigade Infantry. (US) Sharpsburg.
Served from 19 August, 1861 to 27 August, 1864.
(1890-C)

STUDENWALT, Jacob C., (Pvt.) Co. H, 6th Regiment
Maryland Infantry. (US) Age 28. Enlisted at
Hagerstown, 11 August, 1862. Taken prisoner.
Discharged near Washington, D.C., 20 June,
1865. (H.R.M.V., Vol. 1, 242) (MSA-AGR, Vol.
1, 350 and S-936-2))

STULL, John. (Pvt.) Co. I, 7th Regiment Maryland
Infantry. (US) Age 33. Enlisted at
Hagerstown, 25 August, 1862. Killed in action
28 May, 1864, near Cold Harbor, Va. (H.R.M.V.,
Vol. 1, 298) (MSA-AGR, Vol. 1, 354)

SUFFICOOL, Lewis M. (Pvt.) Co. F, 1st Regiment
Potomac Home Brigade Infantry. (US) Clear
Spring. Served from 21 February, 1865 to 29
May, 1865. Transferred to Co. F, 13th Maryland
Infantry. (H.R.M.V., Vol. 1, 515) (1890-C)

SULLIVAN, John. (Pvt.) Co. I, 7th Regiment
Maryland Infantry. (US) Age 22. Enlisted at
Hagerstown, 18 August, 1862. Discharged 31
May, 1865. (H.R.M.V., Vol. 1, 298) (MSA-AGR,
Vol. 1, 353)

SUMMERS, John J. (Pvt.) Co. B, 1st Regiment
Maryland Infantry. (US) Age 23. Enlisted at
Four Locks, 1 November, 1862. Transferred from
Co. G, 7th Maryland Infantry, 1 June, 1865.
(H.R.M.V., Vol. 1, 29) (MSA-AGR, Vol. 1, 324)

SUMMERS, John H. (Pvt.) Co. G, 7th Regiment
Maryland Infantry. (US) Age 19. Enlisted at
Four Locks, Md., 25 November, 1862. Deserted 21
May, 1863. (H.R.M.V., Vol. 1, 294) (MSA-AGR,
Vol. 1, 351)

SUMMERS, Thomas. (Pvt.) Co. F, 4th Regiment
Pennsylvania Cavalry. (US) Smithsburg. Served
from February, 1864 to July 1865. (1890-C)

SUTER, Charles M. (1st Lt.) Co. I, 7th Regiment
Maryland Infantry. (US) Age 24. Hagerstown.
Served from 14 August, 1862 to 31 May, 1865.
Entered service as private; promoted corporal;
sergeant; first lieutenant, 19 December, 1864.
Wounded in action 1 April, 1865. (H.R.M.V.,
Vol. 1, 297) (1890-C) (MSA-AGR, Vol. 1, page
354)

SWAIN, James F. (Cpl.) Co. H, 1st Regiment
Potomac Home Brigade Infantry. (US) Sharpsburg.
Served from 25 October, 1861 to 25 October,
1864. Buried in Mountain View Cemetery,
Sharpsburg. (H.R.M.V., Vol. 1, 528) (1890-C)

SWAN, James. (Cpl.) Co. I, 7th Regiment Maryland
Infantry. (US) Age 22. Enlisted at Hagerstown
28 August, 1862. Discharged 31 May, 1865.
(H.R.M.V., Vol. 1, 298) (MSA-AGR, Vol. 1, 353)

SWARTY, Charles. (Pvt.) Co. I, 7th Regiment
Maryland Infantry. (US) Age 14. Enlisted at
Hagerstown, 18 August, 1862. Discharged as a
minor by civil authorities November, 1862.
(H.R.M.V., Vol. 1, 298) (MSA-AGR, Vol. 1, 354)

SWITZER, John. (Pvt.) Co. I, 4th Regiment
Maryland Infantry. (US) Clear Spring. Served
from 28 August, 1863 to 4 May, 1866. (1890-C)

SWEITZER, John H. (Pvt.) Co. I, 6th Regiment
Maryland Infantry. (US) Age 19. Enlisted at
Hagerstown, 21 August, 1862. Discharged with
physical disability 5 March, 1865. (H.R.M.V.,
Vol. 1, 244) (MSA-AGR, Vol. 1, 350)

SWOPE, John. (Pvt.) Co. A, 7th Regiment Maryland
Infantry. (US) Age 18. Washington Co. Served
from 11 August, 1862 until 3 June, 1865.
Wounded in action 2 June, 1864. Taken prisoner
31 March, 1865. Discharged at Annapolis.
(Sharp, 226) (H.R.M.V., Vol. 1, 280) (MSA-AGR,
Vol. 1, 351 and MSA-S-936-17)

SWOPE, Michael. (Pvt.) Co. E, 1st Regiment
Potomac Home Brigade Infantry. (US) Hagerstown.
Served 14 September, 1861 to 1 October, 1864.
(H.R.M.V., Vol. 1, 509) (1890-C)

SWOPE, Simon. (Pvt.) Co. L, 1st Regiment Potomac
Home Brigade "Cole's" Cavalry. (US)
Leitersburg. Served from 29 March, 1864 to 28
June, 1865. (H.R.M.V., Vol. 1, 697) (1890-C)

-- T --

TABLER, William M. (Pvt.) Co. I, 1st Regiment
"Russell's" Maryland Cavalry. (US) Enlisted at
Williamsport, 17 December, 1862. Discharged 8
August, 1865. (H.R.M.V., Vol. 1, 734) (MSA-
AGR-S-736-38)

TANNER, Dr. Isaac Scott. U. S. Navy; Co. F, 1st
Virginia Cavalry. Staff surgeon to Gen. Joseph
E. Johnston and later Chief Surgeon for Gen.
William Hoke's division. Clear Spring. He
studied medicine under Dr. Perrin, at
Shepherdstown, where he also began his
practice. In 1847 he passed an examination for
surgeon with the U. S. Navy, however, sea-
sickness prevented his anticipated Naval career
from developing. He returned home at the
outbreak of the war enlisting in the
Confederate cavalry. After the battle of First
Manassas he was promoted to surgeon and
advanced to the above positions. (Musser, 384)

TAYLOR, Charles. (Pvt.) Co. D, 4th Regiment
Maryland Infantry. (U.S.C.T.) (US)
Williamsport. Served from 28 August, 1863 to 4
May, 1866. (1890-C)

TAYLOR, James H. (Pvt.) Co. E, 45th Regiment
Pennsylvania Infantry. (US) Hancock. Served
from 16 November, 1864 to 25 July, 1865.
(1890-C)

TAYLOR, James R. (Pvt.) Co. H, 1st Regiment
Potomac Home Brigade "Cole's" Cavalry. (US)
Keedysville. Served from 17 March, 1864 to 28
June, 1865. (H.R.M.V., Vol. 1, 690) (1890-C)
(Williams, Vol. 2, 763)

TAYLOR, William F. (Pvt.) Co. A, 13th Regiment
Maryland Infantry, (US) Downsville. Served
from 15 February, 1865 to 29 May, 1865.
Discharged with heart disease. (H.R.M.V., Vol.
1, 435) (1890-C)

TEACH, Jacob. (Pvt.) Co. E, 12th Regiment
Illinois Cavalry. (US) Pinesburg. Served from
6 October, 1862 to 9 October, 1865. (1890-C)

TEACH, John W. (Pvt.) Co. M, 21st Pennsylvania
Cavalry. (US) Clear Spring. Service dates not
available. (1890-C)

TEARNEY, Leonidas Joseph. (Pvt.) Co. D, 12th
Virginia Cavalry, (CSA) Hagerstown. (Hartzler,
285)

THOMAS, Benjamin. (Pvt.) Co. H, 1st Regiment
Potomac Home Brigade "Cole's" Cavalry. (US)
Boonsboro. Served from 25 March, 1864 to 28
June, 1865. (H.R.M.V., Vol. 1, 690) (1890-C)

THOMAS, Jasper N. (Pvt.) Co. A, 1st Regiment
Potomac Home Brigade Infantry. (US)
Keedysville. Served from 15 August, 1861 to 27
August, 1864. Later transferred to Co. A, 13th
Maryland Infantry. Buried in Mountain View
Cemetery, Sharpsburg. (H.R.M.V., Vol. 1, 491)

THOMAS, John F. (Pvt.) Co. B, 3rd Regiment
Potomac Home Brigade Infantry. (US) Age 20.
Hagerstown. Enlisted at Hagerstown, 18
November, 1861. Veteran. Transferred to Co. F.
Discharged 29 May, 1865. (H.R.M.V., Vol. 1,
579) (Captain Maxwell's roster) (MSA-S-936-23)

THOMAS, Joshua. (Pvt.) Musician. Co. B, 11th
Regiment Maryland Infantry. (US) Hagerstown.
Served from 27 May, 1864 to 29 September, 1864.
(H.R.M.V., Vol. 1, 379) (1890-C)

THOMAS, Michael. (Pvt.) Co. H, 6th Regiment
Maryland Infantry. (US) Age 18. Enlisted at
Hagerstown, 11 August, 1862. Wounded in action
12 May, 1864 at Spotsylvania, Va. Hospitalized.
Discharged 20 June, 1865, near Washington, D.C.
(H.R.M.V., Vol. 1, 242) (MSA-AGR, Vol. 1, 359
and S-936-2)

THOMAS, Michael R. (Pvt.) Co. B, 12th Regiment
Maryland Infantry. (US) Boonsboro. Served from
18 June, 1864 to 6 November, 1864. (H.R.M.V.,
Vol. 1, 425; (1890-C)

THOMAS, William. (Pvt.) Co. C., 15th Maryland
Volunteer Infantry. (US) Washington Co. Buried
in Sandy Hook Cemetery. (WCCR, Vol. 4, 76.)

THOMAS, William H. (Pvt.) Co. G, 11th Regiment
Maryland Infantry. (US) Ringgold. Served from
27 July, 1864 to 21 September, 1864 in Co. B.
(100 days) Reenlisted 22 September, 1864,
serving to 15 June, 1865, in Co. G. (H.R.M.V.,
Vol. 1, 410)

THOMPSON, George. (Pvt.) Co. I, 1st Regiment
"Russell's" Maryland Cavalry. (US)
Williamsport. Entered service 3 September,
1861. Deserted between 30 April and 18 August,
1862. (H.R.M.V., Vol. 1, 734) (1890-C)

THOMPSON, Lawrence P. (Pvt.) Co. A, 7th Regiment

Maryland Infantry. (US) Age 19. Washington Co.
Entered service 16 August, 1862 at Hagerstown.
Served until 30 March, 1865. Wounded in action
31 July, 1864, at Petersburg, Va. Discharged
for disability with surgeon's certificate.
(Scharf, Vol. 1, 226) (H.R.M.V., Vol. 1, 280)
(MSA-AGR, Vol. 1, 356 and MSA-S-936-17)

THOMPSON, Samuel S. (2nd Lt.) Co. D, 3rd Maryland
Infantry. (US) Washington Co. Enlisted 27
February, 1864. Promoted first sergeant 29
February 1864; promoted second lieutenant 14
November, 1865. Veteran volunteer. Mustered out
31 July, 1864. Wounded in left thigh. Buried
in Rose Hill Cemetery, Hagerstown. (H.R.M.V.,
Vol. 1, 125, 131) (WCCR, Vol. 6, 261)

THOMPSON, Thomas H. (Pvt.) Co. I, 2nd Regiment
Infantry. (U.S.C.T.) (US) Boonsboro. (MSA-S-
936-45)

TITLOW, David. (Pvt.) Co. C, 13th Regiment
Maryland Infantry. (US) Hagerstown. Served
from 30 January, 1865 to 29 May, 1865. (1890-C)

TITLOW, John W. (Pvt.) Co. A, 7th Regiment
Maryland Infantry. (US) Age 24. Washington
Co. Served from 16 August, 1862 to 31 May,
1865. Buried at Fairview Cemetery, near
Keedysville. (Scharf, Vol. 1, 226) (H.R.M.V.,
Vol. 1, 280) (WCCR, Vol. 5, 143) (MSA-AGR, Vol.
1, 365 and MSA-S-936-17)

TOMS, Daniel A. (Pvt.) Co. D, 6th Regiment
Maryland Cavalry. (US) Smithsburg. Served
from 20 August, 1862 to 20 June, 1865.
(H.R.M.V., Vol. 1, 234)

TOWSON, J. William. (Pvt.) (CSA) Williamsport. Educated in Washington County and Baltimore. Went south in 1862 with a friend, Baltimore Attorney A. C. Trippe. Enlisted and served in the famous Virginia Black Horse Cavalry under Maj. William F. Randolph, serving as scouts and couriers for Lt. Gen. Jubal Early. Captured at Warrenton, Va, May, 1863; exchanged in June. Participated in the battles of Brandy Station, Gettysburg, Spotsylvania, Wilderness, Cold Harbor and others. Commander of Maryland Confederate Veterans. Later moved to Shelby County, Missouri and elected to the state legislature for two years. Died at Shelbiana, Mo., 23 November, 1920. (CVM Vol. 20, 259 and Vol. 29, 27-28)

TRACY, Hiram. (Pvt.) Co. A, 3rd Regiment Maryland Infantry. (US) Age 24. Enlisted at Williamsport, 15 July, 1861. Discharged 15 July, 1864. (H.R.M.V., Vol. 1, 121) (MSA-AGR, Vol. 1, 359)

TRACY, Washington. (Pvt.) Co. A, 7th Regiment Maryland Infantry. (US) Age 22. Washington Co. Served from 9 August to 31 May, 1865. (Scharf, Vol. 1, 226) (H.R.M.V., Vol. 1, 280) (MSA-AGR, Vol. 1, 364 and MSA-S-936-17)

TRAVER, Zachariah. (Pvt.) Co. B, 13th Regiment Maryland Infantry. (US) Williamsport. Served from 18 June, 1864 to 6 November, 1864. (H.R.M.V., Vol. 1, 425) (1890-C)

TRITCH, Benjamin, K. (Pvt.) Co. B, 11th Regiment Maryland Infantry. (US) Rohrersville. Served from 27 May, 1864 to 29 September, 1864. (H.R.M.V., Vol. 1, 379) (1890-C)

TRITCH, Henry C. (Sgt.) Co. D, 1st Regiment Potomac Home Brigade Infantry. (US) Funkstown. Buried in the Funkstown Public Cemetery. (WCCR, Vol. 4, 17) (1890-C)

TRITCH, Henry L. (Pvt.) Co. A, 7th Regiment Maryland Infantry. (US) Age 21. Enlisted at

Williamsport, 15 November, 1862. Transferred to
Co. C, 1st Maryland Infantry. Discharged 2
July, 1865. (H.R.M.V., Vol. 1, 280) (MSA-AGR,
Vol. 1, 364)

TRITTLE, Daniel M. (Cpl.) Co. A, 7th Regiment
Maryland Infantry. (US) Age 21. Hagerstown.
Served from 18 August, 1862 to 31 May, 1865.
Promoted to corporal 20 August, 1862.
Discharged at Arlington Heights, Va. (Sharf,
226) (H.R.M.V., Vol. 1, 280) (1890-C) (MSA-
AGR, Vol. 1, 363 and MSA-S-936-17)

TRONE, Henry C. (Pvt.) Co. B, 12th Regiment
Maryland Infantry. (US) Downsville. Served
from 18 June, 1864 to 6 November, 1864.
Crippled in shoulder. (H.R.M.V., Vol. 1, 425)
(1890-C)

TRUMAN, John W. (Sgt.) Co. F, 4th Regiment
Maryland Infantry. (U.S.C.T.) (US) Clear
Spring. Served from 28 August, 1863 to 4 May,
1866. (H.R.M.V., Vol. 2, 141) (1890-C)

TROUPE, Joseph C. (1st Lt.) Co. H, 1st Regiment
Potomac Home Brigade Infantry. (US) Age 19.
Farmer. Washington County. Entered service as
private in Co. F; promoted first sergeant;
first lieutenant, Co. H, 1 March, 1865; veteran
volunteer; transferred to Co. H, 13th Maryland
Infantry. (Scharf, 328) (H.R.M.V., Vol. 1,
448, 515, 523) (MSA-S-936-23)

TROUP, Martin. (Pvt.) Co. I, 7th Regiment
Maryland Infantry. (US) Age 24. Enlisted at
Hagerstown, 24 August, 1862. Held for general
court marshall and imprisoned at Ft. McHenry.
Given dishonorable discharge 29 June, 1865.
(H.R.M.V., Vol. 1, 298) (MSA-AGR, Vol. 1, 365)

TROXEL, Levi. (Pvt.) Co. L, 1st Regiment Potomac
Home Brigade "Cole's" Cavalry. (US) Hagerstown.
Served from 31 May, 1864 to 28 June, 1865.
(1890-C)

TSCHUDAY, David. (Pvt.) Co. B, 3rd Regiment

Potomac Home Brigade Infantry. (US) Hagerstown.
Enlisted at Hagerstown, 15 October 1861.
Discharged 15 October, 1865. (H.R.M.V., Vol.
1, 579) (Captain Maxwell's roster)

TURNER, Franklin P. (Major) Co. E, 36th Virginia
Infantry Regiment. Also served on the staffs of
"Stonewall" Jackson and Jubal Early. (CSA)
Sharpsburg. Received his initial education
from his uncle, Rev. John A. Adams, also of
Sharpsburg, and later graduated from Franklin
and Marshall College with a law degree. After
marriage he opened his practice in Ripley,
Western Virginia, serving Roane and Jackson
Counties. As the war neared he was named a
member of the Virginia Secession Convention and
immediately organized two companies of militia,
one from each of the counties he served, and
for his efforts was named captain. He retained
that rank as the war began, entering the 36th
Virginia Regiment, and was later promoted to
major. At Antietam, Turner fought over land
where he had spent his boyhood days. After the
war he settled in Richmond and resumed his law
practice. There, along with Gen. A. L. Long,
he co-authored the life story of Gen. Robert E.
Lee. Turner and his wife, Frances A. Miller
Turner, are buried in Mountain View Cemetery on
the family plot. (Williams, Vol. 2, 1310)
(Hartzler, 293)

TURNER, James W. (Pvt.) Unit unidentified. (CSA)
Four Locks. Served from 18 October, 1862 to 10
April, 1865. (1890-C)

TURNER, Simon. (Sgt.) Co. D, 39th Regiment
Infantry. (U.S.C.T.) (US) Age 28. Weaverton.
Owned by Eli Carpenter. Enlisted at Baltimore
31 May, 1864. Disabled by serious wounds in the
left side and arm, from an exploding shell at
The Crater, near Petersburg, Va., 30 July,
1864. Discharged 10 August, 1864, at Carolina
City, North Carolina, with surgeon's
certificate of disability. (1890-C) (H.R.M.V.,
Vol. 2, 271) (MSA-S-936-51)

UPDEGRAFF, George C. (1st Sgt.) Co. A, 7th Regiment Maryland Infantry. (US) Age 20. Hagerstown. Enlisted at Hagerstown 8 August, 1862. Died at Hagerstown 27 August, 1863, of disease contracted in the service. (H.R.M.V., Vol. 1, 280) (Dorrance collection; letter 19 Aug., 1862) (Scharf, 226) (MSA-AGR, Vol. 1, 368 and S-936-17)

-- V --

VALENTINE, Daniel S. (Pvt.) Co. I, 7th Regiment Maryland Infantry. (US) Chewsville. Served from 5 September, 1862 to 31 May, 1865. Crippled due to action and also blinded in one eye. (1890-C)

VALENTINE, Eli D. (Sgt.) Co. H, 1st Regiment Potomac Home Brigade "Cole's" Cavalry. (US) Keedysville. Served from 29 February, 1864 to 28 June, 1865. (H.R.M.V., Vol. 1, 690) (1890-C)

VANDREAN, Adam. (Pvt.) Co. F, 3rd Regiment Potomac Home Brigade Infantry. (US) Age 39. Hagerstown. Enlisted 19 March, 1864. Discharged 29 May, 1865. (H.R.M.V., Vol. 1, 594) (MSA-S-936-24)

VOGLE, John A. (Pvt.) (CSA) Smithsburg. Unit not known. (Hartzler, 295)

-- W --

WAKENIGHT, John. (Pvt.) Co. A, Davis' Maryland Cavalry, (CSA) Funkstown. (Hartzler, 296)

WAKENIGHT, William. (Pvt.) Co. G, 7th Regiment Maryland Cavalry. (US) Funkstown. Served from 19 August, 1862 to 31 May, 1865. (H.R.M.V., Vol. 1, 294) (1890-C)

WALKER, Charles Wilson Patrick. (Pvt.) Co. I, 3rd Alabama Infantry, (CSA) Hagerstown. (Hartzler, 296)

WALKER, William W. (Capt.) Co. E, 126th
   Pennsylvania Infantry. (US) Hagerstown. Served
   from June, 1862 to February, 1863. (1890-C)

WALLACE, Hiram. (Pvt.) Co. I, 1st Regiment
   Potomac Home Brigade Infantry. (US) Hagerstown.
   (1890-C)

WALTEMEYER. James A. (Pvt.) Co. C, 1st Regiment
   Maryland Cavalry. (US) Age 18. Farmer.
   Hagerstown. Enlisted at Hagerstown,
   7 March, 1864. Discharged 8 August, 1865.
   (H.R.M.V., Vol. 1, 716) (MSA-AGR-S-936-36)

WALTER, Simon. (Pvt.) Co. E, 1st Regiment Potomac
   Home Brigade Infantry. (US) Hagerstown. Served
   from 14 September, 1861 to 29 May, 1865.
   Transferred to Co. E, 13th Regiment Maryland
   Infantry. Sustained bayonet wound in eye.
   (H.R.M.V., Vol. 1, 509) (1890-C)

WALTERS, Samuel. (Pvt.) Co. H, 3rd Regiment
   Maryland Cavalry. (US) Hancock. Served from
   28 September, 1863 to 26 February, 1865.
   Suffered gunshot wound to right hand.
   (H.R.M.V., Vol. 1, 776) (1890-C)

WAMPLER, John W. (Pvt.) Co. B, 12th Regiment
   Maryland Infantry. (US) Leitersburg. Entered
   service 27 June, 1864. Discharged 6 november,
   1864. (H.R.M.V., Vol. 1, 425) (Bell, 67)

WANTZ, Daniel K. (Pvt.) Co. A, 7th Regiment
   Maryland Infantry. (US) Hagerstown. Served
   from 27 August, 1862 to 15 May, 1865.
   (H.R.M.V., Vol. 1, 280) (1890-C)

WANTZ, George. (Pvt.) Co. A, 7th Regiment,
   Maryland Volunteers. (US) Age 21. Hagerstown.
   Died of infection from cut foot. Buried 7
   June, 1863, in Zion Reformed Cemetery,
   Hagerstown. (H.R.M.V., Vol. 1, 280) (Dorrance
   collection: letter 2 Feb. 1863) (Scharf, Vol.
   1, 226) (WCCR, Vol. 6, 35) (MSA-AGR, Vol. 1,
   411 and MSA-S-936-17)

WARD, Joseph C. (Pvt.) Co. E, First Regiment
Potomac Home Brigade Infantry. (US) Hagerstown.
Served from 14 September, 1861 to 1 October,
1864. (H.R.M.V., Vol. 1, 510) (1890-C)

WARD, Robert. (Pvt.) Co. B, 7th Regiment Maryland
Infantry. (US) Age 30. Enlisted at Hagerstown,
16 April, 1863. Transferred to Co. I, 1st
Maryland Infantry. Discharged 2 July, 1865.
(H.R.M.V., Vol. 1, 282) (MSA-AGR, Vol. 1, 441)

WARNER, Frederick G. (Pvt.) Co. F,
1st Regiment Potomac Home Brigade Infantry.
(US) Clear Spring. Served from 4 September,
1861 to 4 September, 1864.(H.R.M.V., Vol. 1,
515)(1890-C)

WARNER, John M. (Pvt.) Co. F, 1st Regiment
Potomac Home Brigade Infantry. (US) Age 19.
Boatman. Williamsport. Enlisted 4 September,
1861. Reenlisted 28 February, 1864.
Transferred to Co. F, 13th Regiment Maryland
Infantry. Veteran. Discharged 28 May, 1865.
(H.R.M.V., Vol. 1, 515) (MSA-S-936-23)

WARNER, John W. (Pvt.) Co. A, 3rd Regiment
Maryland Infantry. (US) Age 31. Breathedsville.
Enlisted at Williamsport, 15 July, 1864.
Veteran. Wounded in right shoulder. Received
penion of $6 per month. (Pensions List, 156)
discharged 15 June, 1865. (H.R.M.V., Vol. 1,
121) (MSA-AGR, Vol. 1, 411)

WARNER, Samuel E. (Pvt.) Co. A, 1st Regiment
Maryland Infantry. (US) Smithsburg. Served
from 28 September, 1864 to 3 June, 1865.
(H.R.M.V., Vol. 1, 24) (1890-C)

WARREN, Daniel, (Cpl.) Co. I, 7th Regiment
Maryland Infantry. (US) Age 22. Enlisted at
Hagerstown 29 August, 1862. Transferred to
V.R.C. 17 October, 1864. Discharged at
Washington D.C., 5 July, 1865. (MSA-AGR, Vol.
1, 253)

WASSEN, Jacob. (1st Sgt.) Co. B, 3rd Regiment

Potomac Home Brigade Infantry. (US) Age 24.
Washington County. Enlisted 23 October, 1861.
Discharged 23 October, 1864. (H.R.M.V., Vol.
1, 578) (MSA-S-936-23)

WATSON, Daniel. (Pvt.) Co. H, 6th Regiment
Maryland Infantry. (US) Age 22. Funkstown.
Entered service 11 August, 1862. Killed in
action 27 November, 1863, at Mine Run, Va.
(H.R.M.V., Vol. 1, 242. (1890-C) (MSA-AGR, Vol.
1, 410 and 936-2)

WEAGLEY, George A. (Cpl.) Co. H, 6th Regiment
Maryland Infantry. (US) Age 21. Enlisted at
Hagerstown 21 August, 1862. Died from
consumption 28 February, 1863, at Harper's
Ferry. (H.R.M.V., Vol. 1, 242) (MSA-AGR Vol.
1, 411 and S-936-2)

WEAVER, David J. (Capt.) Co. B, 3rd Regiment
Maryland Infantry. (US) Washington County.
Enlisted 18 June, 1861; first lieutenant 1
February, 1863; captain 1 November, 1863;
mustered out 7 October, 1864. (Scharf, 328)
(H.R.M.V., Vol. 1, 115, 121)

WEAVER, Hiram S. (Pvt.) Co. C, 2nd Maryland
Cavalry, (CSA) Funkstown. (Hartzler, 300)
(Huntsberry, 92)

WEAVER, Jesse W. (Pvt.) Co. G, 1st Regiment
Potomac Home Brigade "Cole's" Cavalry. (US)
Washington Co. Served from 24 December, 1864
to 28 June, 1865. Buried in Samples Manor
Cemetery. (H.R.M.V., Vol. 1, 688) (WCCR, Vol.
4, 63) (1890-C)

WEAVER, John T. (Pvt.) Co. H, 1st Regiment
Maryland Cavalry. (US) Green Spring Furnace.
Served from 3 December, 1861 to 3 December,
1864. Shot in the right side. (H.R.M.V., Vol.
1, 731) (1890-C)

WEBSTER, George B. (Pvt.) Co. I, 7th Maryland
Infantry. (US) Age 21. Enlisted at Hagerstown,
30 August, 1862. Died 28 May, 1864 of wounds

received in action near Hanovertown, Va.
(H.R.M.V., Vol. 1, 298) (MSA-AGR-Vol. 1, 412)

WEDDLE, Jacob E. (Pvt.) Co. A, 13th Regiment
Maryland Infantry. (US) Smoketown. Served
between 1862 and 1865. Suffered sabre cut to
knee. Discharge date unknown. (1890-C)

WEDDLE, Samuel. (Sgt.) Co. L., 1st Regiment
Potomac Home Brigade "Cole's" Cavalry. (US)
Smithsburg. Entered service 29 March, 1864.
Died 7 July, 1864 of wounds accidentally
received. (H.R.M.V., Vol. 1, 697.) (1890-C)

WEISE, Arthur James. (1st Lt.) Co. A, 7th
Regiment Maryland Infantry. (US) Washington
County. Age 24. Entered 8 August, 1862, as
second lieutenant; first lieutenant 21 January,
1864. (Scharf, 328) (H.R.M.V., Vol. 1, 278)
(Dorrance collection, 20 August, 1862, letter)

WELLING, James. (Pvt.) Co. B, 3rd Regiment
Potomac Home Brigade Infantry. (US) Age 39.
Washington County. Enlisted 7 November, 1861.
Veteran. Discharged 7 November, 1865.
(H.R.M.V., Vol. 1, 579) (MSA-S-936-23)

WELSH, William H. (Sgt.) Co. I, 7th Regiment
Maryland Infantry. (US) Age 24. Funkstown.
Enlisted at Hagerstown 14 August, 1862.
Discharged 31 May, 1865. (H.R.M.V., Part 1,
298) (1890-C) (MSA-AGR, Vol. 1, 411)

WELTY, Jacob. (Pvt.) Co. C, 5th Regiment Maryland
Infantry. (US) Smithsburg. Served from 29
September, 1864 to 9 May, 1865. (H.R.M.V., Vol.
1, 193) (1890-C)

WELTZ, George C. (Pvt.) Co. C, 1st Regiment
Potomac Home Brigade Infantry. (US) Age 26.
Clerk. Enlisted at Hagerstown, 14 September,
1861. Reenlisted 23 February, 1864 at Sandy
Hook, Md. Transferred to Co. E, 13th Maryland
Infantry.

WESSENGER, Leonard. (Pvt.) Co. I, 13th Regiment

Maryland Infantry. (US) Leitersburg. Served
from 24 February, 1864 to 29 May, 1864.(1890-C)

WESTERHOUSE, John H. (Pvt.) Co. F, 1st Regiment
Potomac Home Brigade Infantry. (US) Age 20.
Blacksmith. Washington Co. Enlisted 4
September, 1861. Reenlisted 28 February, 1864
at Frederick, Md. Veteran. Discharged 29 May,
1865. (H.R.M.V., Vol. 1, 515) (MSA-S-936-23)

WHEELER, Frederick. (Pvt.) Co. B, 7th Regiment
Maryland Infantry. (US) Age 39. Enlisted at
Hagerstown, 8 May, 1863. Died 18 May, 1865, at
Harwood Hospital, Washington, D.C. of disease
contracted in service. (H.R.M.V., Vol. 1, 282)
(MSA-AGR-Vol. 1, 411)

WHEELER, Thomas. (Sgt.) Co. A, 1st Regiment
Potomac Home Brigade Cavalry. (US) Age 23.
Hancock. Enlisted 10 August, 1861. Veteran.
Wounded and taken prisoner at Leesburg, Va., 2
September, 1862. Exchanged. Discharged 28 June,
1865. (H.R.M.V., Vol. 1, 670) (MSA-S-936-30)

WHEELER, William. Assistant surgeon, 8th Regiment
Maryland Infantry. (US) Boonsboro. Served from
4 October, 1862 to 30 June, 1864. Discharged
for chronic bronchitis. (H.R.M.V., Vol. 1, 307)
(1890-C)

WHITING, Harold. (Pvt.) Co. I, 1st Regiment
Maryland Infantry. (?) (US) Williamsport.
Served from 12 April, 1861 to 14 May, 1863.
(1890-C)

WHITMORE, George H. (Pvt.) Co. E, 1st Regiment
Potomac Home Brigade "Cole's" Cavalry. (US)
Chewsville. Served from 29 February, 1864 to
28 June, 1865. (H.R.M.V., Vol. 1, 683) (1890-C)

WIDDOWS, Bushrod. (Pvt.) Co. I, 7th Regiment
Maryland Infantry. (US) Age 25. Enlisted at
Hagerstown 30 August, 1862. Died 15 June, 1865
at Rebel prison in Florence, S.C. (H.R.M.V.,
Vol. 1, 298) (MSA-AGR-Vol. 1, 412)

WHITE, Charles W. (Pvt.) Co. A, U. S. Cavalry, Volunteer Rangers. (McNeill's) (US) Clear Spring. Buried at St. Peter's Lutheran Cemetery, Clear Spring. (WCCR, Vol. 2, 143)

WIEBEL, John L. (Pvt.) (Spelled Weavel in HRMV) Co. F, 3rd Regiment Potomac Home Brigade Infantry. (US) Hagerstown. Served from 16 October, 1863 to 29 May, 1865. (H.R.M.V., Vol. 1, 594) (1890-C)

WILBURN, Robert. (Pvt.) Co. H, 1st Regiment Potomac Home Brigade "Cole's" Cavalry. (US) Hagerstown. Entered service 29 February, 1864. Deserted 15 May, 1864. (H.R.M.V., Vol. 1, 690) (1890-C)

WILDERS, James. (Pvt.) Co. A, 1st Maryland Potomac Home Brigade Infantry. (US) Washington Co. (WCCR, Vol. 4, 73) (1890-C)

WILHIDE, Alfred. (Pvt.) Co. G, 11th Regiment Maryland Infantry. (US) Hagerstown. Served from 21 February, 1865 to 15 June, 1865. (H.R.M.V., Vol. 1, 410) (1890-C)

WILKSON, Lauren H. (Pvt.) Co. E, 13th Regiment Maryland Infantry. (US) Boonsboro. Served from 1 March, 1865 to 29 May, 1865. (1890-C)

WILLHIDE, Cyrus. (2nd Sgt.) Co. D, 6th Regiment Maryland Infantry. (US) Hagerstown. Served from 20 August, 1862 to 20 June, 1865. (H.R.M.V., Vol. 1, 234) (1890-C) (Note: The roster lists Willhide as a private while the census indicates the rank of 2nd sergeant)

WILLIAMS, George. (Pvt.) Co. I, 7th Regiment Maryland Infantry. (US) Age 19. Enlisted at Hagerstown, 15 August, 1862. Died 22 December, 1862, of disease contracted in service. (H.R.M.V., Vol. 1, 298) (MSA-AGR, Vol. 1, 412)

WILLIAMS, Lloyd. (Pvt.) Co. I, 2nd Regiment Infantry. (U.S.C.T.) (US) Hagerstown. (MSA-S-936-45)

WILLIAMSON, William Henry. (Pvt.) Co. D or Co. G, Mosby's Rangers. (CSA) Hagerstown. Service length unknown. Died in Hagerstown in 1933. (Herald Mail Jan. 1978, "Do You Remember?" 45 Years Ago feature)

WILLMAN, Julias T. C. (2nd Lt.) Co. H, 3rd Regiment Potomac Home Brigade Infantry. (US) Age 23. Benevola. Enlisted at Hagerstown as a private in Co. B. Promoted sergeant, second lieutenant 22 September, 1862. Transferred to Co. F. Discharged 5 September, 1863. (H.R.M.V., Vol. 1, 597) (Captain Maxwell's roster) (MSA-S-936-23)

WILTSHIRE, Charles. (Pvt.) Co. G, 43rd Virginia Cavalry, (Mosby's) (CSA) Hagerstown. (1890-C)

WILSON, Elias B. Co. I, 34th Pennsylvania Infantry (12th Reserves). (US) Hagerstown. Date and location of enlistment unknown. Later a resident of Huntingdon County, Pa. Captain James Baker's company from Orbisonia vacinity. (Information based on letter on file in Western Maryland Room of the Washington County Free Library, at Hagerstown, Md.)

WILSON, Jacob. (Pvt.) Co. B, 3rd Regiment Potomac Home Brigade Infantry.(US) Age 22. Beaver Creek. Enlisted at Hagerstown, 17 January, 1862. Discharged 17 January, 1865. (H.R.M.V., Vol. 1, 579) (Captain Maxwell's roster) (MSA-(VS-936-24)

WILSON, James. (1st Lt.) Co. A, 1st Regiment Potomac Home Brigade. (US) Sharpsburg. Entered service as second lieutenant 15 August, 1861; first lieutenant 9 February, 1863; mustered out 27 August, 1864. Buried in Lutheran graveyard, Main Street, Sharpsburg. (Scharf, 328) (H.R.M.V., Vol. 1, 486) (WCCR, Vol. 1, 75)

WINCH, Jacob. (Pvt.) Co. I, 11th Regiment Maryland Infantry. (US) Hagerstown. Served from 13 June, 1864 to 1 October, 1864.

WINDER, Daniel Henry. (Pvt.) (Unit unknown) (CSA)
Clear Spring. Enlisted at age 18. Captured
while going home to visit his mother, and
imprisoned at Johnson's Island, Ohio, in 1864.
Died in prison of typhoid fever and neglect.
The shock killed his mother Mrs. Susan Newcomer
Winder. Buried, 21 May, 1864, in St. Paul's
Church Cemetery, at Clear Spring. (Diary in
possession of the late Mr. Frank Mish, Jr., his
great uncle, available at the Washington County
Historical Society in Mary V. Mish's "Temper of
the Times." And information provided to Mr.
Mish by a relative.)

WINFIELD, David. (Pvt.) Co. K, 13th Regiment
Maryland Infantry. (US) Age 29. Shoemaker.
Rohrersville. Enlisted at Funkstown, 10
January, 1865. Transferred to Co. K, 1st
Regiment Potomac Home Brigade Infantry 16
January, 1865. Discharged 29 May, 1865.
(H.R.M.V., Vol. 1, 458) (1890-C) (MSA-AGR-S-
936-22)

WISE, Jacob. (Pvt.) Co. A, 1st Regiment Maryland
Potomac Home Brigade. (US) Sharpsburg. Served
from 8 Dec., 1861 to 27 August, 1864. (1890-C)

WOLF, George. (Pvt.) Co. B, 3rd Regiment Potomac
Home Brigade Infantry. (US) Age 18.
Hagerstown. Enlisted 20 December, 1862.
Discharged 26 June, 1865. (H.R.M.V., Vol. 1,
579) (MSA-S-936-23)

WOLF, John C. (Pvt.) Co. D, 6th Regiment Maryland
Infantry. (US) Leitersburg. Served from 4
September, 1862 to 20 June, 1865. Wounded in
back by shell fragments. (H.R.M.V., Vol. 1,
234) (1890-C)

WOLF, Samuel. (Pvt.) Co. B, 3rd Regiment Potomac
Home Brigade Infantry. (US) Age 41. Laborer.
Washington Co. Enlisted 26 November, 1861.
Discharged 29 May, 1865. Veteran. (H.R.M.V.,
Vol. 1, 579) (MSA-S-936-23)

WOLFORD, Charles H. (Pvt.) Co. A, 7th Regiment
Maryland Infantry. (US) Age 24. Washington Co.
Served from 8 August, 1862 to 17 December,
1864. Discharged with surgeon's certificate.
(Scharf, Vol. 1, 280) (H.R.M.V., Vol. 1, 280)
(MSA-AGR, Vol. 1, 411 and MSA-S-936-17)

WORKMAN, Daniel. (Pvt.) Co. I, 10th West Virginia
Infantry. (US) Millstone. Served from 26
February, 1864 to 22 June, 1865. Shot in right
shoulder. (1890-C)

WORLEY, John T. (Pvt.) Co. F, 1st Regiment
Potomac Home Brigade Infantry. (US) Age 25.
Shoemaker. Williamsport. Served from 4
September, 1861 to 29 May, 1865. Transferred
to Co. F, 13th Maryland Infantry. Wounded in
right forearm. (H.R.M.V., Vol. 1, 515) (1890-
C) (MSA-S-936-23)

WRIGHT, James. (Pvt.) Co. I, 7th Regiment
Maryland Infantry. (US) Age 36. Washington
Co. Served from 20 August, 1862 to 30 March,
1863. Discharged with physical disability.
Injury to abdomen. Received pension of $8 per
month. (Pensions List, 157) (H.R.M.V., Vol. 1,
298) (WCCR, Vol. 7, 443) (MSA-AGR, Vol. 1, 412)

WRIGHT, Joseph H. (Pvt.) Co. F, 36th Virginia
Infantry, The Stonewall Brigade. (CSA)
Williamsport. After the war he served for 40
years as a supervisor on the Western Maryland
Railroad. (Hartzler, 313) (Confederate Veteran
Magazine, Vol. XXXIII, 468)

WRIGHT, William. (Pvt.) Captain Firey's Co. B,
1st Regiment Potomac Home Brigade "Cole's"
Cavalry. (US) Age 19. Farmer. Clear Spring.
Enlisted 4 September, 1861. Veteran.
Reenlisted 14 February, 1864, at Boliver, Va.
(H.R.M.V., Vol. 1, 673) (MSA-S-936-30)

WRIGHT, William E. (Pvt.) Co. I, 7th Regiment
Maryland Infantry. (US) Age 28. Enlisted at
Hagerstown, 20 August, 1862. Reported sick at

Lincoln Hospital, Washington, D. C. Mustered
out at Frederick, Md., 2 July, 1865.
(H.R.M.V., Vol. 1, 298) (MSA-AGR, Vol. 1, 412)

-- Y --

YEAKLE, Lewis. (Pvt.) Co. E, 1st Regiment Potomac
Home Brigade Infantry. (US) Washington Co.
Served from 14 September, 1861 to 1 October,
1864. Buried in Smithsburg Cemetery.
(H.R.M.V., Vol. 1, 510) (WCCR, Vol. 3, 29)

YOUNG, Abraham E. (Cpl.) Co. B, 3rd Regiment
Potomac Home Brigade Infantry. (US) Age 18.
Beaver Creek. Enlisted at Hagerstown, 5
November, 1861. Transferred to Co. F.
Veteran. Discharged 29 May, 1865. Member
Independent Junior Fire Company of Hagerstown.
(H.R.M.V., Vol. 1, 579) (Captain Maxwell's
roster) (MSA-S-936-23) (I.J.F.C. roster)

YOUNG, Henry. (Pvt.) Co. H, 6th Regiment
Maryland Infantry. (US) Age 40. Enlisted at
Hagerstown, 16 August, 1862. Transferred to
V.R.C. 15 April, 1865. (H.R.M.V., Vol. 1, 242)
(MSA-AGR, Vol. 1, 424 and S-936-2)

YOUNG, Jeremiah. (Pvt.) Co. E, 1st Regiment
Potomac Home Brigade Infantry. (US) Age 25.
Laborer. Downsville. Served from 19 January,
1864 to 29 May, 1865. Transferred to Co. E,
13th Maryland Infantry. (H.R.M.V., Vol. 1,
510) (MSA-S-936-23)

YOUNG, Samuel. (Pvt.) Co. H, "Cole's" Cavalry.
(US) Keedysville. Captured and confined to
Richmond's Libby Prison. (Williams, Vol. 2,
803)

YOUNG, William H. (Pvt.) Co. E, 1st Regiment
Potomac Home Brigade. (US) Keedysville.
Served from 14 September, 1861 to 17 February,
1865. Killed in the Battle of Weldon Rail
Road, Va. Buried in the Lutheran Church
Cemetery at Locust Grove. (H.R.M.V., Vol. 1,
510, 540) (WCCR, Vol. 3, 163) (Williams, Vol.

YOUNGER, Harris. (Pvt.) Co. H, 3rd Regiment
Maryland Cavalry. (US) Millstone. Served from
28 September, 1863 to 5 September, 1865.
(H.R.M.V., Vol. 1, 776) (1890-C)

YOUNTZ, William H. H. (Capt.) Co. E, 1st Regiment
Potomac Home Brigade Infantry. (US) Enlisted 23
August, 1861; discharged 1 October, 1864.
(Scharf, 328) (H.R.M.V., Vol. 1, 505)

-- Z --

ZAHN, William C. Co. F, 11th Regiment Maryland
Infantry Regiment. (US) Smoketown. According to
the 1890 Census report Zahn served as aprivate
in Co. F, 1st Virginia Cavalry from 21
September, 1862, to 23 May, 1863. Then on 18
June, 1864, he changed sides and joined Co. B,
12th Regiment Maryland Infantry as a sergeant.
Three months later he was transferred to Co. F,
11th Maryland Infantry Regiment and served
until 15 June, 1865. (H.R.M.V., Vol. 1, 408)
(1890-C)

ZELLER, Joseph R. (Capt.) Co. H, 1st Regiment
Maryland Cavalry. (US) Began service as captain
in 1st Virginia Union Cavalry. Served 9
September, 1861 to 28 March, 1862. Buried in
Salem Reformed Church Cemetery near Cearfoss.
(Scharf, 328) (H.R.M.V., Vol. 1, 728) (WCCR,
Vol. 3, 285)

ZIEGLER, George Frederick. Co. A, 1st Regiment
Potomac Home Brigade "Cole's Cavalry." (US)
Leitersburg. Enlisted 17 September, 1864.
Discharged 25 May, 1865. (H.R.M.V., Vol. 1,
670) (Bell, 67)

ZIEGLER, George H. (Cpl.) Co. A, 7th Regiment
Maryland Infantry. (US) Hagerstown. Age 21.
Entered service 18 August, 1862. Died 28
January, 1865. (Sharf, 226) (H.R.M.V., Vol.
1, 280) (MSA-S-936-17)

ZEIGLER, James R. (Pvt.) Co. A, 1st Regiment
Potomac Home Brigade "Cole's" Cavalry. (US)
Hagerstown. Served from 17 September, 1864 to
31 May, 1865. (H.R.M.V., Vol. 1, 670) (1890-C)

ZEIGLER, John D. (Pvt.) Co. B, 3rd Regiment
Potomac Home Brigade Infantry. (US) Hagerstown.
Enlisted at Hagerstown, 28 January, 1862.
Transferred to Co. F. Veteran. Discharged 29
May, 1865. (H.R.M.V., Vol. 1, 594) (Captain
Maxwell's roster) (MSA-S-936-23)

ZEIGLER, John H. (Pvt.) Co. A, 7th Regiment
Maryland Infantry. (US) Hagerstown. Age 22.
Served from 15 August, 1862 to 31 May, 1865.
(Scharf, Vol. 1, 226) (H.R.M.V., Vol. 1, 280.
(1890-C) (MSA-S-936-17)

ZIMMERMAN, Henry. (Pvt.) 2nd Pennsylvania
Volunteer Infantry. (US) Clear Spring.
Entered the service at age 19 and served until
the war's end. Fought with the Army of the
Potomac at the Wilderness, Cold Harbor and on
many other fields. Wounded at Petersburg and
given an honorable discharge. (Williams, Vol.
52, 1289)

ZIMMERMAN, Henry C. (Cpl.) Co. B, 112th
Pennsylvania Infantry Regiment. (US) Clear
Spring. Served from 8 December, 1863 to 29
January, 1868. (1890-C)

ZITTLE, Joseph. (Pvt.) Co. G, 1st Regiment
Maryland Infantry. (US) Hagerstown. Entered
service 2 November, 1864. Deserted 20 August,
1865. (H.R.M.V., Vol. 1, 209) (1890-C)